Mussolini and Italian Fascism

Giuseppe Finaldi

PEARSON
Longman

Harlow, England • London • New York • Boston • San Francisco • Toronto
Sydney • Tokyo • Singapore • Hong Kong • Seoul • Taipei • New Delhi
Cape Town • Madrid • Mexico City • Amsterdam • Munich • Paris • Milan

PEARSON EDUCATION LIMITED

Edinburgh Gate
Harlow CM20 2JE
Tel: +44 (0)1279 623623
Fax: +44 (0)1279 431059
Website: www.pearsoned.co.uk

First published in Great Britain in 2008

ISBN: 978-1-4058-1253-5

British Library Cataloguing-in-Publication Data
A catalogue record for this book is available from the British Library

Library of Congress Cataloging-in-Publication Data
Finaldi, Giuseppe.
    Mussolini and Italian fascism / Giuseppe Finaldi.
        p. cm.
    Includes bibliographical references and index.
    ISBN-13: 978-1-4058-1253-5 (pbk.)
    1. Fascim – Italy – History.   2. Mussolini, Benito, 1883–1945.   3. Italy – Politics and
government – 1914–1945.   4. Italy – Foreign relations – 1914–1945.   5. Fascism –
Italy – Historiography.   6. Fascism – Italy – History – Sources.   I. Title.
    DG571.F497 2008
    945.091—dc22

2008003307

10 9 8 7 6 5 4 3 2 1
12 11 10 09 08

Typeset in 10/13.5pt Berkeley Book by 35
Printed and bound in Malaysia (CTP-VVP)

The publisher's policy is to use paper manufactured from sustainable forests.

To Daniela

Contents

Author's acknowledgements

Thanks above all to Richard Bosworth for reading and commenting on various drafts of this book but more importantly for trusting me with opportunities I felt had been lost. Gordon Martel gently prodded my writing into shape and the team at Pearson were remarkably efficient. Staff and students at UWA have been a pleasure to work with and when I really needed help Taku Korogi was always available. David Medlen can only be described as the librarian we all dreamed of having but never dared hope for. With Daniela discussions on all the historical issues touched on in this book have been as acrimonious as they have been stimulating, confirming my belief that what makes History so worth studying is the multiplicity of the eyes of its beholders.

Publisher's acknowledgements

We are grateful to the following for permission to reproduce copyright material:

Plate 1 courtesy of Corbis/Underwood & Underwood; plate 2 courtesy of Corbis/Bettmann; plate 3 courtesy of Mary Evans Picture Library/Weimar Archive; plate 4a courtesy of Alinari Archives Management, Florence/Bruni Archive; plate 4b courtesy of Alamy Images/T S Corrigan; plate 5a courtesy of Corbis/Lewis Wickes; plates 5b and 7a courtesy of Alinari Archives Management/Luce Institute; plate 6 courtesy of akg-images Ltd; plate 7b courtesy of Getty Images/Hulton Archive

In some instances we have been unable to trace the owners of copyright material, and we would be grateful for any information that would enable us to do so.

Chronology

1859–71	Process of Italian unification through efforts of old Piedmontese monarchy and Garibaldi's volunteers.
1883	Birth of Benito Mussolini at Predappio (province of Forlí), Romagna.
1896	Battle of Adowa: Italy defeated by Ethiopia.
1902–12	Mussolini active as member of socialist movement in Switzerland, Trent (Austria) and Italy.
1910	Birth of Italian Nationalist Association.
1911–12	Italo-Turkish war; Italy takes Libya as colony.
1912	Prime Minister Giovanni Giolitti extends the parliamentary franchise to include almost all males.
December	Mussolini becomes editor of Socialist Party newspaper *Avanti!* and attempts to radicalize the party.
1913	Catholic MPs support Giolitti's government against socialists.
	Mussolini in contact with broad anti-liberal intellectual movement throughout Italy.
1914	
June	'Red Week': strikes and revolts through much of central and northern Italy.
August	Italy declares its neutrality in the war between Austria and Serbia, which escalates into the First World War.

September	Italian Socialist Party declares its support for neutrality; document drawn up by Mussolini.
18 October	Mussolini attempts to convince the Socialist Party to support Italian intervention in the war.
October–November	Mussolini is forced to relinquish editorship of *Avanti!* and is ejected from the Socialist Party; founds 'interventionist' newspaper *Il Popolo d'Italia*.

1915

January–May	Coalescence of interventionist movement.
23 May	Italy declares war on Austria.
September	Mussolini is called up and on active duty on the Alpine front.

1917

October	Italian defeat of Caporetto.

1918

October	Italian victory against Austrians at Vittorio Veneto.
November	End of First World War.

1919	Beginning of *biennio rosso* (two red years).
March	Foundation of the Fascist movement in Milan.
September	Occupation of Fiume by Gabriele D'Annunzio and his legionaries.
November	First elections with proportional system, liberals lose majority in parliament.

1920	Continuation of working-class and peasant militancy.
	First Fascist squads operating in Po Valley and Italian borderlands.

1921	Upsurge in Fascist squad violence.
April–May	Fascist electoral pact with liberals; election of 35 Fascist members of parliament.
November	Fascist Party (PNF) founded.

1922	Continuation of Fascist squad violence.
28 October	March on Rome.
29 October	Mussolini appointed prime minister.
December	Creation of Fascist Grand Council and Fascist militia (MVSN).

1923

March   Fusion of PNF and Nationalist Association.

July   Acerbo Electoral Law.

1924

April   Elections give Fascists and Allies large majority.

May–June   Matteotti speech and murder.

June–December Aventine Secession and Matteotti crisis.

1925

3 January   Mussolini speech to parliament heralding the dictatorship.

1925–6   Laws reducing freedom of speech, press and abolition of political opposition.

Use of Fascist salute becomes compulsory for employees of state administration; fasces become official symbol of the Italian state.

Launch of the 'battle for wheat'.

Birth of 'afterwork' organization (OND) and Fascist Scouts (ONB).

1928   Launch of land reclamation campaign.

1929   Conciliation with Church (Lateran Pacts).

1931   Abolition of non-Fascist youth groups.

Conflict with Church over Catholic Action.

1933   Hitler comes to power in Germany.

1934   Tension with Germany over Austria.

1935

April   Stresa agreements with France and Britain guaranteeing Austrian sovereignty.

October   Beginning of Ethiopian War; League of Nations declares Italy the 'aggressor' and imposes economic sanctions.

1936

May   Proclamation of Italian Empire.

July   First Italian involvement in Spanish Civil War.

October   Birth of Rome–Berlin Axis.

1937   Italy leaves the League of Nations and joins the Anti-Comintern Pact.

1938

March   Anschluss (German annexation of Austria); accepted by Italy.

30 September   Munich agreements.

November   Racial laws passed.

1939

January   Chamber of Corporations created.

April   Italy occupies Albania.

May   Pact of Steel.

September   Germany invades Poland; Second World War begins.

Period of Italian 'non-belligerence' begins.

1940

June   Italy declares war on France and Britain.

October   Italy invades Greece.

December   Failure of attack in Greece and offensive in Egypt.

1941

April   Italy loses East African empire.

June   German war against the USSR (with Italian participation) begins.

December   Italy and Germany declare war on the USA.

1942   Anti-Fascist parties re-establish bases in Italy.

October   Axis defeat in North Africa.

1943

March   Strikes in Turin and Milan.

May   Axis troops surrender in North Africa.

9 July   Allied forces land in Sicily.

24–5 July   Grand Council meeting votes for removal of Mussolini from control of armed forces.

25 July   Removal of Mussolini as head of government, and arrest.

26 July   Badoglio government formed.

8 September	Armistice with Allies announced publicly; King and Badoglio's flight to Brindisi.
8–10 September	Italy invaded and occupied by German army; Italian army dissolves.
12 September	Mussolini freed by German paratroops.
18 September	Mussolini reconstitutes PNF and announces the creation of the Italian Social Republic (RSI).
1944	Badoglio government recognized by Allies (including USSR).
	Growth of the anti-Nazi/Fascist resistance movement in north central Italy.
June	Allies enter Rome.
16 December	Last public speech by Mussolini in Milan.
1945	Exponential growth of Italian resistance.
April	Anti-Nazi/Fascist insurrections in major Italian cities of the north.
28 April	Mussolini captured and executed by communist partisans.

Who's who

Badoglio, Pietro (1871–1956): Army general during the First World War; present at Caporetto. Chief of Staff 1925–40; commander of the Italian army during the Italian invasion of Ethiopia and proclaimed Marshall of Italy and Duke of Addis Ababa. Scapegoated for the disastrous Italian invasion of Greece in 1940, he plotted Mussolini's downfall with the Italian king. He was made head of government at Mussolini's fall and escaped to Brindisi on 8 September 1943. He was recognized by Allies and resistance as Italian head of government until Allied capture of Rome in June 1944.

Balbo, Italo (1896–1940): Interventionist and decorated officer in the First World War; *Ras* of Ferrara; and an able and determined organizer of some of Fascism's most notorious squads. One of the leaders of the March on Rome, he occupied various positions of power during the dictatorship, most notably minister of the Italian Air Force between 1929 and 1933. He participated as a pilot in the 1933 trans-Atlantic 'raid', for which he was widely acclaimed, although his popularity irked the *Duce*. He was made governor of Libya in 1934. He was killed when his airplane was accidentally shot down by Italian anti-aircraft fire in 1940.

Ciano, Galeazzo (1903–44): Wealthy son of Fascist minister, married Mussolini's daughter Edda in 1930 and made foreign minister in 1936. He was pro-German at first but became disillusioned with the Alliance. He wrote a useful and lucid diary while in office. He voted against his father-in-law in the Grand Council meeting of 24–5 July 1943 and for this he was executed in January 1944.

Corradini, Enrico (1865–1931): Political thinker and founder of the Italian Nationalist Association. He detested *Italietta* and conceived of the idea of Italy as 'proletarian nation'. An interventionist and supporter of his party's fusion with Fascism, he was made a senator by Mussolini but granted no effective power during the Regime.

Croce, Benedetto (1866–1952): Philosopher, historian, politician and liberal thinker of great international standing. He supported Fascism in its early days but became disillusioned with the dictatorship. He put forward an influential interpretation of Fascism as 'parenthesis' in the linear and progressive history of Italy.

D'Annunzio, Gabriele (1863–1938): Avant-guard writer and self-proclaimed decadent bohemian. He was politically active as an interventionist and was the organizer of the Fiume occupation in 1919. He supported Fascism and designed some of its rituals but was politically sidelined (partly from choice) after Mussolini came to power.

Farinacci, Roberto (1892–1945): Interventionist and volunteer in the First World War; a very prominent squad leader during the rise of Fascism. He was *ras* of Cremona, a city he ruled with patronage and an iron fist. He was a radical Fascist, always pushing Mussolini to broke with no forces except Fascism itself, which he interpreted as having been compromised by Mussolini's methods. In general he was sidelined during the Regime. He supported the alliance with Germany and was enthusiastic about Italy's racial laws. He was executed by partisans in 1945.

Gentile, Giovanni (1875–1944): Philosopher disciple of Benedetto Croce. He saw Fascism as a continuation and development of the *Risorgimento* and attempted to construct a coherent Fascist 'doctrine'. He held various ministries and presided over high culture throughout the Regime (e.g. as director and founder of the *Enciclopedia Italiana*). He was shot by partisans during the RSI after publicly supporting the execution of RSI draft-dodgers.

Giolitti, Giovanni (1842–1928): Liberal prime minister of Italy on many occasions before Fascism's rise to power. He was highly influential in broadening Italy's political base in the first two decades of the twentieth century. In an attempt to deal with the rise of the subversive parties, he formed electoral alliances with rising Fascism and hoped to constitutionalize the Fascist movement. He was sidelined on the creation of the Dictatorship but remained in parliament until his death.

Gramsci, Antonio (1891–1937): Co-founder of the Italian Communist Party in 1921 and activist during the rise of Fascism. Arrested in 1926, he wrote a major reinterpretation of modern Italian history while in prison, where he was held for almost ten years.

Grandi, Dino (1895–1988): Interventionist and decorated officer in the First World War; became a Fascist in 1920 and was involved in squadism in the Emilia Romagna region. He participated in the March on Rome, but was a moderate throughout the Regime and favoured a conciliatory attitude to

Britain, where he was Italian ambassador between 1932 and 1939. Mussolini's alliance with Hitler led him to favour a monarchical dictatorship. He was instrumental in Mussolini's fall, after which he wisely fled to Portugal. He returned to Italy in the 1950s and lived to a ripe old age.

Graziani, Rodolfo (1882–1955): Officer in the First World War; participated in the ferocious repression of the Libyan resistance in the 1920s and early 1930s; commander of the southern front in the Ethiopian War and became governor of the colony. He was commander of the Italian forces in North Africa at the beginning of the Second World War, where his army was defeated by the British. In 1943 he chose the RSI, partly out of rivalry with Badoglio. As RSI minister of war he organized the repression of the partisans. He was tried and found guilty of war crimes in 1948 and was imprisoned for a short spell.

Matteotti, Giacomo (1885–1924): Moderate socialist whose speech in May 1924 defended the liberal constitution from Fascism. His murder provoked the Matteotti crisis, which led Mussolini to speed up the construction of the dictatorship. After 1945 he became perhaps Italy's most famous anti-Fascist martyr.

Pope Pius XI (Ratti, Achille) (1857–1939): Pope from 1922. Vehemently anti-communist, he sought to navigate the Church through the difficult post-war years by accepting compromises with both Fascism and Nazism. He was a great protector of Church independence, but less of a spokesman for other victims of Fascism. He signed the Lateran Pacts with Mussolini in 1929.

Starace, Achille (1895–1945): Secretary of the Fascist Party between 1931 and 1939, and responsible for developing much of Fascism's style and choreography through the 1930s. He was removed from power by Mussolini in 1939 and permanently retired, although he was still considered a legitimate target for partisans, who executed him in Milan in 1945.

Togliatti, Palmiro (1893–1964): Communist Party co-founder and leader, and key player in the 1930s Communist International. A loyal Stalinist, he nevertheless was independent minded and was instrumental in forging the broad alliances of all anti-Fascist forces in wartime and post-war Italy.

Victor Emmanuel III (1869–1947): King of Italy from 1900 (at his father's assassination). He espoused a moderate but determined Great Power politics and favoured Italian colonialism. Terrified by the growth of socialism, he was instrumental in calling Mussolini to power and throughout the Regime remained independent of but acquiescent to the dictatorship. He removed Mussolini from power in July 1943, but fled from Rome in September. He abdicated in 1946 in favour of his son, in a futile attempt to save the Savoy monarchy.

Glossary

Arditi: Crack Italian assault troops employed in the trenches in the last year of the Great War. With a powerful *esprit de corps* and ultra-patriotic ideology, they were significant players in the post-war political struggle.

Avanti!: The official organ of the Italian Socialist Party (PSI). It was edited by Mussolini between 1912 and the first months of the First World War.

Azione Cattolica: 'Catholic Action'. Lay organization linked to parishes, which educated the young in Catholic values and provided a locus for a wide variety of social and leisure activities. In the 1930s it lost the right to host sporting activities in an attempt by the Regime to curtail its attractiveness compared to that of the ONB. It survived curtailed until the fall of Mussolini.

Biennio rosso: The 'two red years' (1919–20). A period of intense class struggle throughout north and central Italy, it coincided with the political collapse of liberal hegemony in parliament and in many local councils.

Confino: The sentence of internal exile, normally to remote locations in Italy's south or islands, used to eliminate the threat of those deemed enemies of the Regime.

Corporativism: Means by which Italian society, the economy and politics were supposed to be organized and that was touted as a viable and original 'third way' between liberal capitalism and Soviet-style communism.

Fasci di Combattimento: 'Combat Leagues'. The name of the first political cells of the Fascist movement.

Fasci Femminili: 'Female Fascist Leagues'. The womens' section of the Fascist Party, comprising a variety of organizations including the *Massaie Rurali* (Rural Housewives) and female youth groups. Its *Piccole Italiane* (Girl Guides) section passed to the ONB in 1929.

Interventionists: Cross-party political movement calling for Italian intervention in the Great War during Italy's period of neutrality (August 1914–May 1915).

MVSN (Milizia Volontaria per la Sicurezza Nazionale): 'National Security Volunteer Militia'. The organization that absorbed the Fascist squads and placed them in 1923 under Mussolini's direct command, thus circumventing the local power of the *rases*. The MVSN blended uneasily with Italy's traditional security forces thenceforward and was unable to develop into a respected alternative to them. Although the MVSN formed semi-independent units (the 'Blackshirts') in Italy's military campaigns in Ethiopia, Spain and then the Second World War, their performance was as inadequate as that of the regular army. At the fall of Mussolini in 1943 not one MVSN unit rose in defence of the *Duce*.

Opera Nazionale Balilla (ONB): The Fascist boy scouts organization. It was run by the Education Ministry and became an adjunct to the established school system. It fostered an ethos of military preparedness and devotion to the *Duce*.

Opera Nazionale Dopolavoro (OND): The Fascist leisure association. Aiming to place all public leisure activities in Italy under the Fascist umbrella, the OND significantly modified Italians' taste for entertainment.

Ovra: The Fascist secret police. Its specific task was to track down anti-Fascist activity. Mussolini also used it (his relationship with the *Ovra's* head, Arturo Bocchini, was very close indeed) to monitor and control his Fascist lieutenants.

Partito Nazional Fascista (PNF): The Fascist Party.

Partito Popolare Italiano (PPI): The Catholic Popular Party. Officially launched in 1919, it quickly absorbed much of Italy's Catholic vote. It was considered a 'subversive' party because it fostered peasant organization and challenged the verities of liberalism. Closed down by Mussolini in 1926 with the connivance of the Pope, after 1945 it re-emerged as the Christian Democratic Party and commanded more votes than any other party until the 1990s.

Partito Socialista Italiano (PSI): The Italian Socialist Party, from which Mussolini was expelled in 1914. It became, after the First World War, the largest political party in Italy, but collapsed in the face of the Fascist challenge. Outlawed during the Regime, it was far less effective than the Italian Communist Party in maintaining an underground presence; after 1945 its popular support gradually passed to the communists.

Il Popolo d'Italia: Interventionist newspaper founded in Milan by Mussolini on his ejection from the Socialist Party in 1914. It became the official organ of the Fascist movement and the semi-official voice of the Regime.

Ras: A local Fascist boss. The word was originally encountered by Italians in Ethiopia, where is stands for a military ruler of a province.

Risorgimento: Cultural movement and political-military process that culminated in the unification of Italy in the 1860s.

Squads and squadism: Loosely organized vigilante gangs of the early days of Fascism. They used violence and intimidation to secure Fascist political ends.

Trasformismo: 'Transformism'. A pejorative word denoting the fluidity of political groupings in the Italian parliament before 1922 and the willingness of parliamentary oppositions to support governments in exchange for patronage and political influence.

Vittorio Veneters: Term used in this book to denote the cross-party movements and mentalities that first coalesced after Italy's defeat at Caporetto (October 1917) in defence of the fatherland and in opposition to what were perceived to be the forces that threatened and sapped its vitality. The latter eventually came to include 'defeatists', socialists, Slavs, neutralist liberals, the Versailles peacemakers and Catholics. The term is not synonymous with 'Fascists', although these were a characteristic 'Vittorio Venetist' political force. Vittorio Veneto was the battle in October 1918 that saw Italy defeat Austria.

Part 1

BACKGROUND

1

Introduction

Italy has a long past but a short history, and the Italian Fascist Regime now sits almost exactly half way down the latter. If one takes 1865 as the moment 'modern Italy' began, there is over a century of Italian history that was not Fascist. This should be borne in mind, as much of the way Italian history is thought of hinges on the difficulty of inserting this period within the chronology of the rest. The Italy that came before can be looked at purely in terms of the defects or trajectories that entailed its demise, and the period after can be regarded as an imperfect or a successful coming clean, depending on one's point of view. What is certain is that the hope of the great Italian philosopher and historian, **Benedetto Croce**, that a kind of quarantining parenthesis could be thrown around the whole awkward episode was never realized. Fascism has remained, for better or worse, the central experience of the way in which much modern Italian history is told. But it is also more significant than this.

Italian Fascism made its appearance in world history at a very peculiar moment. Many argue that it could *only* have appeared because of the coming together of a set of unique circumstances. The Great War had exploded the permanence of a European order that had been fairly stable since Waterloo. Some short and very contained wars in the 1850s and 1860s had led to the creation of a unified Germany and Italy, but the post-Napoleon international system remained intact. The Concert of Europe was perhaps not what it had been, but those regarded as beyond the pale still lay outside the confines of a European continent that appeared to have been given permanent possession of the rudder of world history.

Yet even where European rule had never been formalized, in one way or another there was a process that brought the European way of doing things, certainly in international relations, to be the only acceptable one. For the rest, with the important exceptions of China, Japan, Ethiopia, Persia and Siam (Thailand), the world was controlled directly by Europeans or their descendents. In the Old Continent itself much of what had been frighteningly

Benedetto Croce (1866–1952): Philosopher, historian, politician and liberal thinker of great international standing. He supported Fascism in its early days but became disillusioned with the dictatorship. He put forward an influential interpretation of Fascism as 'parenthesis' in the linear and progressive history of Italy.

revolutionary in 1789 was accepted as sound political practice by 1914. The pioneering industrialization of Britain that had been fundamental to Europe's war against Napoleon was now the acknowledged way to go for all civilized nations. Nations themselves were, with some major exceptions, now the justification for the existence of modern polities and the 'people' their ultimate legitimacy.

It would have been difficult for any European to predict in July 1914 that this order was about to plunge into a deep and dark crisis. When some kind of normalcy returned in 1945 much had been irretrievably lost. Europe was sundered along the lines marked by the liberating Anglo-Saxon and Soviet armies. The cracks in European empires were already beyond repair, and others had taken up the world leadership rudder. Tens of millions of corpses, biblical numbers of refugees, great cities reduced to rubble, the knowledge of having murdered, and murdered again and again, and all this among those very Europeans who before 1914 had considered themselves at the apex of the human race, were the bitter legacy of what began in 1914. The three decades between 1914 and 1945 were an extraordinary distillation. In a way they seem to be years that count more than others, or at least they appeared to until the great turning point of the Soviet Union's collapse in 1989–91 brought the 'short twentieth century' to an unexpected conclusion.

Since the end of the Cold War there has been a temptation to drag out Croce's brackets once again, maybe closing them in 1989. The period 1914–89 looks more like an anomaly. Fascism has little to say now and many of its obsessions seem not just absurd but incomprehensible. As Michael Burleigh has put it: 'The regimes established by what have been called "armed bohemians" produced nothing of any lasting moment' (Burleigh, 2001: 812). Mussolini was certainly an 'armed bohemian' (the educated intellectual who felt no compulsion to follow convention and to accept established norms as one's own), and in many ways he epitomises one. Because Italian Fascism became a compass point, an alternative, a possible solution and a fulcrum precisely within this period of European crisis, and Mussolini himself perhaps more than any other individual was the most characteristic product of what the crisis was about, this period of Italian history does not just affect Italy, nor is the biography of Mussolini merely that of a very peculiar Italian. Fascism was emulated by others, and indeed in the late 1930s regimes that in one way or another had looked to Italian Fascism as their inspiration dominated continental Europe. This dominance was only destroyed by the intervention of the liberal Anglo-Saxon powers of the Atlantic and the communist Soviet Union in the course of the Second World War. The radically divided continent that emerged after 1945 was therefore built on the ruins of what had been a Fascist alternative that had begun its life in the short history of Italy.

Bourbons and the pope. Trevelyan concluded his eulogy of Garibaldi with an image that sums up not only the beliefs of many of his generation but some of the most important trajectories of the historiography on the new Italy: '[Garibaldi] had done a mighty labour, and taken his share in a task which the years would soon complete and the long generations ratify – the Making of Italy' (Trevelyan, 1911: 287). This 'ratification' to which the young Trevelyan confidently testified (he published these words in 1911, as Italy celebrated its fiftieth anniversary), has been one of the central concerns of historiography on Italy after unification. It seemed right and fitting that the new Italy should be a liberal and constitutional monarchy, much like Britain, and that from the restrictive franchise established at unification (in 1870 less than 2 per cent of the population acquired the right to vote) it would make democracy, democratic culture and its associated institutions eventually accessible to all. In 1907 it did appear to Trevelyan that this agenda was unfolding. In a letter to the *The Times* of 5 July he stated:

> Nothing is more remarkable – though to believers in nationality and ordered liberty nothing is more natural – than the stability of the Italian Kingdom . . . The building is as safe as any in Europe . . . The power of this great national movement has fortunately been directed only to securing Italian liberty, and not the oppression of others . . . the result has been the unstained purity and idealism of patriotic emotion there.
>
> (In Cannadine, 1992: 69)

But it was Fascism that dispelled the idea that Italy's history since unification was an accumulation of the achievements of the national spirit. The progress of democracy, liberty and development held so dearly by the liberals was suddenly halted and even reversed. The defects that Italy had had at unification and that it was felt liberalism had been slowly but surely dealing with (illiteracy, poverty, underdevelopment, a patriotic deficit, etc.) were now looked at in a wholly new light. Had the *Risorgimento*, national unification and all the rest really been as successful as people like Trevelyan had suggested?

Many, from a variety of points of view, came to very different conclusions. Some Italian intellectuals – often poets, novelists or artists, such as Giosué Carducci, Alfredo Oriani, **Gabriele D'Annunzio**, **Enrico Corradini** and Filippo Marinetti [**Docs 2, 3, pp. 130, 131**], were a constant thorn in the side of post-unification Italian governments: a kind of moral conscience of the nation, an unofficial opposition that consistently chastised Italy and Italians for failing to meet the great objectives that history had obviously prepared them for. If for some Fascism represented a positive strengthening of the national spirit, a great moment or renewal from the Italy of prose that had

Gabriele D'Annunzio (1863–1938): Avant-guard writer and self-proclaimed decadent bohemian. He was politically active as an interventionist and was the organizer of the Fiume occupation in 1919. He supported Fascism and designed some of its rituals but was politically sidelined after Mussolini came to power.

Enrico Corradini (1865–1931): Political thinker and founder of the Italian Nationalist Association. He detested *Italietta* and conceived of the idea of Italy as 'proletarian nation'. An interventionist and supporter of his party's fusion with Fascism, he was made a senator by Mussolini but granted no effective power during the Regime.

followed the poetry of the *Risorgimento* (we see clearly here that Fascism in Italy owed much to a negative interpretation of the present compared with Italy's great past), it was the advent of Fascism itself that heralded the interpretation of Italy's modern history as one of failure or flaw.

For historians such as Trevelyan the destruction of democracy in Italy and the obvious inability of liberalism to defend it was a disconcerting experience. The splendid image of Garibaldi on a white horse leading a freedom-loving Italian people to a liberal paradise was dispelled by cosh-wielding Fascists adulated by a sickeningly brainwashed Italian people. When Italy declared war on Britain in 1940, Trevelyan wrote in *The Spectator* of 14 June that, 'to some of us older men, this is the bitterest day we have yet known in our lives' (in Cannadine, 2002: 85). No longer was Italy becoming more and more like England, but rather its inherent or historical defects consistently came back to trip it up. Its history was its problem. The great school of 'why is Italy not England?' historical enquiry had been born. It has been (and indeed still is) an extraordinarily productive if not always fruitful way of approaching modern Italian history. It has certainly not been exclusively used to understand Italy's move to Fascism but has offered insights and prejudices in understanding Italian democracy after the Second World War, corruption, the Italian south, terrorism, the Mafia and much else besides (Ginsborg, 2000, 2003).

In Italy this pessimistic view was developed by one of the founders of the Italian Communist Party, **Antonio Gramsci**, at almost the same time as Croce was drafting his history of modern Italy. Gramsci, writing in a Fascist prison, considered Fascism to be the fruit of Italy's skewed historical development in the period of the *Risorgimento*. His concept of 'passive revolution' suggested that, unlike France, where the Revolution of 1789 had ousted the old feudal order (and therefore cleared the way for a democratic liberal society), in Italy this moment of class replacement had failed to occur in the proper way. Because in Italy this liberal (or 'bourgeois') revolution had coincided with national unification (France had been welded into a nation in medieval times), Italy headed down a different path of national development. The revolutionary nature of the *Risorgimento* was defective. It had led to no real social upheaval, but only to the political concoction that was the Italian state. The latter was a hybrid based on the ruling classes of the old, almost medieval, south and the more modern and industrializing north. The Italian people itself had never been called upon or had not responded to the more radical elements of the process of unification, and failed (unlike the French people of the revolutionary period) consistently to take the initiative. Moderate conservatives therefore controlled the Italian liberal revolution and it was Italy's stunted social and economic development that in the end gave birth to Fascism (Gramsci, 1967). The history of modern Italy was therefore

Antonio Gramsci (1891–1937): Co-founder of the Italian Communist Party in 1921 and activist during the rise of Fascism. Arrested in 1926, he wrote a major reinterpretation of modern Italian history while in prison, where he was held for almost ten years.

one of anomalies, defects and special paths. Who, though, was responsible for having dragged the peninsula where it ought not to have gone?

Since 1945, Italian history, like all national histories, has been extraordinarily politically orientated, but the irksome legacy of Fascism has intensified and polarized debate. Writers of the left attempted to rescue Italy's people from adherence to the dictatorship and concentrated on pointing out that it was Italy's defective development that led to its political woes, and writers of the right rather blamed the intransigence and uniqueness of the Italian left for Italy's anomalous need to turn to Fascism. Notwithstanding the time that has passed, this still remains the distinguishing mark of historiography on modern Italy (Davis, 1994, 1997). Although much terminology has changed, for example it is now usual to talk about defective 'modernization' rather than 'passive revolution' or 'familism', the questions on the agenda have been refined rather than radically changed.

It was therefore Fascism that mutated the study of modern Italian history and it is specifically to Italian Fascism in historiography that we now turn.

PERSPECTIVES ON THE STUDY OF ITALIAN FASCISM

Trevelyan, as has been said, was bitterly disappointed in seeing his Italy fall to Fascism. He wrote in the late 1930s: 'Fascism was abhorrent to me, because it set out to abolish the easy, kindly temperament of the Italian people that I loved [and sought instead] to drill and bully them into second-rate Germans' (in Cannadine, 1992: 85). Mussolini would have agreed that what Fascism stood for was precisely the eradication of Italians' supposed 'kindliness', and making organ grinders and mandolin players [**Doc. 4, p. 132**] into warriors and empire-builders was the first priority of the Regime [**Doc. 27, p. 148**].

Much historiography on Italian Fascism hinges around the extent to which Fascism really did manage to transform Italians into Germans. The Third Reich looms over Fascist Italy in a variety of subtle and not so subtle ways. At times it drags Italy along, a partner and precursor to its own monstrous barbarity, but at others it is the foil that sets off the relative humanity and mildness of the Italian Regime. To a degree the same can be said of the 'totalitarian' thesis, popular in the 1950s and re-emerging recently but having in the meantime acquired a tendency no longer to take Italy into consideration. The enormity of what was Stalin's Russia and Hitler's Germany rarely appears to need the Italian dictatorship in the totalitarian equation.

Therefore, unlike Hitler's Germany, the Italian dictatorship, while not exactly having out-and-out hagiographers (although even discounting declared neo-Fascists, some accounts of it border on becoming so), certainly does not attract total and absolute condemnation. To be sure, as far as Italian Fascism is concerned the jury of history has pronounced the guilty verdict, but nevertheless the appeal system is always giving it another chance. In its moderate form this means that the Italian population baby is not thrown out with the Fascist Regime bathwater, or that Fascism is boiled down to little more than the hyperbole of the *Duce*. The dictator was a 'sawdust Caesar', as one American journalist memorably put it (Seldes, 1935), and the Fascist Regime made of papier-mâché. More seriously, these views entail placing Regime and people together, making Italian Fascism a perhaps misguided but not altogether unjustified attempt to come up with something positive in an Italy that could easily have fallen into the nightmare of Bolshevism. In any case it was the First World War that made everyone suddenly go mad. Croce's idea of parenthesis tacitly assumed such a scenario. Exceptional circumstances created Fascism, and it was most certainly a one-off.

Marxists, on the other hand, theorized for the first time the idea that Fascism was neither something distinct from capitalist society nor the exclusive property of Italy, nor that it was locked in any particular time-bracket. In 1914 Mussolini, who had been a Marxist himself, was ejected from the Italian Socialist Party and founded a newspaper calling for Italian entry into the First World War. His ex-colleagues in the Socialist Party asked: 'Who is paying you?' Answering this question, with a variety of shades and subtleties, remained for Marxists the key to understanding Fascism. Fascism was not a different 'ism' but a different route that capitalism might travel before its final demise. The challenge presented by the working classes to the capitalist system meant that in periods of crisis 'normal' capitalist states might have to adopt exceptional strategies to ensure their survival. Fascism moved beyond liberalism (the traditional political expression of the capitalist classes) it is true, but it also destroyed any threat to the socio-economic order posed by the left, and the former was the price that had to be paid for the great benefits accrued due to the latter. So Mussolini was paid by the Italian bourgeoisie. Fascism was therefore akin to a declaration of martial law, something that all liberal democracies provide for in their constitutions, suspending the freedoms that capitalist society usually allowed. Fascism was worse than liberalism but very much its sibling – if not its Mr Hyde. Placing Hitler's Germany alongside Italy, as the two dictators themselves sometimes liked to do, was logical. Fascism could crop up anywhere outside the socialist world: it was, in the official communist definition of the 1930s, 'the open terrorist dictatorship of the most reactionary, most chauvinistic, most imperialistic element of finance capital' (in Payne, 1995: 443). The problem though is how to explain the fact that those who bore the brunt of the 'terrorist' dictatorships seemed to support them.

In Italy interpreting Fascism has been the most tortured historical issue since its demise. While Croce's parenthesis seemed the most logical and acceptable path to rebuild social peace in Italy after 1945, it quickly became apparent that the political divisions that wracked Italy in the post-war era could not just be papered over. For a start, in 1946 Italians had to choose whether Italy should be a republic or a monarchy, and in making this choice had to ask themselves in what ways the king had aided and abetted the Regime. Then, as the wartime anti-Fascist coalitions, which had seen an almost incomprehensible alliance between Churchill and Stalin, broke down internationally, Italy found itself with a cold war raging within its borders. It had the largest communist party in the West from the 1940s to the late 1980s. The real bone of contention, and one that still turns up the heat when it is (and it rarely is not) under review, is the place of anti-Fascist resistance in the recasting of Italy during and immediately after the Second World War.

The Italian Republic is officially founded on the resistance to Fascism. Its constitution was drawn up by all those political forces that had been abolished by Fascism, ranging from liberals to Catholics to communists. The only excluded party was the Fascist one itself. In fact in republican Italy it became illegal to form a Fascist party (although neo-Fascists quite easily skirted this provision). In effect, what the new Italy was stating was that to be Italian and to be a Fascist was not only not tolerable but also not actually possible. To be a Fascist meant being beyond the pale; as it was defined after 1945 you could not be Fascist and Italian. To a lesser degree than was the case in West Germany with regard to Nazism, but nevertheless still implicit in this was a denial that the Regime had had any kind of popular mandate, barring a few of Mussolini's black-shirted henchmen. The resistance had been led by communists, and the vast majority of partisans in the resistance movement had been communists too. Yet after 1947, although never actually banned, the Italian Communist Party was stringently prevented from getting anywhere near the levers of national political power. In the Italian Republic before the 1990s there never was a two-party system. Rather there was one, the Christian Democrats with a variety of smaller allies, which ruled Italy for about twice as long as Mussolini did. The small Catholic participation in the anti-Fascist resistance movement hardly justified this monopoly on power, although the importance of Catholicism's long past in Italy's history did. Nevertheless, even among Catholics there was an assumption that, whatever might have happened after 1947, the need to fight what Italians often call 'Nazi-Fascism' between 1943 and 1945 had prevailed over latent conflicts among Catholics, liberals, non-Fascist conservatives, communists, etc. Italy had been reborn and, although non-communists represented the majority and monopolised power, the communists – in return for what they had done to bring down Fascism – were allowed to operate freely, despite American calls to outlaw them.

It was in these circumstances that Italy's reassessment of its Fascist past took place. As Martin Clark has pointed out, in the 1970s there were in Italy 15 institutions specifically designed to study anti-Fascism and none to study Fascism itself (Clark, 1996: 4), something that suggested that the latter was somebody else's history. The spirit of the communist resistance argued that Fascism had been an instrument of class power that succeeded in mobilizing the petit-bourgeoisie (managers, land-holding peasants, teachers, shop-keepers, etc.) and thereby prevented working-class revolution. Non-Marxist anti-Fascists, on the other hand, argued that Fascism did not have a parti-cular class bias but rather that it represented a revolt against the moderate humanism forged in Europe by social Catholicism and moderate liberalism. As such, Italian Fascism could be bracketed with Soviet communism, and of course Nazism in a totalitarian upsurge that was the product of a tragic loss of traditional values and beliefs. Luigi Sturzo, the founder of Italian political Catholicism, had called Fascism 'Bolshevism of the right' (Burleigh and Wipperman, 1991: 8) and this interpretation still has its adherents. These contradictory outlooks nevertheless did agree on one thing: Fascism was a bad, a terribly bad, thing. This small area of common ground had been enough for the international coalition against the Axis and had united dis-parate anti-Fascists in the resistance period in Italy. Marxists saw Fascism in Italy as having failed to taint the working class; non-Marxists saw institutions such as the Church, the family, or the army as having retained their whole-someness by holding Fascism at arm's length.

It was only in the 1970s, and clearly in reaction to the new left that emerged in Italy in the late 1960s, that a real revision of interpretations of Italian Fascism took place. The student and worker revolts that in Italy are labelled simply il Sessantotto (1968) produced a profound intellectual re-evaluation of Italian culture, politics and society. Many looked back at the resistance period with nostalgia and questioned the democratic credentials of the ruling Christian Democrats. They saw and denounced continuities be-tween Fascism and the Republic and often placed part of the blame on Italy's official Communist Party; it had reined in the spontaneous revolutionary upsurge of the Italian masses and had, in a remake of what the radicals had done during the Risorgimento, handed Italy over to the forces of order, to the Church, to the bosses, the bourgeoisie, to the repressive apparatus of the state. In this way of seeing things, Fascists lurked ominously in Christian Democratic disguises waiting to pounce on and to reverse those democratic rights that the resistance had forced out of the Italian ruling class. The Communist Party had forgotten where its roots lay and had become itself part of the corrupt Italian political system. The common ground that the Republic was founded on was being whittled away.

It was in this context that the work of Renzo De Felice began to have an impact. De Felice began the publication of his biography of Mussolini in the mid 1960s and at his death in 1996 it had spawned more than 6,000 pages of text but was nevertheless unfinished. Without drawing too much attention to the book's many shortcomings, what is important about it is that, in its idiosyncratic way, it attempted to re-evaluate Italian Fascism with regard to the historiography that had emerged in Italy since 1945. The first volumes were not particularly controversial, but as the years passed it became clear that what De Felice was mounting was a campaign against what he regarded as the mistaken (and sinister) canons of anti-Fascism. Perhaps what was most disturbing about his argument was that he attempted not only to split Italian from the more radical and malevolent Fascism of Nazi Germany (he more or less rejected the notion of generic 'fascisms') but he placed the Italian people into a relationship of consent with the Fascist Regime. The arguments of the anti-Fascists that had considered the Regime as one imposed on an unwilling people (which rose up when it got the opportunity) was rejected as little more than left-wing propaganda. Rather, that Italians supported and acted in harmony with what Mussolini wanted was proof that Italian Fascism contained many healthy and commendable ideas. In German history, the widely accepted argument that the majority of Germans were generally supporters of what Nazism stood for has made the Third Reich all the more horrifying and unfathomable. But for Italy this same idea aimed rather at reconstructing Fascism as relatively mild and understandable. Italian Fascism succeeded in pursuing the national interest in a way that neither liberal nor Republican Italy ever managed to do: it fostered positive notions of patriotism and its goals remained within the compass of what constituted Europe's most effective bulwark against a dangerous and inhuman left [**Doc. 12, p. 137**].

In this view Italian Fascism therefore contained and put into practice many of the desires that had been central to the critique of liberal Italy by patriotic nationalists, who often represented a rising and modernizing middle class. Those people who had so often been accused of having failed to take the initiative in modern Italian history were not simply tools in the hands of reactionary capitalists but a dynamic force for the transformation of Italian society. They were not always in control of Fascism but remained an important strand within it that re-emerged in the Nazi-sponsored Italian Social Republic of 1943–5, when Mussolini was able to free himself from many of the compromises made with the monarchy, the army and the Church as the price he paid for power. This view took Fascism's ideas and policies seriously. It also linked them to Mussolini's early career as a socialist,

Corporativism: Means by which Italian society, the economy and politics were supposed to be organized and that was touted as a viable and original 'third way' between liberal capitalism and Soviet-style communism.

suggesting that not only was the notion of a 'third way' (between capitalism and socialism) [**Doc. 31, p. 150**] something that could plausibly be associated with Italian Fascism, but that these policies (**corporativism** instead of class-struggle, for example) resonated with large sections of the Italian people. And the resistance? Received knowledge on this score needed debunking argued De Felice. Why should there have been a resistance if the picture painted suggested a consensual relationship between Italians and the Regime? Mussolini's most important biographer saw the resistance as involving minorities, largely controlled by foreigners and certainly not reflecting the will of the Italian people who, in the difficult period of the Social Republic, tended towards 'wait and seeism' (*attendismo*), favouring neither side in the struggle and in the end getting on the winning bandwagon. De Felice argued that he was judging Fascism 'on its own terms' and that moralizing on its supposed evil nature was not the job of the historian. He contended that Italians should stop regarding Italy's Fascist past with blinkered moral outrage and dispassionately assess Fascism's positive as well as negative achievements.

The idea of anti-Fascism being largely a myth and undermining the notion that Fascism's badness was self-evident attacked some of the fundamental ideas sustaining Italian historical identity in the Republic, but in many ways the 'establishment' De Felice attacked was something of a straw man. The Italian university system was certainly not full of anti-Fascists and the 'hegemony of the left' had little to sustain it until the influx of new left-leaning faculties in Italian universities after 1968. De Felice's was not so much an attack on fellow Italian academics – who, as Philip Morgan points, out were mostly very much like himself (Morgan, 2004: 7) – but on the general way of viewing Italian anti-Fascism as a new beginning, no matter how flawed that new beginning might have been perceived to be. Perhaps most characteristic of De Felice's work is his attempt to create a national narrative that, as Trevelyan had put it, 'ratified' not anti-Fascism, or foreign ideologies or powers, but the interests of an Italy understood in the traditional terms of nationalist discourse. Necessarily, it was after Fascism that this positive nationalism went awry.

Many historians and commentators in Italy now follow De Felice's lead. With the break-up of the old party system in the 1990s, and with the relative decline of widespread Catholic and communist subcultures, it has become increasingly acceptable to suggest that Fascism did not symbolize everything wrong with Italian history. Ernesto Galli Della Loggia, perhaps the loudest voice in this school, argues, for example, with regard to democracy, possibly the most vital element of post-1945 Italy's self-justification with respect to Fascism, that if Italian democracy was seriously comparable to that of any other country:

it would have to stand in roughly a half way position between anti-
Fascism and anti-Communism . . . but this has had to be avoided in Italy
. . . anti-Communism has had to be deprived of any democratic legitim-
acy and the only antagonist to democracy must be Fascism, there is
Fascism and there is 'anti-Fascist' democracy to which, [supposedly]
Communism fully belongs.

                                        (Galli Della Loggia, 1996: 121)

Fascism's anti-communist credentials (and it did ally with other forces from
liberal to Catholic in this regard in the period after the First World War)
should be taken seriously and regarded as part of mainstream European culture and politics in this flammable and difficult period. It might have been
undemocratic, but it needed to be to combat that other implacable enemy of
democracy, communism. While Galli Della Loggia's view on this can be
regarded as something of an extreme example of how Fascism is being talked
about now, it does reflect a much wider desire to bring Fascism into the
acceptable fold of national history, or at least to allow it as much (if not sometimes more) legitimacy as the 'anti-Fascist' Republic that followed its demise.

It would be a mistake, however, to suggest that De Felice and his follow-
ers have made a clean sweep of the board. The Australian historian Richard
Bosworth, to take the most important recent example, remains highly critical of De Felician 'revisionism' and its offshoots. According to Bosworth, the
old idea of Italian Fascism as a profoundly inhuman, anti-democratic and
reactionary political regime stands. It was always prepared to use violence in
pursuit of its ambitions, and hundreds of thousands of premature deaths of
some Italians – but mostly of Slavs, Greeks and Africans – are its appalling
legacy. Mussolini was no 'sawdust Caesar' and his Regime no joke. But nor
was the latter a dictatorship comparable in its brutality to Hitler's or Stalin's,
although it should still, Bosworth argues, be held as a precursor and sibling
to the former. Nevertheless, the Regime's pretence at totalitarianism should
be regarded with circumspection. Bosworth is highly critical of those, most
notably Emilio Gentile, who look at Fascism's rhetoric and from it come to
conclusions about Regime, people, consensus or whatever. He is also critical
of those who look at the Italian experience of Fascism solely on the strength
of what people, from party bosses to lowly postmen, said, the uniforms
they wore or the rallies they attended. This wrongly accepts at face value the
choreography the Regime itself concocted. Reality was much more complicated. In Italy (unlike in Germany) the Italian people were not 'working
towards the Duce' but very often, Bosworth argues, it was the other way
around (Bosworth, 2002: 10–11). The picture is one of an Italy in which
Fascism was engulfed by the much greater and ultimately temperate weight
of the myriad experiences of Italian history and civilization. Like Trevelyan,

Bosworth is fascinated by the problem of Fascism's attempt to 'bully Italians into [being] second rate Germans' and more broadly therefore the complex way in which the novel and despicable dictatorships of Europe's twentieth century insinuated (or failed to insinuate) themselves into the age-old social and moral order that European peoples had constructed generation upon generation. Profoundly aware of the political battles raging in post-1945 Italy, Bosworth (1998) nevertheless extricates himself from them and invests in Italy's history, as Trevelyan himself and so many historians before him had done, to further an understanding of the history of us all.

Part 2

MUSSOLINI AND ITALIAN
FASCISM

3

The Origins of Italian Fascism, 1870–1917

LIBERAL ITALY AND ITS DISCONTENTS

When dealing with liberal Italy (1870–1922) it is difficult not to appraise it according to the knowledge of its eventual transformation into Fascism. This 'revelation' thesis has been constructed by authors such as Antonio Gramsci and the British historian Denis Mack Smith (Mack Smith, 1958). In this way of seeing things one must reveal the defects, shortcomings, peculiarities or faults within liberal Italian society, its political culture, its economy or whatever, in order to shunt Italy on to the track that inevitably leads to Fascism. It is true that liberal Italy did eventually spawn Fascism, but it is also true that in the inter-war period much of continental Europe, if it did not adopt out-and-out 'Fascism', turned to some form of authoritarian government. To see liberal Italy as a born failure is a mistake. In the first place, the raw material it had to deal with was not ideal. Before the First World War Italy was shot through with social, economic, regional and political fractures [**Doc. 26, p. 147**], but then in the Europe of this period, where was this not the case? Yet liberal Italy came through the massive effort required to fight the First World War without disintegrating; it performed creditably on the battlefield, and defeated Austria-Hungary, the traditional enemy of Italian unity.

The 'liberalism' of liberal Italy was far more suffused with the moderate monarchism of Britain than the radicalism of republican France. The Italian king maintained much power. He had personal control over the military and could be extremely influential in determining Italian foreign policy. He was also a key figure in the liberal political system as the nominator of the prime minister, no trifling matter as governments could (in theory at least) function without parliamentary majorities. Royal decrees had the force of law, and the Italian upper house, the Senate, was appointed directly by the king. At times of crisis, the king's prerogative could take the place of normal parliamentary government and on occasion (for example, in 1898 after serious rioting in Milan and other cities, and most notably at Mussolini's fall in 1943) an army commander was given effective political power. But it would be going too far to see the Italian monarchy as an autocracy that merely tolerated truncated forms of liberal democracy in what may have been the case in pre-1914 Germany, let alone Russia. The king was the symbolic head of the classes of people that had attached the rest of Italy to Piedmont. These were men, entrenched in local networks of power, patronage and influence, who had been prepared to switch their loyalties from Italy's old ruling royal families (Italian or foreign) to the new Piedmontese order, but who had also expected to be rewarded by economic security, physical protection from insurgencies, and the preservation of their local economic and political control. These were the men who gave themselves (and no one else) the vote at unification and quite naturally never needed to group themselves into political parties. They were all 'liberals', but not members of a liberal party with a defined leadership and structure; parliament was an expression of their collective will and the notorious fluidity of political groupings in the Italian parliament (**trasformismo**) was the reflection not of serious divisions amongst this small and select elite but of an overall consensus for the post-unification status quo. This consensus, however, rested on the exclusion of the vast majority of the Italian people from participation in the parliamentary political process. At best, certainly until the decade before the Great War, Italy's political system can be regarded as an oligarchy, and parliament was only a dim reflection of the true social, economic and political conflicts raging throughout the peninsula.

Trasformismo: 'Transformism'. A pejorative word denoting the fluidity of political groupings in the Italian parliament before 1922 and the willingness of parliamentary oppositions to support governments in exchange for patronage and political influence.

The vast majority of the Italian people was, for this oligarchy, a difficult proposition. Peasant, illiterate, over-abundant, Catholic, rebellious, hungry, criminal, culturally and linguistically fragmented; just to contain (let alone transform) such a morass was a daunting prospect. If the social status quo had to be maintained (something Italy's elites held very dearly), this was to happen without its time-honoured foundations: Catholicism, absolutism, foreign rule and economic stagnation. Modernization had to happen, but without its possible political consequences, and, by the later years of the nineteenth century, the latter did not just mean reactionary Catholicism or radical republicanism but also socialism. Therefore, on the one hand the mass of the Italian people was excluded from the political process; on the other it was expected to participate in Italian social and economic life. Italians were expected to work hard, pay taxes, go to school, be conscripted in the Italian army, and learn what it meant to be a citizen.

The construction of this lop-sided consensus took a wide variety of forms and consisted in a full-scale attempt to transform (or to 'make') Italians. Most importantly the people had to be able to access Italian written culture and the country's disparate economies required integration. Between 1870 and 1914 this integration meant anything from commissioning topographical studies of the peninsula, the adoption of standard weights and measures, a unified currency and legal system to the setting up of statistical collecting agencies to count Italians and what they did, the integration and expansion of the railway network (see Schram, 1997; Patriarca, 1995), administrative integration and the construction of a bureaucracy in provincial cities and of course in Rome. The Piedmontese police force was expanded to the whole of Italy and a prefectural system for the control of law and order in the provinces (following the French model) was put into place. Liberal Italy also created a national education system out of the vast number of already existing, mostly religious, establishments. Its main job, at the elementary level, was to teach Italians to speak Italian and to read and write, and it proved modestly successful.

Being able to read and write meant that it became possible to understand the messages transmitted by books such as Edmondo De Amicis' ultra patriotic *Cuore* (Italy's bestseller throughout the liberal period) [**Doc. 1, p. 130**]. It became more and more possible to come into full contact with emerging national culture: school textbooks [**Doc. 27, p. 148**], for example, glorified Italy's *Risorgimento*, Italy's Roman and renaissance past, plotted national aspirations and reiterated the perceived achievements of the country since unification. They showered praise on the monarchy and bore witness to Italy's supposed reacquisition of military prowess; they romanticized Italy's colonial ventures and depicted Italy as a new and dynamic nation seeking a place in the world, inferior to none and contending for primacy in the club of Europe's civilized nations.

But with the expansion of this national patriotic culture, dissent and disappointment also modernized and in many ways offered alternative readings of the Italian nation. For the liberals consensus proved elusive, mostly because economic development, which was actually considerable, was nevertheless unable to ensure most normal Italians an adequate standard of living. Emigration statistics for the years before the First World War bear out how poverty stricken Italy really was. Between 1870 and 1910 more than 10 million Italians left the peninsula, never to return, and many millions more spent prolonged periods working in other national economies. Being an organ grinder or shoeshine boy in New York or Paris ensured a better standard of living than being a peasant in the Veneto or Sicily. Italy's population totalled 35 million in 1914; it had stood at 25 million in 1861. Adding also the 10 million who emigrated permanently means that the population almost doubled in this period and that a rise in gross domestic product was likely to be absorbed without seriously amending living standards. Throughout the

period covered by this book Italy remained essentially an agricultural economy and one that was relatively backward and poor compared to much of
Europe [**Docs. 21, 25, pp. 144, 147**]. To use a label of the times, it was the
persistence of 'the social question' that ensured continuous political dissent,
and that meant many Italians did not see liberal Italy as somewhere in which
they could feel at home and at ease. Many left, but others felt that an alternative Italy would provide what the liberals had failed to provide. One of the
latter was born at Predappio near the small town of Forlì in the Romagna
region, into a working class but comfortably off family in 1883. He was
named by his socialist father Benito (after Benito Juarez, the Mexican revolutionary) Amilcare (after Cipriani, the Italian anarchist who had fought for the
Paris Commune) Andrea (after Andrea Costa, the first socialist to enter the
Italian parliament) Mussolini.

As his names suggest, Mussolini was brought up in an ambience of
opposition to the liberal verities passed down by the Italian state. Socialism
was emerging as a powerful force in Italian society in the decade before 1900
and represented an alternative to both liberal nationalism and the Christian
monarchism that still had its adherents throughout Europe. Even before the
quantum leap of Fascism, Mussolini was to move from the moderate socialism of his father, to its radical and revolutionary variety; he was to be
attracted by syndicalism, aspects of anarchism, and understood the power
of popular and radical nationalism. Other forces of opposition to the liberal
political system would also be important in Mussolini's formation. These
were, in particular, what could be called Italy's 'new' nationalism, as well as
the force of the traditional dissatisfied nationalism of the liberal era: irredent-
ism aspired to 'complete unification' by absorbing into Italy those territories
with Italian speakers still under Austrian rule. The 'new' Italian nationalism
had its roots in a series of intellectual journals published, for the most part
in Florence, at the beginning of the century. Enrico Corradini, who became
the leader of the Nationalist Association before the war, transposed Marx's
notion of class struggle into the sphere of international relations. Italy, he
maintained, was the 'proletarian' nation [**Doc. 4, p. 132**]. To break out of its
situation of poverty underdevelopment and 'mediocrity' it needed a new
moral consciousness and a refusal of the pragmatic brokerage that was a
central requirement of liberal democracy. Other opposition groups, like the
artistic movement of the Futurists, intellectuals who glorified war, speed and
modernity, also contributed to the general disaffection many people felt
towards the liberal state and the promises it had not fulfilled [**Doc. 3, p. 131**].

Between 1902 and 1904 Benito Mussolini, secondary-school educated
and a qualified primary school teacher, lived in Switzerland; in this period
his political career can be said to have begun. His 'genetic' sympathy for
socialism had already become a tradition in his native Romagna, and was

immediately given over to its more intransigent brand which would, hoped Mussolini in 1902, 'return to its old methods of struggle, demonstrate its implacable hostility to all constituted authority without, whatever [socialist] congresses or deliberations might decide, ever coming to terms or selling out' (in De Felice, 1965: 29) From Switzerland Mussolini returned to Italy and, after a stint in Trent (an Italian town under Austrian rule) as Socialist Party secretary, threw himself into the radical politics of his native Romagna. Here he became well-known as an uncompromising young radical, rejecting any form of socialist collaboration with the liberal state, and it was to be this intransigence that propelled him to fame and prominence within the socialist movement. The launch by **Giovanni Giolitti** (Italian prime minister on and off in the two decades before 1914) of a military campaign against the Ottoman Empire for the acquisition of a colony in North Africa (it would eventually be called Libya) in 1911 was the occasion in which Mussolini emerged from the local politics of his region to centre-stage. Giolitti's thrust for colonies sought to satisfy many of his critics: nationalists who accused him of lacking virility and some socialists who were convinced that colonialism might solve aspects of Italy's social question. But none of these ideas swayed the young Mussolini. He was one of the most outspoken critics of what, he believed, was a ploy to divert the working class from its real interests. Yet in war, contradictions might emerge that would benefit the revolutionary socialist cause: 'war between nations will become a war between classes' he sloganned (De Felice, 1965: 105) [**Doc. 5, p. 00**]. The general strike that took place against the war and that the future *Duce* organized in the Romagna was very successful and he saw it as a proof of the wisdom of his extreme approach. Yet, as far as Giolitti was concerned, the war achieved many things. Although the effective occupation of Libya was to take decades, in the eyes of the world Italy had won a war, reversed the humiliation of its defeat by the Ethiopians at Adowa in 1896 and, as Croce so approvingly put it,

> was no longer what she had been fifteen years before, but was now able and ready to organize a military expedition and carry it through to victory [. . . the Libyan war] gave proof of the unanimity of national feeling, which in the [Ethiopian] war had been hesitating and divided.
>
> (Croce, 1928: 261–2) [**Doc. 4, p. 132**].

Clearly Mussolini was fighting in the opposite direction and for a while intransigence in the Italian Socialist Party (PSI – *Partito Socialista Italiano*) swept all before it.

From the platform of his rejection of Italian imperialism Mussolini launched a successful attack on the PSI leadership which saw him become

Giovanni Giolitti (1842–1928): Liberal prime minister of Italy on many occasions before Fascism's rise to power. He formed electoral alliances with rising Fascism and hoped to constitutionalize the Fascist movement. He was sidelined on the creation of the Dictatorship but remained in parliament until his death.

Partito Socialista Italiano (PSI): The Italian Socialist Party, from which Mussolini was expelled in 1914. It became, after the First World War, the largest political party in Italy, but collapsed in the face of the Fascist challenge. Outlawed during the Regime, it was far less effective than the Italian Communist Party in maintaining an underground presence; after 1945 its popular support gradually passed to the communists.

Avanti!: The official organ of the Italian Socialist Party (PSI). It was edited by Mussolini between 1912 and the first months of the First World War.

editor of **Avanti!**, the official newspaper of the Socialist Party and Italy's first real national daily, and gain a place on the party executive. The struggle against reformism swung his way because of the realization among many members of the PSI that Giolitti's concessions and his colonial war had changed little in the situation of the workers at grassroots level. But what Mussolini was to discover in his years as editor of *Avanti!* was that between intransigent socialism and actual revolution gaped a huge abyss. He opened up the pages of *Avanti!* to eminent syndicalists and started an intellectual journal appropriately labelled *Utopia*. Yet, although throughout this period (1912–14) he was able to radicalize some parts of the party, he never acquired enough support to expel reformists altogether, nor to actually set the revolution's date. As usual, the actual class struggle meant strikes, agitation, concessions and the occasional *eccidio* (the police killing protesters or strikers), but there was no real revolutionary breakthrough. This tense situation ensued for two years, saw Mussolini's *Avanti!* double its readership, but entailed no substantial change in the unfolding of the class struggle; this was the case even when the dream of revolution in Italy appeared about to come true. The 'Red Week' of June 1914 was sparked off by a series of police killings in response to strikes and agitations in the Marche and Romagna. Throughout Italy, economic hardship, poor working conditions and the militancy that had emerged over Italy's Libyan war were ignited in many places into a full-scale revolt. In Rome barricades were thrown up, in the Romagana whole areas became police no-go areas, in some cases officers were 'arrested' by revolutionary groups, and throughout Italy a spontaneous general strike was called and adhered to. In many places the government was forced to declare martial law. If the revolt had a leader it was the anarchist Errico Malatesta and not the revolutionary socialists, including Mussolini. The decision to turn the spontaneity of 'Red Week' into a full-scale socialist revolution was never taken and the struggle remained divided and factional. The government held on, used force in some areas, parleyed in others and made concessions in yet others, but saw the moment through.

From Mussolini's point of view, 'Red Week' was the greatest achievement and disappointment of his guidance of the PSI. It was the high point of radical class struggle in Italy before the war, but for a revolutionary of Mussolini's ilk its conclusion in a *status quo ante bellum* was an abysmal failure. He knew that without an actual revolutionary takeover of power even the mass-mobilization and mass-violence of 'Red Week' could achieve very little except reformist concessions from the government, which themselves had the tendency to stabilize class relationships. On the whole, the PSI remained distant and cut off from the centres of violence and action and was forced to follow events rather than directing them and bringing them to a more serious conclusion. The socialist trade union organization, the

Confederazione Generale del Lavoro, was instrumental in bringing 'Red Week' to an ignominious conclusion. Although in the pages of *Avanti!* Mussolini hailed 'Red Week' as the beginning of the end of capitalist Italy, it was also clear for many that rebellion, general strikes and revolutionary 'myths' were not the same thing as revolution.

INTERVENTIONISM

Only a few days after 'Red Week' the Sarajevo assassination took place. It was a crucial moment in the career of Mussolini as well as of so many of his generation. Mussolini's inability to transform 'Red Week' into an actual revolution had left him perplexed as to what was needed – what 'myths' were required – to mobilize the proletariat in an attack that would topple Giolitti's hated political system. The first thing that happened when the European powers went to war was the collapse of the Socialist International. No European socialist party had called the working class out in a general strike against the war and the German SPD (by far Europe's most powerful socialist party) had in early August 1914 unanimously voted its government war credits; the French followed suit. Socialist workers were aligned by their parties behind the war effort of each European government and socialist internationalism revealed itself to be a myth. But the situation in Italy proved to be radically different.

As the Russians, Germans, Austrians, British and French all marched to war, the other supposed Great Power remained on the sidelines. Italy had been bound by treaty to Germany and Austria but had also signed a series of accords and made unofficial promises to the British and French that it was unlikely that Italy would go to war on the side of Austria or Germany. In reality Italy remained substantially outside the Great Power system. The conflict, as it unfolded in July 1914, was not particularly threatening to Italy. Austria hardly wanted to stir up old rivalries with its southern neighbour as it faced a titanic struggle against Russia for control of the Balkans and Germany braced itself for a bid to control the European landmass north of the Alps. What was in it for Italy? It could stick to its Triple Alliance partners (Germany and Austria) and take Corsica and Nice as 'unredeemed' Italian territory, or it could on the other hand turn against the Central Powers and redeem Trent and Trieste. Colonial expansion might be favoured by joining either side, although it seemed very unlikely that British naval hegemony in the Mediterranean could be seriously challenged by Italy. The fact that there was no obvious side on which Italy felt compelled to join was a clear sign of its international inconsequence. That the Central Powers had not included Italy in their plans, although an ally, also made this all too clear. The only possible logic, in the end, of keeping to its alliance partners was the likelihood of them winning, but after the battle of the Marne in September 1914 it was clear that this was not going to be a repeat of Prussia's easy victories at the expense of France in 1870. The Italian government, headed by Salandra (although Giolitti still maintained a majority in parliament, which, however, was in recess) therefore simultaneously declared Italian neutrality and opened up bids to the belligerents for Italian involvement or non-involvement. In practice neutrality was doing the Central Powers a favour as they were already coping with two fronts and it became quickly apparent that Austria would probably be prepared to offer 'quite a lot' (in Giolitti's notorious phrase) for Italian neutrality. But as Russian offensives ground to a halt in the Carpathians, the Central Powers felt less inclined to give away bits of Austrian territory to keep Italy out. In the event, Italy joined the Allies and a secret treaty guaranteed it the 'unredeemed' areas of the Habsburg Empire, a share in the redistribution of Germany's colonies and in the break-up of what remained of the Ottoman Empire. The Allies had the advantage of promising Italy what was not theirs.

The time lag between the outbreak of war and Italy's joining it was to be of fundamental importance in defining political struggle in Italy far beyond 1918. David Stevenson has rightly noted that Italy's entry into the war was unique in being preceded by a domestic crisis (Stevenson, 2005: 112). For example, in France and in Germany immediate belligerence meant that a consensus of political forces (including socialists, liberals, Catholics and the right) was achieved almost unexpectedly. The *union sacrée* or *Burgfrieden* (a sinking of all political difference under the banner of the fatherland in danger) of the first few months of the war in France and Germany coincided in Italy with this unique political crisis and the failure to construct a political consensus at Italy's eventual entry was to have profound repercussions.

As has been suggested, at the outbreak of war Giolitti's majority liberals saw no reason why Italy should become involved, at least not immediately. The recent granting of a wider suffrage and national insurance schemes, growing industrial production, the shock waves of 'Red Week' and financial exhaustion due to the Libyan war all called for a period of consolidation where their far-reaching implications might find a viable equilibrium. Giolitti's carefully constructed parliamentary majority, his success in having brought some moderate socialists and Catholics into the political fold, and his continued reliance on the precarious votes of his southern supporters meant that from the outset war did not appear, as it did in other European countries, as a solution to profound internal and external problems.

In the country at large this was also very much the case. Catholics had only very recently directly entered the Italian political fray. For them a patriotic war behind a liberal government against ultra-Catholic Austria held no particular attraction. Pope Benedict XV was famously to describe the Great War as a 'useless slaughter' that pitted Catholic against Catholic. The PSI too, possibly for the first time, found itself in general agreement with the government. For a while Italian socialists were able to avoid the tortuous choice between the fatherland and internationalist principles faced by other socialist parties. Like the Church, the PSI separated its faithful from the Italian state but at the same time did not require them to stand against it; 'neither adherence nor sabotage' was the PSI's slogan throughout the war. This stance entailed a strange congruence with the majority liberals who, even after war was declared, looked on the PSI with some circumspection, and it was possibly this idiosyncratic nature of Italy's experience that not only pushed Mussolini into a permanent break with the Italian Socialist Party, but that began the odd coalescence of forces that was to form the nucleus of post-war Fascism.

Who, then, wanted war? The actual decision to join the conflagration was made by a remarkably small number of men. Parliament was not consulted and even most of the military were unaware that negotiations were going on between the Italian government and the *Entente* concerning the terms of Italy's entry into the war. Prime Minister Antonio Salandra (who had been regarded as a stop-gap between two Giolittian governments) and Foreign Minister Sydney Sonnino negotiated with the *Entente* (Britain, France and Russia) and made the decisions. The Treaty of London (signed in April 1915), in exchange for Italian belligerence, promised Italy vast tracts of Austrian and Turkish territory, as well as a say in the redistribution of German colonies.

The clamour for Italy to become involved in the war had begun with the assassination at Sarajevo. The nationalists of Corradini were willing to consider remaining true to the Triple Alliance: war was war and it was surely the energetic young German nation that was taking on the decrepit old nations of France and Britain. But it was the desire for entering the war on the side of France that accumulated the most adherents. Italian republican volunteers were already fighting on the western front in December 1914 under the leadership of Peppino Garibaldi (the great man's grandson). 'Irrendentists' saw the opportunity to realize their aims of joining the Italian-speaking parts of the Habsburg Empire to Italy. The **interventionists** also included men like Gabriele D'Annunzio, Futurist artists and many student and non-Catholic youth groups. They believed war would lift Italy out of Giolittian mediocrity, as the Libyan war had begun to do, and launch it on to a trajectory of glory and power. D'Annunzio, already a famous poet, hedonist, womanizer and arch-poseur, stood against all things that smacked of compromise as far as Italy's honour was concerned; he headed back home from Paris at the

Interventionists: Cross-party political movement calling for Italian intervention in the Great War during Italy's period of neutrality (August 1914–May 1915).

outbreak of war and gave all his support and his considerable propaganda skills to the interventionist campaign. It was in Paris, too, that the Italian Futurists had launched their diatribe against the Italy of museums, tourism, guidebooks and the crushing weight of its past. Mandolin playing was, in the opinion of many Italians of the chattering classes, an embarrassment to be ruthlessly repressed. The Futurists adulated 'speed' and the crackle of machine-gun fire [**Doc. 3, p. 131**]. Like D'Annunzio, Marinetti, the Futurists' founder, hurried to Italy in 1914 and pushed for its entry into the war. Many Futurists were to die in the trenches, as they exchanged their pens and paint-brushes for shells and shrapnel.

On the left of the political spectrum many syndicalists, who Mussolini had been in contact with for years, also desired Italian entry. Filippo Corridoni was a typical revolutionary of this ilk. He looked on the outbreak of war from the prison in which he was held for revolutionary activity, as one that the Italian proletariat could not just sit out. But he also felt that, with war, the popular classes could not rise beyond their own limited and blink-ered economic interests [**Doc. 7, p. 134**]. Mussolini himself, did not, at first, turn away from the official stance of the PSI. As editor of *Avanti!* he carefully maintained the official line of the party, threatening the government should it actually bring Italy into the war. Indeed, the official document stating the PSI's position with regard to the war was written by Mussolini himself and even after his 'conversion' remained the official PSI policy document throughout the war. But it was precisely because the Giolittian majority and the PSI's outlook dovetailed over this issue that the future *Duce's* discomfort began to emerge. He knew that Giolitti's system was satisfied with neutrality because it depended on a precarious stability that would be torn apart by war. Only the 'national' syndicalists and the nationalists had understood this fact and in the end it was logical that Mussolini should join them in calling for intervention. The revolution was certainly not going to come in opposi-tion to the war for the simple fact that the liberal majority did not want it. Had Italy intervened on the side of the central powers, as the Triple Alliance demanded, Mussolini would have remained a revolutionary socialist.

In what was to be his last important article for *Avanti!* Mussolini spelled out the reasons why he believed the PSI should move from what he called 'absolute' to 'relative' neutrality. To begin with he argued that the PSI's neutrality had never been absolute; there had always been a tacit preference for the *Entente*. Belgium's fighting for its 'freedom' from German aggression should not have attracted the overwhelming if passive sympathy of the Italian left. If Belgium had a right to exist then it followed that socialists should support that country's war against Germany and join the great European socialists who had rallied to the cause of the *Entente*. Once it was accepted that there could be a right side and a wrong one, according to Mussolini, it followed that the PSI should push for Italian intervention on the side of good, i.e. the *Entente*.

Mussolini's party comrades refused his logic and the PSI remained true to its neutralist position. The future *Duce* was accused of treachery and collaboration with the warmongering bourgeoisie and he retorted by blaming the party directorate for never having been revolutionary enough. At a meeting called in Bologna on the day after the *Avanti!* article (19 October 1914) the party directorate heard Mussolini's argument that 'I would understand absolute neutrality if you had the courage to go all the way, that is to provoke an insurrection, but this possibility has been discounted by you *a priori*' (OO VI: 406). The future *Duce* believed he had made the most revolutionary and socialist decision and it was the spineless Giolittian bourgeoisie backed up by an equally supine PSI who feared Italian entry into war. The new newspaper Mussolini was to launch a month later, *Il Popolo d'Italia*, was still 'socialist', as it proclaimed on its masthead, but although he failed to convince any other prominent PSI activists he also stated to his old comrades (at the turbulent meeting in Milan when he was expelled him from the party) that 'you only hate me now because you love me . . . and that although my membership card is being torn up, my socialist faith is not being taken away and you will never stop me fighting for the socialist cause and for the revolution' (OO VI: 40–1).

Il Popolo d'Italia: Interventionist newspaper founded in Milan by Mussolini on his ejection from the Socialist Party in 1914. It became the official organ of the Fascist movement and the semi-official voice of the Regime.

THE GREAT WAR AND ITS AFTERMATH

Mussolini was now on his own as far as the official Socialist Party in Italy was concerned, but the abandonment of one set of comrades did not mean political ignominy. He was greeted with open arms by many others and was counted as a superb catch by the warmongering camp, although interventionists of Salandra's ilk felt that Italy's entry should be exclusively a decision of the executive (whose orders the populace should obey without question) and not the result of the socialistic rabble-rousing at which Mussolini was such a dab hand. However, there was enough common ground to warrant unspoken alliances, and if people like D'Annunzio could pack theatres and piazzas without the help of the future orchestrator of 'oceanic' crowds, what Mussolini had was his newspaper; and it was around the latter that interventionist coalitions could be formed. Apart from the now utterly detested Germans and Austrians, Giolitti was the main enemy, as was the official Socialist Party, but Salandra's government seemed more likely to bring Italy into the conflict and was therefore more leniently treated. Along with men like De Ambris and Michele Bianchi, the first *fasci d'azione rivoluzionaria* were

formed, uniting some of Mussolini's left-wing interventionists but avoiding
the creation of a new political party. As would be the case for Fascism after
the war, this wanted to be a catchall that comprehended the left's many factions over the war issue. Its manifesto stated 'Not to cooperate in the victory
of the [the powers that fight for freedom] will benefit the other side.
Revolutionaries have no choice but . . . to take up the cause of the European
revolution against barbarism, authoritarianism, militarism, German feudal-
ism and perfidious Austrian Catholicism' (OO VII: 118–19). *Il Popolo d'Italia*
took the line that it was the great desire of the Italian people to join the
conflict and it was the PSI who no longer understood the former's 'infallible
intuition [that] distinguishes between wars and wars' (OO VII: 122). Like so
many socialists of his generation, in the raging of hatred for Germany and
Austria, Mussolini no longer saw the revolution exclusively in terms of class
but now assigned progressive and regressive roles to particular nations. From
here, some hesitated at joining with out-and-out nationalists; others, and this
was eventually to be the case for Mussolini, cleaved to them in an embrace
that was to be final.

But the martial spirit of the Italian people could be found in the pages of
Il Popolo d'Italia much more easily than in the streets, and if Mussolini had
failed to bring about a revolution by resting his case on the traditional concerns of the working classes he was equally unsuccessful using his newly discovered 'myths'. On the whole there was no widespread desire for Italian
intervention. However, as has been said, this did not mean that Italy did not
enter the war. The traditional diplomacy of the Italian elites brought the
country into the conflict and, like everybody, barring a minuscule group of
diplomats and policy-makers, Mussolini had no idea what the secret clauses
of the Treaty of London stated. Although many (including Mussolini) were to
claim that Italian entry was brought about by a pro-war popular consensus
that had finally coalesced in May 1915 ('the radiant days of May'), the
Giolittians, the Catholics and socialists stood firm on their old positions.
Mussolini wrote on the day Italy finally declared war: 'The working class
masses are convinced of this war's necessity and holiness . . . to you Mother
Italy, we offer our life and our death' (OO VII: 419). Many were still to be
convinced that the decision was the right one.

The Great War can be divided into two as far as Italy is concerned: that
which took place from intervention in May 1915 to the Italian defeat of
Caporetto in October 1917, and then the post-Caporetto year to the final
victory. Richard Bosworth has labelled the former 'Liberal and dynastic' and
the latter 'popular and national' (Bosworth, 2005: ch. 2–3) to point out that
there was something of a character shift in the conflict and in the way it was
envisaged in Italy in these two time periods. The first was a war that rested
on the Treaty of London, decided by elites and searching for territorial

expansion; the second was one of national defence, which pitted the entire resources (physical and psychological) of the nation in the outcome of the struggle. The 'dynastic' war itself went more or less in the same way as the all-too familiar stalemate on the western front, except that instead of the corpses being strewn in the mud-choked fields of Flanders they collected in the crevices and jagged precipices of the Alps. There were, for example, 12 battles of *Isonzo* with none achieving much, and some peaks changed hands dozens of times. But when the line did finally break it was the Italian one that did so.

After two and a half years of stalemate and hundreds of thousands of casualties the Italian front gave way in October 1917. The disintegration of Russia in that same month provided the Central Powers with the opportunity to plan and execute a knockout blow on the southern front, and a gigantic offensive passing through Caporetto was immensely successful. Germans and Austrians cascaded into the Po Valley and Italians retreated deep into their own territory. Udine, the residence of the Italian High Command, was taken and Venice looked like it was about to return to the Habsburgs. In total there were 40,000 dead, 280,000 Italian prisoners were taken, and 350,000 Italian soldiers simply fled in disorder. In just a few days, much of the Italian military edifice that had swollen to huge proportions over the past two years burst like a bubble. Caporetto left behind it a poisonous legacy that even the final victory over Austria did not cure. Had Italians done their duty on that day? Had they simply given up? Were all the values that they were fighting for of no consequence in the face of a determined enemy? Had the war, fought for king and country, for territorial acquisition and dynastic prestige, for the greater glory of the *Patria*, been, in the eyes of the peasant soldiers who cast their weapons (and the Italian flag) into the nearest crevice, nothing but humbug? Caporetto might be taken as a sign that Italian unity, under the aegis of liberalism, had failed [**Doc. 8, p. 134**].

The dynastic war had physically wounded Mussolini in an artillery exercise. He survived and now had the added kudos of battle scars, even if they had been the result of friendly fire. Like Hitler, who was to receive the news of Germany's surrender in November 1918 in a hospital bed, Mussolini was in convalescence when Caporetto happened. *Il Popolo d'Italia* had continued to publish during his stint in the trenches, but it now lacked the punch it had in the interventionist period. Mussolini and what his newspaper stood for worked much better when fulminating against internal enemies, or with a grand (and rebellious) project to give it some fire, but in the first years of war, as has been said, it printed hate against the external foe and continued its anti-PSI stance, but in practice the exigencies of winning the conflict meant pulling together with the official backers of the Italian war effort. De Felice argues that Mussolini's abandonment of socialism only really took place after

Caporetto (De Felice, 1965: 392). But it was already clear to the future *Duce* before then that, to win the war, the interests of the working classes had to be suppressed in favour of national unity and that therefore his view of what constituted the political way forward for Italy had already changed dramatically. With Caporetto this conviction was doubly confirmed. From now on Mussolini was, according to De Felice, no longer merely a propagandist for intervention, an able agitator of the left whose political possibilities remained circumscribed, but a mature politician capable of forging alliances with a whole variety of forces that transcended the restricted milieu in which he had been immersed since his youth. The new path adopted by Mussolini at this point was that which led to the fashioning of the political alliance between moderate liberals (including Giolitti) and the social and economic forces they represented in Italian society in the early 1920s, and the gamut of ex-combatant associations that saw in the year of warfare after Caporetto the locus of their birth, and therefore marked the real beginning of Fascism.

There is no doubt that Caporetto reconfirmed the existence of a major fracture in Italian society. The tens of thousand of Italian soldiers who surrendered to the Austrians, and those who fled, casting aside their arms and wishing for an end to the war (won or lost), were none other than an Italian equivalent of the Russian peasants to whom Lenin promised peace at any price, propelling, thereby, the Bolsheviks to power. But Italy did not go the way of the Tsarist Empire because the liberal regime mustered just enough legitimacy to rally broad swathes of the Italian people to itself, and British and French divisions could be rushed into that theatre of war. But in order to create something of a *Union Sacrèe* in Italy (as had not been the case in 1915) the basis on which the war was being fought needed to be radically altered. This was no longer to be a war of secret treaties (they were in any case no longer secret, since they had been published by the Bolsheviks) but one of national defence, of the rights of national self-determination, and for a deep and lasting renewal of Italy itself. After Caporetto liberal Italy mortgaged itself to the Italian people. The latter fought and won the war, but after the conflict expected repayment, and liberal Italy's failure to honour its debts goes a long way in explaining the crisis that led to Fascism.

4

Fascism as Movement, 1917–21

THE BIRTH OF THE FASCIST MOVEMENT

Closing the breach opened up by Caporetto involved pinpointing and isolating those deemed responsible for it in the first place and constructing a consensus around the need to resist the invader. There were many contenders who fitted the bill for the former: Pope Benedict XV of 'useless slaughter' fame; the rioters who halted production in Turin just before Caporetto and forced the government to occupy the city militarily; Bolshevik sympathizers; the socialists who, even after Caporetto, continued to support neutrality; Catholic peasant movements like that headed by Guido Miglioli, who wrote a book called *Terra non Guerra* (Land not War); the neutralists who were also lurking in parliament; and the threat of a Giolittian majority that always loomed.

Mussolini and *Il Popolo d'Italia* came into its own once again: parliament should be shut down; the pope was an out-and-out traitor; the socialists were German spies. After a moment of deep depression as the enormity of Caporetto sank in, Mussolini found himself propelled back to stardom as the man who might be able to amass widespread support for the war effort. The type of journalism favoured by the future *Duce* was just what was required. When it came to making the war popular the government was at a loss: the old royalist slogans were hardly what the famished peasant soldiers wanted to hear, but the left interventionists were brimming with ideas. For Mussolini the post-war state would belong to the combatants and their staunch allies at home, the 'producers'. Internal enemies would be silenced for good and, as he put it in an article, the war should be given social content. 'Land to the peasants', the future *Duce* wrote in November 1917, 'this is the moment in which the time has come – in order to win the war – to bring the peasantry into the nation's orbit. For the peasant he that says land says Fatherland' (OO X: 57). Miglioli's 'land not war' had become 'victory then land'; the government made rash promises in the terrifying atmosphere of post-Caporetto

Italy, but it had to or the disaster might have engulfed the whole edifice of state and nation, as was happening in Russia.

In the end the Germanic advance was checked. The Piave river became the new front line and, with the entry of the USA into the conflict and the shifting of some British and French divisions to the Italian theatre, Italy was able to hold on as Austria and then Germany cracked under their own internal contradictions. The Italians took advantage of the situation and pressed for victory. The Vittorio Veneto offensive marked the end of Austro-German resistance south of the Alps and concluded the war triumphantly for Italy [Doc. 11, p. 136].

Mussolini's newspaper could justly congratulate itself. It had contributed much to Italy's entry and to maintaining momentum when it flagged after the short-war illusion was dispelled, but most importantly the paper had stood firm after Caporetto and had thus gained the respect of the whole pro-war camp, not just its initial leftist supporters. Mussolini and *Il Popolo d'Italia* were now one of the most important focal points for all the disparate organizations that made the war (and the victory) their most treasured possession. According to their own rhetoric they were the virile Italy of Vittorio Veneto that had stood against the Italy of Caporetto, of the defeatists, the shirkers, the anti-patriots. The newspaper itself dropped the word 'socialist' from its masthead in August 1918 and now stated that it was the organ of 'combatants and producers', which, as Mussolini argued, 'is fundamentally different to saying soldiers and workers . . . "Combatants" means Diaz [the commander of Italy's armed forces] all the way down to the lowliest private . . . and "producers" is all those who work and not just those engaged in manual labour . . . Defending producers means allowing the bourgeoisie to fulfil its historic mission' (OO XI: 243). The enemy was no longer 'the bourgeoisie' as such (as had been the case in Mussolini's now distant socialist days) but 'parasites', who could be socialist, liberal, Catholic or anything else. There now existed a group of hardened war veterans, proud of their victory and in no way tied down to liberal legal niceties with respect to those they regarded as the nation's enemies. Any patriotic deficit, any denigration of the victory, anything that smacked of compromise were watched with clenched fists. In 1918 Mussolini was not the leader of this new caucus, indeed it had none, but he was a significant voice within it and, as always, he had his newspaper. Fascism eventually came to power because the Italian state as embodied in the old liberal order was unable to capitalize on the victory and to become the unimpeachable custodian of the values held so passionately by those who can loosely be called the **Vittorio Veneters [Docs. 9, 10, 11, pp. 135, 135, 136]**.

At the Versailles settlement Italy gained little compared with what it had been promised in the Treaty of London. Orlando, the Italian prime minister,

Vittorio Veneters: Term used in this book to denote the cross-party movements and mentalities that first coalesced after Italy's defeat at Caporetto (October 1917) in defence of the fatherland and in opposition to what were perceived to be the forces that threatened and sapped its vitality. Vittorio Veneto is the battle in October 1918 that saw Italy defeat Austria.

stormed out of the conference when, to his horror, he realized that Italy's booty consisted only of the old unredeemed territories. No colonies were granted, no Dalmatia, and certainly no bits of Turkey. How was he going to tell his countrymen that this was all that the blood spilt in the Alps and on the Piave had managed to buy? The interventionists (and Orlando had been one) must have felt their own blood run cold; Italy's war had, after all, been their big idea. The victory was rapidly becoming, in D'Annunzio's words, a 'mutilated' one [**Doc. 12, p. 137**].

In Italy's mixed-language borderlands, the situation threatened to slip out of the government's hands because the latter was seen to be incapable of standing up for the rights of the Italian population there. The most notable event was the occupation of the small Italian-Croatian town of Fiume in September 1919 by Gabriele D'Annunzio and a motley crew of ex-servicemen, among whom the *Arditi* [**Doc. 9, p. 135**], crack Italian storm troopers, were overrepresented. This small town, in itself of no great significance, symbolized the dilemmas that Italy was facing immediately after the conflict. The American president, Woodrow Wilson, had rebuffed Italian claims to the town at Versailles, as the majority of the population was not ethnically Italian, but some of its Italian speakers clamoured for absorption into Italy. When it was decided that Fiume's fate should be decided by an Allied commission and Allied soldiers should be replaced (temporarily) by British policemen to avoid clashes between different national groups there, D'Annunzio and his legionaries made their move. Much of the paraphernalia and symbolism of early Fascism came together during the poet's 12-month occupation of the town. The *Arditi*'s black shirts (their Great War uniform), the Roman salute, the slogans and rhetoric were inventions of the poet or emerged from the veteran mêlée rather than from the mind of Mussolini, firmly at his desk in Milan. The Italian government, headed now by Francesco Saverio Nitti, failed to intervene against D'Annunzio in Fiume because it felt the heat of the Vittorio Veneters, whose motivations it fundamentally shared but whose methods it did not. However, it could hardly act directly against Allied wishes, and so stalled until it did eventually occupy the town, clearing out D'Annunzio but making Fiume independent of both Italy and Yugoslavia. In other areas such as Trieste, Italy's greatest prize for having intervened in the Great War, the mixed ethnicity of the population made it a hotbed of rival nationalist associations and gangs. Fascism, as the final inheritor of the Vittorio Veneter spirit, was to have one of its most vociferous and powerful sections in this Adriatic port.

In Milan, where Mussolini was busy with his veterans and combatants' newspaper, the first *Fascio di Combattimento* (Combat League) was formed at a meeting in March 1919. Its adherents were very similar to the men who would later become D'Annunzio's legionaries at Fiume and who had made

Arditi: Crack Italian assault troops employed in the trenches in the last year of the Great War. With a powerful *esprit de corps* and ultrapatriotic ideology, they were significant players in the postwar political struggle.

the myth of the 'radiant days' of May in 1915: left-wing interventionists, Futurists, radical nationalists, who were now joined by *Arditi*, army officers and army veterans. Their initial programme was 'national socialist'. It called for the eight-hour day, a minimum wage and for worker 'technicians' to be given a greater role in industry; uncultivated land was to be expropriated from landlords and a one-off progressive tax was to redistribute ownership of the means of production. The support of workers for 'a foreign policy aimed at expanding Italy's will and power in opposition to all foreign imperialisms' (in Schnapp, 2000: 3) was obviously being sought here. These were the *Fascisti*, the first association of Vittorio Veneters headed by Mussolini [**Doc. 13, p. 138**]. It had no more than a couple of hundred members and its initial impact was minimal. In just over three years, what turned this small group of men into a movement that took power was the inability of the state to deal with an upsurge in working-class militancy that not only transformed relationships of power in the workplace but swept away liberal control in parliament and in many localities throughout northern and central Italy. At first Fascism was nothing more than the most well-organized group of Vittorio Veneters and became the banner under which the reaction against the social and political revolution of 1919 to 1920 coalesced.

THE *BIENNIO ROSSO* AND FASCISM'S REACTION

Biennio rosso: The 'two red years' (1919–20). A period of intense class struggle throughout north and central Italy, it coincided with the political collapse of liberal hegemony in parliament and in many local councils.

The period from the end of the war to the end of 1920 is called in Italian historiography the **biennio rosso** (the two red years). There is debate as to whether similar conditions existed in Italy at this time to those that led to revolution in Russia earlier and why Fascism emerged out of the crisis rather than a new Soviet Union on the shores of the Mediterranean. But whatever the answer to these questions it is certainly incontestable that in these two years it was as if the Italian peasantry had suddenly woken up. The war had drafted them by the million and they had suffered most of its casualties. After Caporetto the 'defend Italy and it will be yours' slogan, was interpreted by many as a promise of land; nothing of the sort materialized, even though peasants in uniform provided the bulk of those who held the Piave. Unlike the pre-war years, when land-hunger and violence in the Italian countryside had been endemic but disorganized, the PSI and the new Popular Catholic Party (*Partito Popolare Italiano* – PPI) as well as new peasant and worker unions ensured that a much more coordinated and dangerous attack on power relations in the Italian economy took place. The latent discontent evident in Italian society since unification was expressed through every means made available by the newly democratized state. In 1919 there were

500,000 strikes, in 1920 over a million. The PSI's network of peasant leagues and worker organizations spanned Lombardy, Emilia, Romagna, Tuscany, Piedmont and more restricted areas of the south. In national and local elections in these same areas the PSI and PPI swept all before them. Throughout the Po Valley the red flag flew over city halls, and in parliament the largest single political party entered the chamber after the 1919 elections [**Doc. 14, p. 139**] singing 'Red Flag'. The PPI could now command more than a hundred MPs (as the papal ban on participation in politics was definitively lifted). Strikes in factories in all the important northern industrial areas brought the workers higher wages in a period when profit margins were strained to the utmost. In Turin in 1920 the factories were occupied and Soviets on the Russian model debated the pros and cons of revolution versus 'mere' worker control of industry.

Mussolini's tiny **Fasci di Combattimento** languished for much of the *biennio rosso*. By the middle of 1920 they had 20,000 members, almost all concentrated in Italy's northern cities, and the mix of veterans, artists and *Arditi* that had coalesced in Milan a year before did not look like it had a particularly bright future. What happened to transform Fascism's plight, as has been said, was the radicalization of the class struggle throughout north and central Italy and the ethnic struggle in Italy's borderlands. In practice, Fascism became the umbrella under which a whole series of diverse political and social movements (nationalist in Trieste, anti-socialist in Tuscany, anti-PPI in rural Veneto, etc.) manoeuvred themselves in the concerted reaction to the changes that characterized Italy during the *biennio rosso*. From being Mussolini's political brainchild, an offshoot of his journalistic opinions, the *Fasci*, their paraphernalia, their uniforms and what they stood for were adopted by a wide range of local interests as an adhesive to bind them together in tackling what were essentialy local problems. Thus Fascism, as it developed in 1920–2, was not a political party, with a programme and an internal structure headed by Mussolini who sent proselytizing disciples into the provinces, but a catch-all movement that, loosely speaking, would have met with the approval of many who saw themselves as belonging to the very widespread political and social environment of the Vittorio Veneters. The ingredient that was (almost) unique to Fascism and which gave it an edge over traditional patriotic parties was its willingness to employ violence for political ends. Its ability to give a semblance of political coherence and a plausible set of symbolic reference points to what was essentially reactionary vigilantism allowed the process of law and the functioning of democracy, which was favouring the forces of subversion, to be sidestepped with panache. Fascism's phenomenal growth in these months consisted in welding local power interests to the new men who rejected traditional liberal or other party affiliations in the spirit of the Vittorio Veneters. As

Fasci di Combattimento: 'Combat Leagues'. The name of the first political cells of the Fascist movement.

such, the Fascist movement was only partly connected to Mussolini himself [**Doc. 15, p. 139**].

If one surveys the Fascism in the localities at this point it is easy to see how this peculiar movement articulated itself. In Florence the local (and somnolent) branch of the *Fascio di Combattimento* was suddenly transformed by the involvement in its affairs of the town's association of landlords, which had in the past been a stalwart of liberalism. It provided the *fascio* with funds necessary to recruit its dashing Vittorio Veneters in its own struggle against the peasant leagues and, in so doing, had also to undermine its own traditional and legally sanctioned institutional power. But the success of the Fascist **squads** was such that it must have seemed money well spent. The effectiveness of throwing Fascist squad violence into the class struggle, from the landlords' point of view, was little short of miraculous:

> Throughout the spring and summer [of 1921] the eight provinces [of Tuscany] witnessed an unending succession of raids by Fascist squads against town halls with recently seated socialist councils, against the branches of the socialist and popular parties; against the offices of the subversive press; and against homes of union officials. Activists were harassed, assaulted, and murdered. When resistance was offered, whole villages were plundered and set aflame.
>
> (Snowden, 1989: 70)

Squads and squadism: Loosely organized vigilante gangs of the early days of Fascism. They used violence and intimidation to secure Fascist political ends.

The use of terror pushed many socialists to abandon their political activity, and the normal functioning of administration on which the gains made in the *biennio rosso* rested was often halted.

All over northern and central Italy the story repeated itself. Where socialists (or in some areas the PPI) had made real gains, Fascist squads with the connivance of local (and sometimes state) authority were able to mount violent campaigns of intimidation. In Ferrara a *fascio* had been set up on Mussolini's radical Milanese model in 1919. Its leader, Olao Gaggioli, was a radical nationalist who espoused many of the syndicalist traits of Fascism's first programme; but the *fascio* proved unattractive to the peasantry, who were staunchly socialist, and it failed to get off the ground. However, when here too, as in Tuscany, local landowners hoped to use the movement's youthful energy in their struggle, Gaggioli was sidelined and **Italo Balbo**, socially respectable and personally connected to the wealthy of the city, emerged as leader. His squads, equipped with lorries, guns, cudgels and castor oil, became anti-socialist *arditi* whose lack of numbers was offset by mobility and shock and awe tactics. But by September 1921 manpower problems were over too; he could muster 3,000 men in a raid on nearby and socialist-controlled Ravenna (Bosworth, 2002: 151).

Italo Balbo (1896–1940): *Ras* of Ferrara and organizer of some of Fascism's most notorious squads. He was minister of the Italian Air Force 1929–33 and participated as pilot in the 1933 trans-Atlantic 'raid'. Made governor of Libya in 1934, he was killed when his airplane was accidentally shot down by Italian anti-aircraft fire in 1940.

In the south of Italy, with the exception of a few areas, the *fasci* were not needed. In 1919–20 the liberal permanence in power survived and the new mass political parties that did so much to destabilize the political administrative system in the north failed to win many adherents. Once again, the differing history of Italy, north and south, was reinforced by both the absence of the major characteristics of the *biennio rosso* and the reaction against it. In some areas this was not the case: Puglia for example, where similar dynamics in the agricultural economy to those prevalent in areas of the north were in operation had its Fascist movement before 1922, but even there the employment of mobile armed squads to crush peasant solidarity was not an invention of the *biennio rosso*, but had been standard practice well before the First World War (Snowden, 1986).

From Mussolini's point of view the rise in squad violence represented a mixed blessing. Much of the movement was in practice nothing at all to do with him, except that he was a prominent Vittorio Veneter. The fact that Mussolini's *fasci* were not a political party meant that they could grow in a way that would have been impossible had they been firmly organized inside an apparatus loyal to the future *Duce*. Rather, the loose associations and programmes of each *fascio* allowed them to operate in a wide diversity of locales. The Genoese *fascio's* founding document merely stated that it stood for: 'defence of the last National war to the bitter end, for the exploitation of the victory, for the resistance and opposition to the theoretical and practical degeneration of politicizing socialism' (in Lyttelton, 1973: 69). This was the basic programme of the Vittorio Veneters and even its anti-socialism was couched in terms not of socialists representing a threat to the established order but that they had supposedly betrayed the Italian war effort. So it was that in each of its strongholds, by the end of 1921, Fascism was a mix of local *fasci* bosses (called *rases* after Ethiopian military rulers) intermeshed with local economic interest groups, each having a loyal set of troops adept at destroying socialist or other targets. The *rases* owed a spiritual allegiance to Mussolini as the man in whom their values as Vittorio Veneters were best expressed, and his newspaper would have been available in their *fascio's* headquarters, but they did not owe their new positions of influence and power in their base areas to the future *Duce* – in some cases they had never even met him. However, Mussolini did his best to locate himself at the head of the movement through *Il Popolo d'Italia* and very importantly he was to become its spokesman when the Italian government, or major Italian interest groups, from businesses to trade unions wanted to deal with it at the national level. The nature of Mussolini's spiritual and distant, rather than actual leadership of the movement was to have profound consequences on how Fascism came to power and on the eventual structure of the Regime. In order to be appointed prime minister, Mussolini had to sideline the movement and come to terms with the Italian political establishment and to ditch many of the early syndicalist aspects of the Fascist programme. With his appointment as Italian premier the tables were reversed, and rather than Mussolini needing to coax and to satisfy the unruly *rases* and to argue that he had much to offer them, he was suddenly transformed into being the arch dispenser of patronage, and the bows and curtsies had to be made by the *rases* themselves.

It was Mussolini's relationship with the traditional centres of Italian power (as they had emerged after unification) that led to him becoming the *Duce* rather than there being a revolutionary takeover on the part of 'his' *fasci*. How had the Italian government observed and pondered the rise of the Fascist squads? As has been said, at the local level there was much collusive satisfaction in seeing the *biennio rosso* turned around, but contradictory orders were also issued through Italy's prefects to keep the peace. What the government did do was allow the growth of the paramilitary squads and to forego what should have been its monopoly over the use of violence throughout the country. The Italian state had never really been blessed with such a monopoly, but the flouting of its authority by the Fascist squads was not taken seriously enough. The latter were after all Vittorio Veneters and as such they were surely upholders of the national values that liberal Italy had tried so hard to inculcate in its people; in any case their enemy was not the Italian state but those who would drag it in the mud. Even as liberal a commentator as Luigi Albertini, senator of the kingdom and editor of Milan's *Il Corriere della Sera*, the closest thing Italy had to national 'public opinion', regarded the squads as a necessary evil. The occupation of the factories, the fruits of the great fear sparked by the *biennio rosso*, were enough for him to explain that Fascism was, after all, the socialists' own fault. 'Whose fault is this?' he asked in an important article of November 1920, 'whose if not the socialist party who aspires to an Italian civil war. It is the socialist party that wants this environment of savage warfare . . . they should not complain when they too get some knocks' (in De Felice, 1965: 662). For Albertini, once the socialists were given a dose of their own medicine and were very much in retreat, his ideal scenario would have been for Fascism to fade away and the spirit of the Vittorio Veneters to swing in behind a new and strengthened liberal patriotic order [**Doc. 17, p. 141**]. This did not happen.

In November 1921 it was liberal Italy that placed an unknown Italian soldier's body found in the trenches of the Alps within the massive base of the vast monument that had been built in the middle of Rome to honour Italy's founding father, Victor Emmanuel II, as if to bring together the two Italies, the 'real' and the 'legal', the dynastic and the popular, the pre and the post-Caporetto. But however poignant and pregnant with meaning this act was it remained something of a gesture. Although the entombment of the

unknown soldier in the dynastic monument led, according to some historians, to a moment of heightened 'and mystical patriotism' (Pini and Susmel,
1973: 146), throughout (north and central) Italy the people continued to
vote socialist or PPI. This fact was enough for the inheritance of the Vittorio
Veneters to slip through the liberals' fingers as parliament and, in some areas,
local power continued to be in the hands of the anti-systemic (and anti-
Vittorio Veneter) parties, even if the Fascist squads had temporarily ejected
them. In Fascism's strongholds, without the (illegal) squads the reality was
that power would immediately devolve to either the socialists or the PPI. In
practice democracy, as it stood in 1919–22, could not work if the liberals
regarded themselves as the only legitimate ruling party [**Doc. 14, p. 139**],
and if the socialists, and after 1921 the PPI, saw any kind of power sharing
as undermining what they stood for. In order to get a longed-for majority
Giolitti was prepared to include the Fascists in an electoral coalition
[**Doc. 17, p. 141**]. His interlocutor could be no one except Mussolini, and
the failure of even the 'national bloc' in the elections of May 1921 to dent
the support Italy's people gave to the anti-systemic and anti-Vittorio Veneter
parties meant that liberal Italy, as the liberals themselves envisaged it, was
now doomed.

5

The Road to Dictatorship, 1921–6

THE MARCH ON ROME: MYTH AND REALITY

The decision on the part of Mussolini's old nemesis Giolitti, who was prime minister between June 1920 and July 1921, to bring the Fascists into the 'legitimate' political fold was to transform the future *Duce* from being the leader of a movement that was linked to him only in spirit, to his heading a real political party. In the face of strikes, agitation, factory and land occupation during the *biennio rosso*, the Italian government was not always capable and willing to take the side of the established order. Giolitti, as was his wont, sought compromise; he hoped that moderation would convince at least some socialists that it was possible to collaborate with liberal governments, and in the process, of course, preserve the latter after the electoral catastrophe of 1919. Giolitti's decision to include Fascists in his 'national bloc' in elections that he called in May 1921 is, on the face of it, surprising. But it was in reality just another attempt at classic *trasformismo*. Mussolini, who had had 15 years of political experience to understand the Giolittian method, leapt on to the bandwagon fully aware of what he was doing: he would benefit from the blessing of the aged politician to stabilize his own position within the Fascist movement.

At the May 1921 election the Fascists won 35 seats; the PSI and the PPI maintained the support of the electorate, however, and together were still the majority in the house [**Doc. 14, p. 139**]. For the Fascists, sheltering politically under the liberal umbrella worked well. In many small towns of the north the unspoken alliance between the wealthy, who had always been liberal, and the Fascist squads had in any case been forged over the previous months in the anti-subversive struggle. Walking now arm-in-arm meant merely an open recognition of what had previously been an illicit but still public relationship. But at the national level, in parliament, Mussolini made it quite clear that his MPs were not just 'transformism fodder': they sat on the far right of the house and neglected to give Giolitti their votes. The latter's last gamble had failed. By allying with Fascists, the chances of a coalition of the centre that included moderate socialists could hardly now come about and, apart from his southern deputies who still delivered votes for governmental patronage, Giolitti's parliamentary position tottered. He resigned (in July 1921), for the last time in his career. The dreamed-of majority had not coalesced and parliament remained as hung as it had before the 'national bloc'. Giolitti was replaced by Ivanoe Bonomi who headed a minuscule reformist (and interventionist) socialist party. He was an old acquaintance of Mussolini's and had praised the Fascists loudly in their stemming of what he believed was an unstoppable Bolshevik tide in his native Mantua.

With his entry into the national parliament, Mussolini himself was now the undoubted spokesman of the Fascist movement, particularly when important politicians in Rome wanted to deal with it. The continual violence of the squads though, reflected in parliament too by the beating up by Fascists of a communist deputy who had proudly been a deserter during the war, was hardly the way to behave in such a locus. Even though Vittorio Veneters would have thoroughly supported the exclusion from parliament of traitorous deserters, continuing violence in the provinces was no longer within acceptable limits. To a great degree the threat from the left had now dissipated, certainly in the provincial class struggle, and for many it was time for Fascists to go home. Some kind of control needed to be asserted by the government and Bonomi went directly to Mussolini. Could Mussolini organize a return to peace in provincial Italy? Could he rein in the squads and therefore leave Italy once again to the rule of law? The soon-to-be *Duce* grasped the opportunity in Bonomi's request. The Fascist movement needed to be normalized as a disciplined political organization in order to be brought under his command. Its violence would then not operate in favour of this or that local **ras**, or his local paymaster, but could be a veiled threat with which to consolidate Mussolini's own political position at the national level. The March on Rome only a year later, was to confirm the wisdom of this policy, but at the end of 1921 Mussolini had to take a very difficult decision. By agreeing with Bonomi that a reining in of the squads had to take place, Mussolini was risking the crumbling of the very precarious unity that the Fascist movement had acquired through two congresses and the break into parliament. The 'Pact of Pacification', a ceasefire between socialists and the Fascist squads, was Mussolini's answer to Bonomi's proposition. It was Mussolini himself who had to bring this policy, which appeared to be a betrayal, to his black-shirted *rases*, and it very nearly cost him the position of pre-eminence that he had acquired in the movement.

Interpreted as Mussolinian duplicity, Balbo reacted by his March on Ravenna, and Marsich, the leader of Venetian Fascism, 'occupied' Treviso.

Ras: A local Fascist boss. The word was originally encountered by Italians in Ethiopia, where is stands for a military ruler of a province.

There was much talk of the spiritual leadership of the movement being granted to D'Annunzio. The *rases* in the localities had their own agendas. Not only was the re-emergence of socialism the most likely outcome if the squads suddenly laid down their arms, but the circumscribed popular support local Fascists had acquired from the working class and the peasantry would very likely disappear if privileged access to jobs and patronage from employers were not guaranteed. Mussolini, however, argued his case forcefully and posed as a true Vittorio Veneter, having the interests of Italy as a whole to heart. He referred to Fascism as his 'child' and argued that some salutary correction of it was required, for the child's own benefit. We must not alienate everybody except ourselves, he said, 'the votes of the veterans, and of the mothers of the wounded are "moral" factors, that a movement cannot ignore, if it is true that we want to connect to Vittorio Veneto and its meaning in the history of Italy' [**Docs. 10, 11, p. 136**]. Mussolini was now suggesting that only he, as the movement's founder, had the total vision; that which could rise above the needs of the petty interests of the localities. The *rases* had even dared to see Rome as deserving of the 'scorn of the people', as if Rome was not something so much greater than their trivial concerns (OO XVII: 80). What was Bologna or Cremona or even Venice compared to Rome? And Rome was, symbolically, Mussolini himself.

The Pact of Pacification proved a non-starter with the movement and was wholeheartedly rejected by his *rases*, but for Mussolini it still proved to be the launch pad to the conquest of power at the national level. He resigned from his position in the Fascist movement's central committee and became merely a rank-and-file member. The ball was in the *rases'* court now. If they wanted him back, they would have to have him on the terms that he dictated. After D'Annunzio refused to be the *rases'* new symbolic head, it was clear that either Mussolini must be accepted as Fascism's boss by the *rases* or their movement was destined to remain nothing more than the whipping boy of the left in provincial Italy. In Sarzana, Liguria, a few weeks earlier Bonomi's government had ordered the police to block a Fascist raid, and it had all ended in a bath of Fascist blood. Without Mussolini, local Fascists could hardly stabilize their new prominence in the provinces. No matter what the situation might be in Bologna or Cremona, the *rases* were expendable if they did not have the permanence guaranteed by the blessing of Rome. They needed Mussolini as much as he needed them. There was no alternative leader on a par with Mussolini, and he was necessarily recalled. At the same time the Fascist movement was transformed into a political party of which Mussolini was the undisputed chief, and in return the Pact of Pacification was quietly forgotten.

From the point of view of Bonomi and the politicians in Rome, who observed what Mussolini was up to, the return of Fascist violence after the short lull of the pact could hardly be blamed on the future *Duce*. He had done his best, and his creation of the Fascist Party (*Partito Nazional Fascista* – PNF) was taken as a sign that he was getting the movement under control. Mussolini emerged out of 'Fascism's crisis' strengthened immeasurably: he had earned the respect of the liberals in Rome, who considered him to be the only man who could deal with grassroots Fascist turbulence without recourse to the ugliness of bloodshed between Vittorio Veneters; he now controlled a large political party; and, when violence did occur in the provinces he was free to endorse or to distance himself from it depending on his audience. It was an enviable position to be in; perhaps it had not been planned, but Mussolini had certainly navigated the turmoil of those months with extraordinary skill.

The March on Rome, as the prelude to Mussolini's appointment as prime minister came to be called in Fascism's own retelling of its 'revolutionary' seizure of power, was the logical conclusion of this exceptional strategic position into which Mussolini had manoeuvred himself. As Fascist squads sabre-rattled, occupied different towns and called for a takeover of state power, Mussolini negotiated with the government, now headed by Luigi Facta, but still largely controlled by Giolitti. The wily Piedmontese statesman had nothing in particular against Mussolini being given some sort of authority in government, and Mussolini was prepared to negotiate when it came to creating yet another coalition government. Although he still aimed to be prime minister, Mussolini had only 35 members of parliament and would need to negotiate with all the usual people in order to form a government. The prospect was not as bad as it seemed: Mussolini could unite some of the factions of the liberal right and bring Vittorio Veneter feeling firmly behind a national government. The unruly provincial Fascists would be assuaged and grant their full support to a coalition that their leader headed. From this position of strength, further elections might then be held which would, once and for all, end the Italian parliament's being held to ransom by the subversive parties. Also, by being given real responsibility, it was presumed that the Fascist squads would lose their raison d'être. Mussolini would be able to work through the prefecture and the normal channels of state authority to protect Italy from the possible resurgence of subversion [**Doc. 17, p. 141**].

At this point (the beginning of autumn 1922) the blacksmith's son from the provinces must suddenly have felt the giddiness of how close he actually was to power, fame and glory. The lust of that moment was surely overpowering, but he kept his eye firmly on the prize. He reassured the king that the Fascists, as he understood them, were proud of the Italian monarchy (and its great national achievements) and menacingly reminded **Victor Emmanuel III** that his cousin, the far more dashing Duke of Aosta, had nothing against the Fascists. Even the new pope, **Pius XI**, a staunch anti-socialist, was

Victor Emmanuel III (1869–1947): King of Italy from 1900 (at his father's assassination). Terrified by the growth of socialism, he was instrumental in calling Mussolini to power and throughout the Regime remained independent of but acquiescent to the dictatorship. He removed Mussolini from power in July 1943, but fled from Rome in September to avoid falling into German hands.

Pope Pius XI (Achille Ratti) (1857–1939): Pope from 1922. Vehemently anti-communist, he sought compromises with both Fascism and Nazism. He signed the Lateran Pacts with Mussolini in 1929.

comforted by Mussolini's proclaiming the Church (but not the PPI) to be a bastion of order and fundamental to what it meant to be Italian. The radical economic policies of the first Fascists, which were still supported by some of the *rases*, were officially abandoned and replaced by Mussolini's new-found love of the free market, assuaging the doubts of industrialists. A hastily arranged meeting between Mussolini and General **Pietro Badoglio** made it clear that the armed forces had nothing to fear; the March on Rome was a coming together of veterans in defence of the values of the fatherland.

Pietro Badoglio (1871–1956): Chief of Staff 1925–40, commander of the Italian army during the Italian invasion of Ethiopia, and proclaimed Marshall of Italy and Duke of Addis Ababa. He plotted Mussolini's downfall with the Italian king and was made head of government at Mussolini's fall. He escaped to Brindisi on 8 September 1943.

As Fascism's *rases* marched (or rather walked) their poorly armed men towards the capital in heavy rain, Mussolini waited in Milan. Since no one who had the authority to do so was prepared to call out the guard, disperse the marchers, and take the complicated consequences that would have ensued, the only alternative available was to offer Mussolini the post of prime minister in a coalition government. He, rather than the army, would have to deal with the Blackshirts slogging their way to the place all roads lead to, and he too would have to decide on how far, as Giolitti would have put it, he remained within constitutional limits. Consequently, on 29 October 1922 Mussolini was proffered the invitation to form a new government. From Milan he took the train and arrived in a still rainy eternal city the following morning. This was no revolution, nor a heralding of dictatorship. More plausibly it was what Italian schoolchildren were to be taught for the next two decades: with Mussolini's appointment as prime minister, the Vittorio Veneters had finally come home.

THE 'BIVOUAC' THAT MIGHT HAVE BEEN: THE *DUCE* AS PRIME MINISTER, 1922–4

It is difficult to decide, at this stage, if Mussolini's rise to the premiership was the first step to a premeditated dictatorship. In retrospect, of course, it would appear that this was the case. Hindsight is the tantalizing prerogative of the historian, but discerning an inexorable road to the Regime is, even in the first period after the March on Rome, not a clear-cut exercise. In his first speech to the Italian parliament as prime minister, Mussolini reiterated the unique strategic position he now occupied. He 'could have' made the chamber a 'bivouac' for his troops, he proclaimed, but had chosen to not do so. He would remain within the limits of the constitution, for the time being anyway [**Doc. 16, p. 140**]. As usual, Mussolini stated his policies by giving opposition the chance to come to terms and at the same time making veiled threats if they refused. He promised that his government would operate 'above the shades of party affiliation and unite all those who want to save the nation . . . A warm homage is to be paid to the king . . . who by his actions has avoided civil war'. On foreign policy he assuaged international concerns about his appointment by promising to stick to treaties signed by Italy, while insisting that pledges made to Italy should be respected. Italy would be tolerant of others, would stick by its wartime allies but would, if necessary, 're-take its freedom of action and defend its interest by other means' (OO XIX: 18–20) [**Doc. 16, p. 140**].

However, what characterized the first period of Fascist rule was essentially a contamination of what Fascism stood for with an array of ideas held by other political forces, who were themselves enriched by the dynamism and the agendas proposed by Fascism. If Mussolini had really gone to the king in 1922 and stated that what he was bringing to power was 'the Italy of Vittorio Veneto' there was clearly a vast area of Italian political life over which Fascism could throw its mantle and in so doing be transformed beyond recognition itself. Apart from the basic programme of the Vittorio Veneters, Mussolini did not have to implement immediately any clear political agenda; his only real constraint were the *rases*, but they were now dealing not with a Milanese journalist but the Italian prime minister, who could employ the force of the state itself. Mussolini made it quite clear that he would honour his debts to them, but for the time being they should shut up. His first government can therefore hardly be called 'Fascist'. Mussolini held the Foreign and Interior Ministries as well as the premiership, and Fascist Party members Acerbo and Finzi received only under-secretariats. The right-wing philosopher **Giovanni Gentile** was given Education, and the leader of the Nationalist Association, Luigi Federzoni, was given Colonies. The War Ministry went to General Armando Diaz, who had been commander of the Italian army after Caporetto, and the Exchequer went to the Fascist but free-market orientated De' Stefani. A right-wing PPI member, Stefano Cavazzoni, got the Ministry of Public Works. This alliance of forces was hardly a revolution. It was a conservative ministry that expressed the collective will of industry, the monarchy, even of the Church, and that sought to stabilize, across a broad spectrum of the right's many factions, a coherent and more permanent government after the long period of political instability following the war. At least until the next election, this would have to do. In practice the great novelty of Mussolini's first government was that for the first time in modern Italian history the coalescence of a serious conservative party, with real popular appeal, appeared to be on the verge of realization [**Docs. 14, 17, pp. 139, 141**].

The most obvious novelty introduced by Fascism's coming to power, apart from the anti-parliamentary rhetoric sometimes indulged in by Mussolini, was the establishment of the Fascist Grand Council and the transformation of the squads into a legally defined militia. The former was filled with the

Giovanni Gentile (1875–1944): Philosopher disciple of Benedetto Croce. He saw Fascism as a continuation of the *Risorgimento* and attempted to construct a coherent Fascist 'doctrine'. He held various ministries and presided over high culture throughout the Regime. He was shot by partisans during the RSI.

rases who had not been given cabinet jobs, and could clearly be interpreted as an alternative government in the making. However, it was not given a constitutional function and its relationship with normal parliamentary institutions remained undefined; yet it was not meant to be just the executive committee of the Fascist Party in the sense of that possessed by other political parties. It met frequently, at least in the first period of Mussolini's rule, and often made policy that was then presented to the cabinet for rubber-stamping. For example, the transformation of the squads into a legally recognized militia (known as the **MVSN**) was decided in the Grand Council and then approved by the cabinet and eventually enshrined in law, giving the Fascist Party, uniquely, an armed wing that was theoretically outside the state's control. In 1922 the only person who had executive power in both the cabinet and the Grand Council was, of course, Mussolini himself, and the creation of this new specifically Fascist body could be interpreted as the continuation of the policies the *Duce* had been pursuing for more than two years – making himself the indispensable bond between the geographically circumscribed power of the Fascist base and the broader forces who did find representation in the organs of the state. This was as much a sign of Mussolini's understanding that, in the final analysis, he only possessed a relatively small mandate throughout Italy, as evidence of there being a master plan for the establishing of a personal dictatorship. Nevertheless the situation that was to characterise the next 20 years was already apparent. The *Duce* was able to forge alliances between very disparate groups that were broadly on the Italian right (and which did include the liberals) and to blend them within a redefined conception of what Fascism was. He did eventually replace much of the leadership of the Italian state with people who had emerged in the Fascist movement in the years after the First World War, but this did not imply an abandonment of his consensual relationship with Italy's pre-Fascist elites. The big losers in the establishment of the Fascist Regime were the forces who had been subversive in liberal Italy: the Catholic popular movement, the socialists and their subculture, the young Communist Party, the trade unions and the peasant leagues. Those opposed to the Vittorio Veneters were silenced for good. The story of Mussolini's dictatorship can be read as his making himself indispensable to the broad forces of the right and then manufacturing support for this alliance among the rest of the Italian population. How successful he was in this is a hotly debated issue.

In the initial period after Mussolini became prime minister two events in particular were of crucial importance in the blending of Fascism with the broader right. The first was the absorption into the Fascist Party of the Nationalist Association. The latter had been of great significance in the panorama of Italian politics since its foundation in 1910. Although it had never acquired a significant popular base, its militants were highly respected

MVSN (*Milizia Volontaria per la Sicurezza Nazionale***):** 'National Security Volunteer Militia'. The organization that absorbed the Fascist squads and placed them in 1923 under Mussolini's direct command, thus circumventing the local power of the *rases*. The MVSN formed semi-independent units (the 'Blackshirts') in Italy's military campaigns in Ethiopia, Spain and then the Second World War, yet at the fall of Mussolini in 1943 not one MVSN unit rose in defence of the *Duce*.

figures. Their desire for an authoritarian renewal of Italy through a strengthening of the executive (monarchist in many cases) and a more assertive foreign policy laced with imperial ambition had had some resonance in the south and even more importantly was looked on with favour by many influential people in the armed forces, the royal family and the diplomatic corps. Federzoni, as Mussolini scathingly remarked, was not a man to go out for a roll of toilet paper without donning a 'dark suit' (Bosworth, 2002: 178) but it was precisely the Nationalist Association's impeccable respectability that made it so attractive and useful to Fascism as it moved from its provincial and plebeian origins into the higher echelons of the Italian political and administrative system. Notwithstanding the inability of the nationalists, since 1910, to get their patriotic message across to broader strata of Italian society, they were thinkers of the highest calibre and eventually gave (or attempted to give) Fascism, and certainly the Regime, something of an ideological underpinning as well as a political programme that went beyond the simple platform of the Vittorio Veneters that was, after all, still all that united Mussolini's coalition. The absorption of the Nationalist Association into the PNF in March 1923 was something of a watershed for Fascism too: it was an endorsement of the movement by an older and more respectable section of the right, but also the final consummation of a relationship Mussolini had started when he called for the Socialist Party to pledge its support for Italy's entry into the Great War. What Mussolini was exceptionally good at was acquiring new allies to offset reliance on the old, and the entry of the Nationalist Association into the PNF partly freed the *Duce* from being shackled to the *rases*. The radical programme of the Fascist movement was being rendered irrelevant and the entry into the party, and at its top, of men like Federzoni, Alfredo Rocco and Giuseppe Bottai, who hailed from the nationalists, was not greeted with enthusiasm by the Fascist old guard, although it must have been less worrying to the new members of the Fascist party who had been flooding in since October 1922. From 300,000 members at the time of the March on Rome, Party membership had almost tripled in less than a year (Clark, 2005: 69).

But unification with the nationalists was only the start of Fascism's transformation. If it had provided the *Duce*'s rag-tag following with respectability at the national level, the organization of elections that were eventually held in April 1924 cemented Mussolini's relationship with the liberal establishment and achieved popular endorsement of the March on Rome and the stabilization of his leadership of the whole anti-subversive coalition. The Acerbo Law, which was passed by a still 'liberal' parliament, before the election took place, made certain of a governmental victory. It stated that the political grouping that gained the most votes (provided a quorum of 25 per cent was reached) would be rewarded with two-thirds of parliamentary seats.

Opposed by the subversive parties, this piece of legislation, amounting to a constitutional revolution, was supported by liberals of all shades, right-wing Catholics, nationalists and of course the Fascists themselves. Why, in particular the liberals, including Giolitti, should have supported this law is difficult to understand. Yet its aim was not the construction of a Mussolinian dictatorship but to prevent the subversives from hamstringing parliament and to attain a secure majority of the right. It was the final answer to all the woes that had emanated from the electoral disaster of 1919. From this point of view it represented for liberals such as Giolitti a constitutional way of preserving the centrality of parliament in the running of the country [**Doc. 17, p. 141**]. What the liberals wanted above all was that the institutions of the state be used to stabilize the country, and this included both the ending of the latent subversive threat and also the permanent reining in of the squads; if Mussolini was the man to do this then the dividends of seeking protection under his umbrella were likely to be good.

So, when the *listone* (the big list of candidates selected by the government) was drawn up for the 1924 elections, the situation of May 1921, when Fascism's 35 members of parliament had won their seats, was turned on its head: the liberals were now in the train of Mussolini and not the other way round. The election itself was a startling triumph and a vindication of Mussolini's tactics. The Acerbo Law was not even required to ensure a huge government majority in parliament, although it had, for obvious reasons, forced candidates to get on the government list to have a chance of actually being elected. Overall, 65 per cent of the vote went to the *listone* and for the first time since the war the subversives could not hang or destabilize parliament. What had happened?

This is not a simple question to answer. To be sure in some areas it had been impossible for people to vote freely and Fascist coshes had forced the voter's hand. For example, in parts of Ferrara province Fascist candidates received 100 per cent of the vote (Morgan, 2004: 90), but coercion had not been universal. The government list swept the south and represented Fascism's first significant inroad into the massive electoral potential of this area. Yet the majorities attained there were not a great victory for Fascism directly but rather a movement of traditional client networks to the shade of the Fascist umbrella, and therefore carried the usual price tag: jobs, patronage and not too much ideological and political interference. The left remained divided and had failed to mount an effective campaign. The PPI had been undermined by Mussolinian overtures to the Vatican from 1922 on, and its leader, Luigi Sturzo, had been forced to resign as party leader in the summer of 1923. With the Catholic Church hierarchy now clearly in favour of the government coalition and a rudderless PPI, Catholics too shifted away from the old 'subversive' party: the PPI won only 9 per cent of the vote.

Mussolini had been remarkably successful in coalescing support for order, stability and the broad values of the right. Not that this meant Italians were voting for a dictatorship; they might have simply wanted an end to the turmoil that had wracked Italy since 1918. Mussolini capitalized on the widespread desire for order. He had won over a good part of the Catholic vote, had dragged the southern 'liberals' into his coalition and had become the only legitimate inheritor of the broadest platform of the Vittorio Veneters. The *rases* occasionally barked, but were now more or less under control and were in any case swamped by the massive influx of other groupings into the Fascist movement. Mussolini could look with immense satisfaction on his achievements: the impossible had happened and the subversives were now a defeated and insignificant minority. Without need of a master plan Mussolini had forged a new rightist coalition and had offset his reliance on the unruly Fascist movement as his only locus of support. He had succeeded where Giolitti and all the other liberals from Crispi to Salandra had failed, and he appeared now to be the indispensable pivot of the new Italian political system. Yet only a few months later the inherent weakness of his position became apparent: his alliances tottered and it seemed that he, too, like so many Italian politicians before him, would be the head of yet another short-lived coalition. But what emerged rather than a further crisis and a realignment of the political parties of the right was the Italian dictatorship.

THE MATTEOTTI CRISIS

When the new parliament met, the situation remained tense. Mussolini had a huge majority and for a while even put out feelers for some kind of co-option of the more moderate socialists, or at least the more practically minded trade unions, but a *trasformismo* of the subversives was not to be and they appeared in the chamber licking their wounds, bruised, down but not out. It would be going too far to suggest that one of the roots of the dictatorship lay in the refusal of the subversives to recognize the legitimacy of the 1924 elections, but it is inescapable that their uncompromising attitude to their defeat complicated Mussolini's relationship with his Vittorio Veneter allies and made it less likely that he would remain within constitutional limits. In an electrifying speech [**Doc. 18, p. 141**] in parliament on 30 May the high-profile reformist socialist **Giacomo Matteotti** made it clear that this parliament and the Fascist victory were the product of violence, intimidation and corruption. Mussolini may have been posing now in top hat and tails, but the reality was that his power rested on castor oil and the cosh, and his fellow travellers were passionately invited to abandon him as the

Giacomo Matteotti (1885–1924): Moderate socialist whose speech in May 1924 defended the liberal constitution from Fascism. His murder provoked the Matteotti crisis, which led Mussolini to speed up the construction of the dictatorship.

thuggish head of a thuggish movement. Even after Matteotti's murder, a few days later, the aim of the subversives was to split Mussolini's majority and to press the monarchy to dissolve the government. When the evidence pointed to Mussolini himself having ordered Matteotti's brutal killing, the coalition did indeed tremble and many of the *Duce's* fellow travellers asked themselves if this was really a man who could be trusted over the long term, but as his main accusers were the old liberal-hating subversives, keeping Mussolini was always preferable to a return to 1919–20.

Mussolini held on, distanced himself from the killing, and ostensibly made sure he showed himself to be utterly fair-handed in investigating the real cause of a murder that shook Italy to its core. Perhaps most importantly he gave up the Interior Ministry and passed it to the respected (nationalist) Federzoni. Many liberals and the press turned against Mussolini. The king and the army watched the situation and took no action, although the latter provided the MSVN with a huge cache of arms at this very delicate moment, as if to suggest that come what may the Matteotti affair was not to be used as an excuse by the subversives for renewed militancy. The Fascist Party, or at least sections of it represented most vociferously by the radical, but highly self-interested, Cremonese *ras* **Roberto Farinacci**, called on Mussolini to cease his compromising with the establishment and to carry out a full-scale Fascist revolution. The subversives doggedly called on the king to oust Mussolini, a prime minister who would not tolerate opposition in parliament and who murdered his political enemies. In June 1924 they withdrew from parliament altogether (known as the Aventine Secession, after some ancient Roman 'precedents'), taking the moral high ground and leaving the majority coalition to disintegrate by itself. An order from the king would have been enough for Mussolini's majority to dissolve. But the order never came. Most liberals, who by now were a vital prop to Mussolini's position, took the view that Fascism was better than a return to the impotence of the 1919 and 1921 parliaments [**Doc. 17, p. 141**].

This was the situation of the March on Rome over again and once more it was Mussolini who played the situation to his benefit and eventually re-emerged as the pivot of the Italian political system. But something had changed: it was now clear to Mussolini that he could demand much more than before and the likelihood of his being sidelined or ejected from his nodal point in the political alignments that he had done so much to create was actually rather slight, particularly if demands for his removal came from the subversives. Yet it had also become apparent that any future crisis might mean that the anti-subversive consensus to his pivotal political location could melt and then recoalesce elsewhere (around the monarchy, for example) if he did not move quickly to make himself indispensable. The dictatorship was therefore Mussolini's attempt to crush the subversives, remove them

Roberto Farinacci (1892–1945): Prominent squad leader during the rise of Fascism and *ras* of Cremona, a city he ruled with patronage and an iron fist. He was a radical Fascist and in general he was sidelined during the Regime. He supported the alliance with Germany and was enthusiastic about Italy's racial laws. He was executed by partisans in 1945.

from Italian politics, and prevent any future alliance between them and his moderate supporters. That no such alliance emerged until July 1943 testifies both to the absence of a serious anti-Fascist movement in Italy after 1925 and to Mussolini's relative restraint in pursuing a real 'fascistization' of Italian society.

On 3 January 1925, in a parliament still bereft of the subversives, Mussolini made possibly the most important speech of his career thus far. In it he did not specifically admit to Matteotti's murder, but stated that he claimed responsibility for the 'historical, political, and moral climate that [he had] created from interventionism to now'. Violence was justified and the silencing of the subversives was the only way forward. After Matteotti's death they had attacked him in the press, murdered Fascist sympathizers, removed themselves from parliament and proven themselves to be a revolutionary and unconstitutional force: 'if Fascism was [as the subversives argued] just castor oil and clubs, and not the passionate pride of the best Italian youth . . . if Fascism was nothing but an association of criminals, then he was the head of this criminal association'. To be sure, Mussolini continued, he could have unleashed his Blackshirts, but this was not necessary because the government 'is strong enough to fully and definitively destroy the Aventine sedition'. For the love of Italy, of peace, and tranquillity (which is what all Italians wanted), Mussolini stated, the time had come to 'clarify the situation' (OO XXI: 238–40) [Doc. 19, p. 142]. He was greeted by the subversive-free parliament with roars of approval, prolonged applause, shouts of 'long live Mussolini' and a large number of members of parliament pressed around the flushed prime minister to shake his hand.

ESTABLISHING THE REGIME

Mussolini's 'clarification of the situation' meant above all the outlawing of the political parties that had carried out subversive practice and the organs that expressed their opinion, but it also entailed the foreclosure of the institutions that had allowed them to operate relatively freely and that were embedded in the framework of the liberal state. In practice the subversives could not be dealt with permanently without the dismantling of certain key sections of the liberal order too, and in this way Fascism did radically transform the Italian political system and in doing so encroached on the entrenched power of traditional elites. But this appeared to be a price that these traditional elites were willing to pay – at least until Mussolini's alliance with Hitler threatened to let the subversives back on to the Italian political scene via the back door of Italian military defeat.

The dictatorship was not a period of martial law but a real alternative to the liberal democratic state as it had developed in Europe since the nineteenth century. However, only some areas of Italian society were radically transformed, while others remained substantially untouched. As has been shown, Mussolini had no blueprint for the construction of a Fascist Italy except the basic platform of the Vittorio Veneters. This may well have been enough to unite a whole series of disparate forces in the face of the subversives, but it was hardly a programme for dictatorship or a guideline for future political action. The Vittorio Veneters wanted national self-assertion, the glorification of the First World War dead and veterans, possibly a larger African empire and intolerance towards other ethnic groups on Italy's borderlands, but there was little here on which to base the actual running of a very large and complex European country. Much of what Fascism tried to do and what it left alone in the 15 years after 1925 was of course about readying Italy for future 'self-assertion' (including full-scale military engagement in Europe) but, apart from the tell-tale sign of Italy's appalling performance in the Second World War, which rated much below that of Giolittian Italy's in 1915–18 and which seriously calls into question the seriousness of this plank of the Fascist Regime's raison d'être, Fascism's malleability can also be put down to Mussolini's need to reassert himself as the keystone of the political system he had created.

The permanent elimination of the subversives involved as its first step the closing down of the liberal order in terms of the functioning of democracy and the unhindered run of free speech and press. In the months that followed his January 'clarification', Mussolini put some punch into his posturing: all political parties were outlawed except for the PNF, and openly anti-Fascist newspapers were closed down. Although the overseeing role of the state, at first through newspaper ownership 'readjustments' and occasional coercion by the prefecture of the Interior Ministry, ensured that no deviation from prescribed opinions found its way into print, there was clearly much willingness to come to terms with what the Regime stood for on the part of hundreds of newspapers up and down the peninsula. The destruction of the Socialist Party political press, which had a vast array of local newspapers throughout Italy, must have been welcome news to many a newspaper owner competing for readers in a circumscribed market. From the ad hoc control of the early Fascist period, the press was eventually *inquadrata* (to use the buzz word coined by the Regime and meaning something like 'regimentation') via a tightly monitored register of journalists and by the mid-1930s by a full-scale Ministry of Press and Propaganda.

The actual political constitution of liberal Italy was transformed too. The newly invented position of 'head of government' (Mussolini, of course) became accountable only to the king and could issue decree laws. Parliament, now deprived of opposition, was emasculated to the point that, by 1926, the losers were the Fascist deputies who had had a clear run in the chamber ever since the Aventine Secession. Local government, whose socialist councils had been such a thorn in the side of the Italian state in the *biennio rosso*, was transformed by the abolition of representation. From 1926 mayors were no longer elected but appointed by the prefecture. In practice, the designation of a local political chief by the state had the tendency to undermine the position of local Fascists who, certainly in some areas, had had it all their own way in local government for a considerable time. There was no wholesale fascistization in this regard throughout the Regime, and for the most part local government officials came from the same oligarchies that had been in control since unification. As far as they were concerned democracy, as espoused by Giolitti, had only opened the floodgates to the plebeian subversives and Mussolini had readjusted the situation. To be sure there was often now a vociferous set of Blackshirts demanding a slice of the local pie, but there was usually enough to go around – especially as so much time, effort and money no longer needed to be invested in holding off the subversives. Mussolini was the lynchpin once again, and he made sure he did enough to alienate neither the Fascist movement nor the old elites, who did not mind joining the party but were not prepared to hand over the levers of local power to a bunch of blackshirted parvenus. Mussolini knew this and worked hard to continue to preserve the balance. What was most important in this equilibrium was the relationship between the state, Fascism as movement, and society in general. That Mussolini hung on to power for so long testifies to his remarkable capacity nearly always to work the system to his favour.

6

The Fascist Regime, 1926–36

THE STRUCTURE OF THE FASCIST REGIME

It is no coincidence that the Fascist philosophy of the state was drawn up by thinkers of the old Nationalist Association such as Alfredo Rocco and Giovanni Gentile. For them, Fascism was the means by which their programme of national renewal, debated over a prolonged period of disillusionment with the results of liberal Italy's failure to tackle what they regarded as fundamental flaws in state and society, could be put into practice. They had long despised democracy, hated the left and regarded the parliamentary wheeling and dealing and the compromises of Giolitti and his ilk as profoundly damaging to the greater good of the nation. They had, of course, wanted Italian intervention in the Great War and saw in the more authoritarian governments that had marshalled Italy's resources during that conflict an inspiration for the future. It was not the state's job to mediate between contending and competing individuals and political forces (as liberals might have argued), but to forge a nation where each individual worked as cog, gear or rivet in the locomotive that was the fatherland. United and regimented at home, Italy would be fit enough to succeed in the international struggle and accrue to itself the resources required for development and further expansion. To say that this agenda had not been part of Italian liberalism would be going too far, but it had coexisted and competed with the more progressive pluralism that was the other pulse of the post-unification order: according to the nationalists, it was now time for their programme to take the upper hand, and Fascism would provide the means to do so.

The decision to grant the ex-nationalists the right to draw up the blueprint for the Fascist state was, from Mussolini's point of view, yet another ploy in his divide-and-rule tactics. It forestalled the Fascist movement, the PNF above all, from making too many demands. As De Felice put it:

> While in 'classic' totalitarian regimes (the Soviet Union and Nazi Germany) the party was the cornerstone in the conquest of power . . . and

the state apparatus became subordinated to it . . . for Mussolini and therefore the Fascist Regime, the opposite was true: the fulcrum, substance and
leadership of the Regime was to be only and exclusively the state and the
party was to be subordinated to it.

(De Felice, 1968: 298)

The secretary of the party in 1925, Roberto Farinacci, had a more radical
vision: he saw the PNF as being a kind of vanguard, spearheading a real
social remodelling of Italy, and voiced the widespread resentment of many
early Fascists who had hoped that Mussolini's coming to power would have
guaranteed them more influence. The squads were at work throughout the
period of the Regime's construction, but when their attention turned from
subversive remnants to the establishment – for example, prominent free-
masons in the state bureaucracy were targeted from early 1925 – it was clear
that Mussolini needed to make some quick decisions. Already in January
1925 an order had gone out from Federzoni's Interior Ministry banning
spontaneous political demonstrations, be they held by subversives or Fascists,
and the police were even instructed to arrest the latter if the need arose. The
way Mussolini would go was already apparent and during a speech given at
the Scala opera house in Milan in October 1925 he was to make his stance
explicit: 'everything in the State, nothing outside the State, nothing against
the State' (OO XXI: 425) ran the slogan, and the process, already begun in
October 1922, of incorporating the Fascist movement into the now very
stretched confines of the liberal state picked up momentum.

In the same way that Rome had mattered more to Mussolini than
Fascism's northern Italian provincial towns and their various *rases* in 1922,
so now the *Duce* clung to the nationalists, held off the Fascist Party, co-opted
the pre-existing institutions and personnel of the liberal state, and in the
process refashioned Italy into a Mussolini-dependent hybrid. In this new
creation the party was to become the choreographer of the Regime; primarily
busy with the incorporation of ever-broader sections of the Italian public,
through its cultural and flanking activities, into the state's overall aspirations.
It would never come close to monopolizing power. By the late 1930s, PNF
membership had ballooned to more than 3 million and a majority of Italians
belonged to one of its many social and cultural organizations (Dogliani,
1999: 86). Its very size precluded the party occupying a privileged place in
Italian society. Mussolini constantly exchanged the limited support of the
Fascist movement for the institutions of the established Italian state, while
allowing the former an expanding space in the marshalling of the people.
Throughout the Regime he would play one force off against the other and
ensure that it was his arbitration that held final authority. On many occasions
the *Duce* withheld a decision and preferred to let the two sides balance
each other indefinitely. As a way of running a large and complex country it

was inefficient, but for Mussolini it had the great advantage of making him irreplaceable.

Although Fascist Italy was not the well-oiled machine that propaganda cracked it up to be, this did not mean that it was unable to deal with opposition. The tools of repression, police powers and the legal system, were intensified and unshackled rather than radically changed, and characteristically it was a non-Fascist and southerner, Arturo Bocchini, who was given command of the repressive apparatus. The **Ovra**, a political and secret police force, was set up in 1927, although a similar body had existed under the liberals, and remained answerable to the Interior Ministry but was financed by secret funds. Its activities ranged from sniffing out the communist underground to spying on high-ranking Fascists. That even Mussolini's phone calls were tapped indicates that the *Duce's* control over his police chief was not total. Prefects continued to be appointed from out of the civil service, and as late as 1943 only 37 out of 117 were political appointees whose credentials rested on their power in the Fascist party (Clark, 1996: 235). *Rases* never became prefects automatically but operated uneasily alongside them and, when conflicts occurred, Mussolini usually favoured the latter [**Doc. 23, p. 145**]. After a series of attempts on the *Duce's* life in the mid-1920s, a 'Special Tribunal for the Defence of the State' was set up with the power to apply the death penalty, and did so 26 times before 1943. However, it liberally dished out **confino** sentences (more than 15,000), which meant the removal of political activists (including disgraced Fascists) to remote locations in the south of Italy or the islands. The practice of the latter confirmed that political subversion was of no consequence whatever if it occurred in the south, and as official policy it stood in glaring contradiction to the idea, much mooted by Fascism, that under its aegis Italy had become one. A spell in a village south of Eboli was for the Italian political class tantamount to having been banished to Botany Bay. Alfredo Rocco's new legal code came into force in 1931. It strengthened the powers of prosecution as well as in principle curtailing individual rights in favour of state security; it also increased the number of offences punishable by death. That the *Codice Rocco* remained in force into the 1970s testifies to the fact that its underpinning logic did not necessarily require a Fascist Regime for it to work, but it should be taken in its specific context as one pillar in the general overhauling of the liberal order. One of the most important other ones, indeed one of the few real innovations Fascism made in the restructuring of the Italian state, was corporativism.

Much touted as a 'third way', superseding both capitalism and socialism, corporativism represented the synthesis of the nationalist ideal of a state that subsumed class division by recognizing as 'producers' all economically and socially active individuals, whatever their function or position in the

Ovra: The Fascist secret police. Its specific task was to track down anti-Fascist activity. Mussolini also used it (his relationship with the *Ovra*'s head, Arturo Bocchini, was very close indeed) to monitor and control his Fascist lieutenants.

Confino: The sentence of internal exile, normally to remote locations in Italy's south or islands, used to eliminate the threat of those deemed enemies of the Regime.

productive process. Institutions such as trade unions, employer associations, committees of landlords and peasant leagues which, according to Fascism, exacerbated and institutionalized class division, were to be replaced by state agencies whose mandate was to guarantee and streamline production for the benefit of the nation as a whole. Class conflict was written out of the constitution. Strikes (but also lockouts) were made illegal in 1926 and independent trade unions were also abolished. The Fascist Grand Council issued a much-vaunted Charter of Labour a year later, which set the parameters for industrial relations. Worker representation was at first left to the Fascist syndical organizations, which could appeal to the state when conflict arose, but their growing power – they had over 3 million members by 1929 (De Bernardi and Guarracino, 1998: 522) – and autonomy led eventually to their being broken up and swallowed by the corporations.

In one sense corporativism was an answer to the fact that, notwithstanding legislation, workers' interests were still difficult to reconcile with industrialists' or landlords' profits, particularly in the 1930s with the contraction of the Italian and international economy. Fascist syndicalists like Edmondo Rossoni found themselves having to fill the yawning gap left by the destruction of the socialist and Catholic trade unions, and had to do so with something concrete. In 1925, for example, there had been a series of major strikes led by the Fascist trade unions that made the willingness of bosses to accept the end of the socialist unions in exchange for Fascist ones highly unlikely. Mussolini had to keep both sides happy, and corporativism got the go-ahead. Rossoni was sacked and the Fascist syndicates subdivided into occupational categories. Particularly after the onset of the depression and through the carefully drafted decrees of Giuseppe Bottai, minister of corporations in the early 1930s, what appeared at first to be merely the enshrining in law of the desire of industrialists and landlords to make money without any interference from their workers, became a fully fledged alternative productive system, at least on paper.

In practice, corporativism did not significantly change the operation of the Italian economy. It did not even mean the expansion of state involvement in it, because when this did occur it did not do so through the corporations but via a series of agencies that were erected alongside them. IRI, the Institute for Industrial Reconstruction, was founded in 1933 to provide government money to shore up Italian industries and banks that had been severely affected by the depression. This state-holding company intervened with loans in exchange for assets throughout the Italian economy and quickly became a major shareholder in a significant proportion of Italian banks and companies. The logic of corporativism led in 1939 to the replacement of the Chamber of Deputies (the Senate remained, as its abolition would have meant an unacceptable encroachment on the king's prerogative), which had in any case become a rubber stamp for governmental decrees, with a Chamber of Fasces and Corporations. Appointed members from the corporations therefore replaced territorial representatives and the new institution became another cumbersome part of the state bureaucracy, which provided jobs and an audience for Mussolini's speeches but was insignificant in running the country.

The actual decision to transform the Chamber of Deputies into the Chamber of Corporations was made in the Fascist Grand Council. In 1928 the latter had acquired official status as a state institution and was no longer merely an organ of the Fascist Party as it had been since 1922; it had the power to present a list of names to the king in case the head of government needed replacing, and was meant to provide Fascist continuity in government should something happen to Mussolini. The *Duce* could hardly argue that Fascism would die with him if his Regime were to be taken as a serious (and internationally exportable) 'third way', but as head of the Grand Council he made sure no list of plausible successors was ever drawn up. The Grand Council, too, only had consultative functions; it was appointed by Mussolini and only had as much power as the *Duce* chose to give it, which was very little. Most importantly, it was up to Mussolini to convene it and in the 1930s it very rarely met. Although in 1943 it was this body that gave Mussolini a vote of no confidence and precipitated his fall, it did not have the constitutional power to remove him from office; the authority to do this remained exclusively in the hands of the king.

In fact, from Mussolini's point of view, the principal weakness of the Fascist Regime as it evolved over the late 1920s and through the 1930s was the role of the monarchy in the hybrid Italian 'constitution'. During the March on Rome and the Matteotti crisis it was the king's willingness to call to and then sustain Mussolini in office that allowed the *Duce* to overcome the qualms of the liberals, parliament and, importantly, the Italian army, and what had been given to the Romagnol parvenu might at any point be taken away [**Doc. 38, p. 156**]. This sword of Damocles continued to hover over the *Duce*, no matter how he tinkered with the political system he had inherited, and sapped the possibility of a sustained and radical transformation of Italian state and society in a Fascist direction. Mussolini remained a hostage to the weakness of his initial position when he came to power in 1922, which itself was also responsible for his adoption of a 'statist' interpretation of his dictatorship [**Doc. 20, p. 143**]. By working through the prefecture, the bureaucracy and the survivals of the old liberal state as opposed to launching a real Fascist revolution and resting his mandate exclusively on the Fascist movement, Mussolini chose perhaps the only real option that was open to him, but it meant that he was always vulnerable to a loss of support from the establishment. In part the destruction of the subversives (and the setting up of the dictatorship itself) had been precisely to do with the fact that they had been capable, not of defeating Fascism on their own, but of driving a wedge between Mussolini and his allies among Italy's elite. In Fascist Italy there was no SS that owed its privileges to the Fascist 'revolution', partly because the construction of a similar body would have meant a confrontation with the army that Fascism was likely to lose, but also because Mussolini himself preferred to trust in his ability to negotiate, to divide and rule rather than to put all his eggs in the Fascist basket. With Mussolini's full support, the Fascist militia had a precarious identity and fell under state, rather than party, regulation early on in the Regime, and never became the bodyguard of the PNF.

Fascism's victory over Italian state and society might have been patchy, but the *Duce* considered that he had an ace up his sleeve that would in the end render the compromises of the past irrelevant. He understood that having made Fascism, his complicated and wobbly system required for its long-term survival that he should make Italians Fascist. In other words he needed to convince the public at large of the veracity and plausibility of his vision, to make all Italians aware they were truly experiencing and contributing to a moment of radical and positive change. Mussolini knew perfectly well that he was a master at this kind of game and the journalist in him was confident he could leapfrog the bargaining and compromise, paper over the shoddiness of his dictatorship's totalitarianism, and reach out to the real people who would respond to his orchestration; after all, in the past, with little more than a newspaper and his voice he had achieved miracles. What might he not do with the apparatus of the Italian state at his disposal?

FASCISM AND RELIGION

When liberals and the kingdom of Piedmont had unified Italy, the task of bringing into the fold the multiplicity of cultures, the diversity of 'Italian' life, had been a daunting but essential key to their project's success (see Lanaro, 1988). Yet their agenda had been limited: they recognized that other identities, such as being Catholic or Jewish or socialist, might coexist with being 'Italian'. The travails of liberal Italy were associated with the difficulties encountered during the implementation of this limited agenda. As had been the case for the liberals, the question of how far it was possible to be both 'Fascist' and something else at the same time quickly became a vital one for the Regime. The *Duce's* need to justify his grip on power in the absence of electoral mandates and an opposition played itself out as a constantly narrowing definition of what identities were deemed acceptable. This was the essential difference between Fascist and earlier forms of dictatorship. Patriotism was not enough.

Emilio Gentile has suggested that:

> Once in power, Fascism instituted a lay religion by sacralizing the state
> and spreading a political cult of the masses that aimed at creating a virile
> and virtuous citizenry, dedicated body and soul to the nation. In the
> enterprise of spreading its doctrine and arousing the masses to faith in
> its dogmas, obedience to its commandments, and the assimilation of its
> ethics and its life-style, Fascism spent a considerable capital of energy,
> diverting those energies from other fields that might have been more
> important.
>
> (Gentile, 1996: 159)

While the fascistization of Italian society may well appear as a remarkable
new and potent religion, there were more prosaic impulses at work, chief
of which was Mussolini's need to establish and then maintain a special relationship with the Italian people as his trump card vis-à-vis the old elites.
To see the *Duce* as a kind of messiah deeply convinced of his own mystical
role in leading the people to a 'body and soul' dedication to Italy is mistak-
ing tactical opportunism for religious fundamentalism. Above all, the dynamic
of Italian Fascism in power was a Mussolinian balancing act.

Nowhere is this juggling more apparent than the way in which the established religion of by far the majority of Italians was dealt with through the
Fascist Regime. Much of the uniqueness of Italian history since the fall of the
Roman Empire had been related to the fact that Rome hosted the spiritual
head of Christendom, while the Eternal City's temporal power exhausted
itself a hundred or so miles beyond its walls. While this tension was perhaps
a defining characteristic of all Europe before the Reformation, in Italy it
was a particularly pressing issue at all times. The liberals had never solved
the contradiction of having to sculpt the nation against the wishes of the
papacy, with a block of marble that was almost entirely Catholic. Yet, as
has been shown, the Church was not averse to condoning national identity,
provided that the adoption of the latter did not imply the squeezing out of
Catholicism. The Church's ideal scenario was one in which a large part of
what being Italian meant was actually being Catholic. This was not something liberals could ever have fully accepted, but strangely enough the
anti-clerical Mussolini, at least on paper, eventually did. How was it possible
for Fascist Italy to come to terms with Catholicism and the papacy, and to
accept the latter's definition of Italian identity, and still presumably continue
to aspire to a 'body and soul' conversion to Fascism of the Italian people?

In reality, the Church and Fascism had much to offer each other [**Doc. 20,
p. 143**]. On the one hand, the consecration of Mussolini's Regime would
mean a massive leap of legitimacy in the eyes of undecided Catholics, and,

on the other, it would herald a return of Catholicism into the apparatus of the state in a way that the papacy only dreamed of after 1870. Mussolini swallowed his visceral odium for prelates and did what all prime ministers had failed to do since the walls of Rome had been breached by Italian troops more than a half-century before: he recognized Catholicism to be an integral and unavoidable part of the essence of being Italian.

In early 1929 protracted negotiations between Italy and the Vatican resulted in the long-awaited mutual recognition. The Church finally accepted Italy's existence and in return the Vatican became a fully fledged and independent state. But this was only one part of the deal: the Church was given the duty to teach religion in Italian schools all the way to university level; its marriages were recognized by Italian civil law; and the existence of Catholic Action (**Azione Cattolica** – a lay organization educating and mobilizing Italians outside the recreational and educational networks of the state) was guaranteed at least for the foreseeable future.

Azione Cattolica: 'Catholic Action'. Lay organization linked to parishes, which educated the young in Catholic values and provided a locus for a wide variety of social and leisure activities. In the 1930s it lost the right to host sporting activities in an attempt by the Regime to curtail its attractiveness compared to that of the ONB. It survived curtailed until the fall of Mussolini.

What Mussolini had gained from the reconciliation was immense prestige and a further tangible connection with the majority of the Italian people. His brother Arnaldo, running the *Duce's* old newspaper *Il Popolo d'Italia*, could not help but conflate Fascism, Italy and Catholicism in what must have seemed a liberal's nightmare. 'We Fascists,' he wrote in the aftermath of the treaty, 'as Italian Catholics who were born and educated according to Christian principles, baptised in our churches, which are full of national memories, are transported with joy by the resolution of the "Roman Question"' (*Il Popolo d'Italia*, 12 February 1929, in Pollard, 1985: 62). The bells were rung throughout the peninsula (and beyond) on the day the concordat was signed and, to many, their ringing seemed to herald a new era where the travails of the past, the fraught choices that had previously had to be made in terms of loyalty to nation and Church, were dispelled for good. For the ex-socialist Mussolini this was no mean feat and he could be satisfied that, while he may have been accused of flip-flopping, the bells peeled as much for the *Dux* as for the *Pontefix Maximus*. The great losers were the radical anti-clerical Fascists, but also defeated were the exiled leaders of the disbanded PPI and its many supporters, who were glumly forced to witness their pope proclaiming their nemesis, Mussolini, as a 'Man sent by Providence'. As for Italian liberalism, the bells must have sounded like the mocking laughter of the licentious old priest, so dear to liberal anti-clerical propaganda, once again whispering into the ear of the powerful. But with the conciliation, had the 'real' Italy finally entered the national fold? It is difficult to argue that this is not the case, as far as Fascism was concerned, and many of its active cadres lamented the fact, since it entailed an extreme, almost unbearable dilution of the masculine and gung-ho frissons of the old days of squadism and the trenches. The pope had been no Vittorio Veneter.

As usual, Mussolini was not averse to playing off the humble village sexton and housewife against the blackshirted activist, and both against the elites of Italian society. A plebiscite gauging the Italian people's feeling towards the general direction Fascism was taking was held in March 1929, and for the first time the Church openly and fully endorsed the Fascist Regime. Some of the few who voted against the government may have been old supporters of the PPI, but the bulk of Catholics endorsed Fascism's programme on the basis of the common-sense assumption that there was nothing wrong with being both Italian and Catholic. Here we are talking about not a new 'state religion', as Emilio Gentile might have put it, but yet another Mussolinian 'working towards the Italians'. While there was plenty of opportunism in Fascism ploughing itself into the deep Catholic loam of Italian society, Fascist philosophers rose to the occasion and justified this choice in terms of the state attuning itself to the innermost spiritual identity of the Italian people.

However, no sooner had the ink dried on the conciliation documents, than the signatories began to dispute the meaning of what had been signed. The 'marriage' between Fascism and Catholicism was characterized by plate-throwing, tantrums, domestic violence and adultery. Yet it was only death that in the end parted the two parties. Predictably, it was the Church that outlived the Regime and after 1945 a quick remarriage was arranged for the surviving spouse without the formality of a decent period of mourning. For Pope Pius XI, the PPI and the Catholic trade unions had been expendable, but Catholic Action for a variety of reasons was not. The latter had never been a political party but was the means by which the Church connected with the Italian lay people over and above the day-to-day administration of the sacraments. Catholic Action was the main pillar of Italian Catholicism's dynamic re-entry into the field of education in the face of the catastrophic ejection it had suffered in the construction of the Italian school system in the 1870s. But it was also much more than this. Its overall aim was to make the parish the focal point of the socialization of the Italian people in a moment when the traditional relationship between the Church and civil society was undergoing rapid change. Therefore, Catholic Action developed an intricate network of parish-based groups teaching Catholic morality but also provid-ing a locus for social interaction. For example, at the same time as learning the catechism, the mysteries of football might also be imparted, or films might be screened in the parish hall. It was the attractiveness of the social side of Catholic Action's activities that in the end proved to be the major bone of contention between the latter and the Fascist Regime. But even here the strategy of Mussolinian juggling seems to have been important. Notwithstanding the conciliation (in fact, because of it), a wave of Fascist agitation, in the squadist tradition, was unleashed on the premises and activities of Catholic Action, prompting the pope, who had so recently showered the *Duce* with blessings, to make an extraordinarily powerful statement drawing the line as to the limits of how far Fascism might go in relations with the Church and the family. The papal encyclical issued in 1931 in defence of Catholic Action was far from being a call to rebel but it affirmed categorically that the idea that the 'rising generations belong to [the state] entirely . . . cannot be reconciled [with being] a Catholic' ('On Catholic Action in Italy', 1931). 'Totalitarianism' butted up here against a formidable barrier and the sudden Church–state conflict of 1931 resolved itself as an uneasy draw. The Church did indeed relinquish many of its parish-based social and sporting activities, but Catholic Action remained standing almost as an alternative government-in-waiting.

MAKING ITALIANS FASCIST?

The 1931 dispute with the Church had been one of the consequences of what was to be a very serious test for the longevity of the dictatorship: the great depression. The fine-tuned political balance achieved by Mussolini by the late 1920s had rested on the economic policies of that decade, which had generally been positively received by Italian industry and finance. Under the slogan the 'battle for the lira', an exchange rate of 90 lire to the British pound had been aimed at and achieved by 1927. By this date the Regime had laid the foundations for the protectionism of the 1930s, with a 'battle for wheat' where more land was given over to the growing of this staple and tariffs were imposed on its import. However, lower wages and higher food prices resulted. Despite the trumpeting of the conciliation, the Fascism that had been born in the exuberance of the triumphant Vittorio Veneter moment risked settling down into a comfortable middle age. There appeared to be few serious threats and, to the rising generations, even the *biennio rosso* and the war were now distant and intangible forces.

Italian anti-Fascist exiles lamented the success of the Regime and were disgruntled with what they perceived to be the passivity of the Italian people before its agendas. **Palmiro Togliatti**, the leader of the Italian Communist Party, understood that there was something afoot in the persistence of the Regime in the difficult conditions of the 1930s that could not be put down to 'open violence and terror' alone. He argued that it was the dictatorship's attempt to cope with the world economic crisis that precipitated and intensified the campaign to win over the hearts and minds of Italians and to make them fully 'Fascist'. '[G]oing to the people' (*L'Internationale Communiste*, 5 October 1934, in Togliatti, 1973: 468–88) was about stabilizing elite power through, once again, conceding to Fascism the authority to

Palmiro Togliatti (1893–1964): Communist Party co-founder and leader, and key player in the 1930s Communist International. A loyal Stalinist, he nevertheless was independent minded and was instrumental in forging alliances of all anti-Fascist forces in wartime and postwar Italy.

develop the institutions connecting the Italian people to the state. According to Togliatti, if the rise of Fascism could be accounted for by the crisis that followed the Great War and the class struggle of the *biennio rosso*, its intensification and survival through the 1930s was tied to its usefulness in the economic crisis of that decade. If Hitler's dictatorship was a direct product of the depression, Italian Fascism's 'going to the people' or the transformation of Mussolini from the almost bourgeois politician of the 1920s, not averse to wearing top hat and tails and mixing with Roman high-class society, to the granite-like and distant dictator nearly always in military or blackshirt uniform with no equals within Italy, was the way Fascism repackaged itself in the transformed circumstances of the 1930s.

Making Italians Fascist depended on a definition of what being Fascist actually meant. There was no consensus, even among Fascist leaders, on the basic tenets of Fascism. No thinker of unquestioned authority had ever come up with an agreed definition and even official Fascist attempts at making a concrete statement of principles – for example, the entry for 'Fascism' in the *Enciclopedia Italiana* of 1932, written by Mussolini and Giovanni Gentile (in Delzell, 1970: 91–106) – were convoluted and vague. Mussolini was too astute a politician to tie himself down to a detailed set of dogmas. However, this is not to suggest that there were not some overarching principles that would have seen all Fascists in agreement: the subordination of all classes and individuals to the collectivity as embodied by the state; ultra-nationalism of the 'my country right or wrong' variety; and the acceptance that international conflict for the capture of limited world resources was not only inevitable but beneficial to the strengthening of the 'national community'. In theory anything that purported to further these goals was good, anything that hindered them was bad. It is difficult to see this as an original and novel political doctrine. Rather it was the alive and kicking Vittorio Veneter programme writ large, and in its essentials the agenda of late nineteenth-century nationalism. What Mussolini rightly defined as new was the level of activism and participation expected of the people: above all, he wrote, 'The Fascist disdains an "easy" life' (in Delzell, 1970: 93). For Mussolini to have something to offer, for his Regime to dispel rumours of middle-aged redundancy, 'going to the people' meant dispelling the Regime's and the *Duce*'s built-in obsolescence. Even in Mussolini's own definition of Fascism his greatest fear was a lapse back to liberalism, as if, by default, crises having been overcome and emergencies solved, Italy would, like any civilized country, automatically return to the liberal fold. Mussolini was aware of his own expendability if, as he stated, '[liberalism is classified] as outside the judgement of history, as though history were a hunting ground reserved for the professors of Liberalism alone – as though Liberalism were the final unalterable verdict of civilization' (in Delzell, 1970: 102).

In practice, the way in which most Italians understood Fascism as it was fed to them and as they themselves developed it in the 1930s was very much as an activation or an intensification of those agendas of the 'nationalisation of the masses' (Mosse, 1975) that had been such a central feature of Italian life since unification. There had already been parades, there had already been uniforms, drill, speeches, patriotic songs and celebrations. There had already been cults of national heroes, the myth of ancient Rome, the construction of national monuments and preparation for war. There had already been empire in Africa. There had already been much talk of the benefits bestowed by Italy's great economic leap forward since unification [**Doc. 23, p. 145**]. In Fascism's 'going to the people', these aims and achievements, though, became more and more pervasively dwelled on and snaked into loci where they had previously been (almost) absent. If the liberal state had, for example, made it (theoretically) compulsory for all to go to school and had conscripted men into the army, Fascism was to continue in the same vein but at greater depth. There was nothing specifically to compare in liberal Italy with the role assigned to the dictator who, according to one Fascist slogan, 'was always right', but even here there had been individuals who appeared to rely on their visionary charisma and a patriotic 'religious faith' to control the peninsula (Duggan, 2002) and the hyperbole attached to the figure of the monarch often verged on the cult of personality. Of course, a major difference with liberal Italy was that under Fascism the platforms from which a political opposition could legally challenge the authority of the established regime were all dismantled.

By the mid-1930s Fascism had created a series of new institutions that sought to establish and then maintain the link between people and state as a permanent and 'total' one. The mesh of liberal Italy's net had been relatively loose. Over and above a few years of school and a stint in the national army, it relied on the spontaneity of civil society to generate organizations or cultural media that instilled the virtues of patriotism, or the benefits of modern economic discipline. Liberal Italy's hands-off policy (De Grazia, 1992) was in reality no different from that of most of western European states before 1914, but the peninsula's economic backwardness constrained the capacity of civil society to reach out to the people.

This boosting of a programme that was already embryonic prior to Fascism's coming to power is perhaps best exemplified by the *Opera Nazionale Balilla*. The ONB began life as a youth annexe to the party but its influence and importance remained circumscribed before 1925. Unlike the Hitler Youth in Germany, which had tens of thousands of members before Hitler came to power, the ONB was really invented with the Regime itself under construction, and developed as a corollary to the fascistization of the Italian school system. The ONB eventually created sections catering

Opera Nazionale Balilla (ONB): The Fascist boy scouts organization. It was run by the Education Ministry and became an adjunct to the established school system. It fostered an ethos of military preparedness and devotion to the *Duce*.

for children between the ages of 6 and 18, of both sexes (in separate organ-izations), and replaced all other associations that provided recreational and social activity for young people and children. The ONB did not remain a party organ but in 1929 was absorbed by the Ministry of Education. It therefore became an adjunct of the school system, used its premises and its staff, and gradually took over the running of all extracurricular activities ranging from sports to hiking, art competitions, essay-writing champion-ships and so on. It gave its members a uniform (in Italy, school 'uniforms' had been little more than aprons to keep normal clothes clean) and therefore fostered a sense of belonging. Although membership was not compulsory until 1939, children who did not join were likely to be discriminated against by their peers, and parents had to provide a written explanation of why their child did not belong. By the early 1930s state employment required a past in the ONB. With the parishes losing the right to host sports activities and with the closing down (or absorption) of all other social youth clubs, the alternative to the *Balilla* was either the insipid catechism of Catholic Action or the streets (Koon, 1985: 94). Notwithstanding compulsion, in 1939 50 per cent of Italian youth preferred the freedom of the latter (De Beranardi and Guarracino, 1998: 329) and ONB membership tended to tail off as the age of 18 approached. To most Italians, who were still peasants in the mid-1930s, a state job was unimagineable and it would have been more important for a Sardinian shepherd's child to be sent up to the mountains to guard sheep than to learn what it meant to be a 'son of the [Roman] she-wolf' (as the very young members of the ONB were called) **[Doc. 26, p. 147]**.

So what was the ONB expected to do? Produce 'Fascists, Fascists . . . Fascist soldiers . . . conservators of national values . . . the secure military garrison of the new Italy' (Koon, 1985: 94) went one answer. But what is meant by 'Fascist' is here not stated. Male children were regarded as the soldiers of the future, hence the growing pedagogical obsession with phys-ical as opposed to mental education. Although physical education had been part of the Italian school curriculum since the 1870s it had often amounted to little more than a weekly kick-about with a football in a dusty yard, or being forced to attempt a vault over some rickety apparatus in a tiny 'gym-nasium' (usually a classroom). The 'playing fields' and sporting traditions of Anglo-Saxon education simply did not exist. Therefore, in most cases, the ONB's activation of a wide variety of sports as fostering the physical qualities necessary for the soldier was in fact often not about Fascism taking over pre-existing sports organizations but inculcating an interest in sport for the first time. The ONB also provided cheap holidays in purpose-built 'colonies', such as *Sciesopoli* (ski town) in the Lombard Alps, to which thousands of members of the ONB were sent by their parents.

But what did the little *Balilla* do during their summer vacations, for example, at the 'Rosa Maltoni Mussolini' (the *Duce's* mother) colony built between 1929 and 1933 near Livorno? Contemporary newsreels convey a typical 'day in the life' of the children: first we see them march out in the morning beneath a huge and billowing Italian flag against the backdrop of the extraordinary futurist-inspired architecture of the site; they then perform a series of gymnastic exercises in unison and are marched down to the beach. We are then given a view of the ultra-modern kitchens and laundries of the colony and their contented and neatly dressed female staff as the vast crowds of children splash into the sea. What appears to be a hearty lunch is followed by play in a large and modern games room. A ballet of the little female *Balilla* beneath the colonnade of the 'Rosa Mussolini' building then gives way to a serried rank of girls praying before going to bed in a large and clean dormitory (newsreel, *Giornale Luce B0310*, 14 July 1933). Whatever the truth in this rather innocent depiction of a 'Fascist' holiday, a trawl through the hundreds of newsreels showing the activities of the ONB gives prominence to athleticism, the health and vigour of outdoor activity, cleanliness and efficiency, and what George Orwell called in *Nineteen Eighty-four* 'physical jerks' (Orwell, 1990: 33), the precursor of aerobics.

The aspiring 'totalitarian' societies of the 1930s (and beyond) could never resist the vision of thousands of young and healthy activists performing physical exercises in unison – usually in a stadium – and imbued with simple but deep symbolic meaning. The typical image, of which there are an endless variation in Italian newsreels of the 1930s, is that of the dictator (or his representative) on a podium looking down on thousands of weaving athletes forming with their unified bodies the letters of the word *Dux*, or an airplane, or the lictor symbol, or a Fascist slogan. Whether these ceremonies created 'Fascists' may be debated [**Doc. 25, p. 147**] but they were collective expressions of identity and their preparation took long hours of drill for teachers and children alike. There was clearly a sublimation of the potentially challenging vigour of youth at work here, but far more significant was the way these events symbolized the way society was supposed to function for the people involved in the mass 'physical jerks', for those who might only see them on a newsreel, or for the dictator himself, who would feel that his spiritual reorganization of society was taking place before his eyes.

Running around a stadium in uniform under the eyes of a self-satisfied *Duce*, however, did not necessarily mean that those who participated were undergoing a radical metamorphosis; rather these were the duties required of ONB members. In an Italy, where the family tended (especially for females) to be the exclusive locus of social interaction, being forced out of the home by the requirements of fascistization could be a liberating experience. Holidays in a Fascist *colonia* were so popular because, for the vast majority of Italians, a vacation by the sea or in the mountains was something rare. The experience of women in particular needs to be seen in this light. To say that Fascist policies pushed women back into the home is true but misleading: Victoria De Grazia argues that in Fascist Italy, 'women's lives were a disconcerting experience of new opportunities and new repressions' (De Grazia, 1992: 1) and that the way women related to the Regime depended on a range of factors from class, to region, to the kind of employment held. Making generalizations out of case-studies is often deceptive (see Wilson, 1996).

Fascism's 'going to the people' was gendered: it was different for males and females. What Fascism wanted was for both sexes to feel that their lives gained meaning through their relationship to the aims of the state. To make the personal political was part of the way Fascism departed from liberalism, in which the personal and the political were meant to occupy strictly separate spheres. But Fascism also aimed to transform politics from an institutionalized form of social conflict. The politicization of the personal meant imbuing all activity with a meaning that was provided from the top by the burgeoning apparatus for the implementation of Fascist social policy. What was expected of women in this context?

The 'battle for births' had been inaugurated with Mussolini's 'ascension day' speech in May 1927 in which the *Duce* had pointed out that 'in order to count, Italy has by the second half of the 20th century to have a population of no less than sixty million inhabitants' (OO XII: 364). Comparing Italy unfavourably in terms of population size (40 million in the late 1920s) with the Anglo-Saxon countries, Germany and 'the Slavs', it was clear that pretensions to permanent status as a Great Power would require not falling behind in the demographic stakes. Suddenly, from being regarded as *the* overpopulated country *par excellence*, Italy was being depicted as in grave danger of losing what had seemed its almost unchallengeable dominance in this area. As Mussolini highlighted in his speech, it was now only the southern regions that kept Italy's birth rate reasonably high. He praised Basilicata for its leadership in this field. The *Duce* was referring to the emancipation of women when he ambiguously paid tribute to this poverty-stricken and almost entirely agricultural region as 'not yet sufficiently infected by all the pernicious currents of contemporary civilization' (OO XII: 366). In Basilicata the patriarchal family of traditional peasant society continued in its overabundance of children.

Demographic concerns were not particularly 'Fascist', but actively fostering larger families and granting mothers a heroic role in the affirmation of the fatherland on the world stage was new. Yet even here there were many ambiguities. A woman dedicated to the family and the hearth, whose primary role was to procreate, to bring up as many children as God sent her and to be at her husband's service at all times, submissive and totally dedicated to the household was much the same as what the Church had propounded over the course of the centuries (with obligatory visits to the parish, of course), but perhaps what the Great War had done was to significantly raise expectations. From 1914 Europe populated itself with bereaved mothers as the death toll of their sons (and husbands and lovers) rose to dizzying heights. Women were expected to bear the loss with stoic resignation, imbued with the firm belief that their 'sacrifice' had been worthwhile and willingly made. The demands on all European states in fighting the Great War went a long way to break the boundary that separated the private sphere of the family from the incursions of the fatherland. The process of politicizing the personal was well under way before Mussolini came to power.

The dichotomy of the experience of women in Fascist Italy was the fruit of exactly this tension. On the one hand Fascism reinforced traditional female gender roles in its quest for a bigger population and perhaps 'consensus' from men and the forces of tradition throughout Italy. On the other it wanted to get into the minds of women in a way that had never been envisaged before 1914, and to do so it had to politicize and therefore push them out of the confines of the family. Perry Wilson has gone so far as to characterize the Fascist period as one where

> attention to defining the female contribution to the state meant that women were brought on to the national stage *for the first time*. Women's roles became more visible and new spaces opened up for them in the public sphere. In this respect Fascism should be considered as innovator and the interwar period a watershed in Italian women's history.
>
> (Wilson, 1996: 81)

What is being referred to here is the panoply of women's organizations that came into being in the Fascist period, and some of the possible emancipatory effects of economic modernization in the 1930s, as well as the consistent presence of women in Fascist public utterances from Mussolini down. Prolific mothers received prizes for their fecundity and might even be paid to go to Rome where, pointedly, they would receive the personal blessing of both *Duce* and pope. Incentives to procreate were also made in terms of tax reductions (and later loans) for men in exchange for births, and a bachelor's tax shifted a modicum of wealth from the male and single to the married with children. Mussolini, father of five legitimate children himself, was fond of saying that 'a man is not a real man unless he has sired children' (in Dogliani, 1999: 244).

The *Fasci Femminili*, a women's section of the PNF, was founded in the 1920s but had languished during the rise of Fascism. 'Going to the people' in the 1930s gave the organization a new life and it quickly became one of

Fasci Femminili: 'Female Fascist Leagues'. The womens' section of the Fascist Party, comprising a variety of organizations including the *Massaie Rurali* (Rural Housewives) and female youth groups. Its *Piccole Italiane* (Girl Guides) section passed to the ONB in 1929.

the primary channels through which welfare was administered to poorer citizens. A neat uniform and a bustling activism connected the PNF to ordinary women and provided a new model of activism to which to aspire. Although Catholic women's groups continued to meet and administer the charitable bounty channelled through the coffers of the Church, the *Fasci Femminili* took over much of the middle-class do-goodism that had been particularly active in Italy's northern cities before 1922. It was in the countryside that the presence of middle-class party members must have been much more surprising. The *Massaie Rurali* (Rural Housewives) party section was set up in 1933 to carry Fascism's ideals to women outside the cities and it specialized in bestowing the benefits of modern hygiene and household management, as well as acting as a vehicle of propaganda for the pro-natalist policies of the Regime. There were benefits in joining, such as subsidized insurance policies, courses on a variety of domestic skills, receiving the organization's publications and attending meetings. Belonging also meant an occasional visit to Rome where certain days and celebrations aimed specifically at women (as long as they belonged to one or another of the state's or the PNF's women's subsections) were a real innovation of the Regime. On 20 June 1937, for example, the launching of an exhibition on the summer *colonie* and on childcare attracted more than 60,000 women to the capital (Dogliani, 1999: 102). A glimpse of the *Duce* might also be had and this, in itself, could provide a moment of fame on returning home.

By 1940 the *Massaie Rurali*, the *SOLD* (an equivalent organization aimed at women factory and domestic workers), and the *Fasci Femminili* each boasted more than half a million members. But the majority of 'uniformed' women were by the late 1930s within a Fascist organization not because they were female but because they were young. Here perhaps contradiction seems most apparent. Why take girls out of their families and launch them into the intense social world of the camps, marches, hikes and holidays of the Fascist youth organizations only to redirect all their energy back into domesticity? The contradiction is only an apparent one. For both women and men the Fascist youth organizations, as has been said, were liminal and formative rather than a permanent institutionalization into the Fascist state. Boys would progress from the youth organizations into the party proper as well as the militia and, of course, the national army, but would also marry, get a job, etc., and girls would be expected to be forming their own families. Their 'own' families is important to stress here, as acquiring the status of wife (and eventually mother) was for many women a real step up from being daughters, a position far lower down in the pecking order of the Italian family [**Doc. 28, p. 149**].

As has been suggested, the reality of women's experience in the Fascist era was one of great diversity and contradiction. The party and state poured scorn on the *donna crisi* (perhaps translatable as a 'woman on the edge of a nervous breakdown') – thin, cranky, ever-searching for fulfilment, with short hair, smoking, barren of course and utterly unresponsive to the sculpting of one man – and lauded the rosy-cheeked and big bosomed peasant girls crying out to be turned into mothers, who still tend to be found on minor Italian pasta manufacturers' packaging. But both these images were unrepresentative clichés. In Italy's towns Hollywood permeated culture and the starlets of American cinema were avidly copied, magazines followed fashion and the wealthy continued to live a lifestyle not very different from their counterparts across the Alps, with Edda Ciano, Mussolini's daughter, fulfilling all the expectations of the ultra-modern bourgeois woman: an open marriage with a successful, rich and influential husband, children who did not spoil her looks and a life that consisted of an endless tour of Europe's resorts. In Italy's rural areas there was no great Fascist spiritual revolution. The Church continued to provide an alternative, if anything increasing its influence on women because '[the Catholic women's movement] was not oppositional; to the degree that its very impetus was in reaction to the same emancipatory trends to which the Regime was opposed' (De Grazia, 1992: 243–6). In southern Italy outside the provincial capitals women were largely unaffected, and continued to be outside Mussolini's 'pernicious currents of contemporary civilization', although he had not, of course meant to include Fascism among these.

The concerted effort to assign political significance to all activity in Fascist Italy, to make the personal political, extended also to 'free' time. *Dopolavoro* (afterwork) was a much more fitting and politically pregnant term than *tempo libero* (free time), which implied that the relationship with, and obligations to, the state and society ceased on clocking off, and its adoption when referring to leisure signified a desire to liquidate the border separating work and non-work time. The idea of spending 'free' time on what was dubbed in the Anglo-Saxon world a 'hobby' (a word that has no equivalent in Italian and is in fact used in Italy in its English original) would have been anathema to Fascism. Yet the concept of leisure itself was still a novel one in inter-war Italy and one should understand Fascist policies in the context of a society where traditional forms of 'afterwork' activity – tied to the parish, the religious confraternity, or to the *festa* – still existed alongside, or were being co-opted in, more 'modern' forms of social interaction spanning the workingman's club, the political party section, the bourgeois literary association, or the shooting club. As such, Fascism was picking up on a longer-term process that had been initiated in liberal Italy of inserting the secular state in those areas of society that were being emptied by the changing imperatives of the Italian economy.

The **Opera Nazionale Dopolavoro** (the Fascist leisure association) was founded by royal decree on 1 May 1925. The means and the date are very

Opera Nazionale Dopolavoro (OND): The Fascist leisure association. Aiming to place all public leisure activities in Italy under the Fascist umbrella, the OND significantly modified Italians' taste for entertainment.

significant. The achievement by the industrial working class of Europe of its 'own' holiday had been a rallying cry and a mark of an independent identity since the end of the nineteenth century. One of Fascism's major goals was not so much the destruction of working-class identity but the latter's blending with what it considered to be the overarching agendas of the nation, symbolized by the law being a royal decree. The OND was therefore the logical adjunct to corporativism and of the pressing need to fill the vacuum that came into being once most independent political and social networks affiliated to liberal Italy's political parties and to the Church were abolished. Another vacuum was the product of Fascist legislation on working hours. The eight-hour day had been introduced in 1924 and *sabato fascista* (the 'Fascist Saturday', granting the afternoon off) made almost the whole weekend available to many Italians for the first time in the mid-1930s. The idea of workers' time being organized by their employers beyond the hours put in at the workplace was not new, but the shape the OND eventually took differed significantly from the precedents established in the USA in that it ultimately comprised not only the mushrooming social organizations of Italy's big companies such as FIAT (cars), SIP (telecommunications and energy) or Pirelli (tyres) of the 1930s but also a large apparatus affiliated first to the Economics Ministry and later (1927) to the Fascist Party. By the late 1930s the OND constituted the umbrella under which all organized social interaction outside the workplace was to take place. In 1937 it was placed under the direct command of Mussolini as a public utility; by 1939 it had 4.5 million members in 25,000 factory and local sections (De Bernardi and Guarracino, 1998: 416).

According to De Grazia, the OND was an attempt

to manipulate those tendencies, endemic to capitalist development, that would potentially cut across class and regional lines; such were the expansion of a mass consumer market and the growth of the mass media. Fascist organizers were able to capitalize on the fact that the development of a mass consumer market in interwar Italy demanded regulation to compensate for the highly unequal levels of consumption.

(De Grazia, 1981: 151)

Italy's relative poverty and massive social differentiation (between, for example, the industrial north and agricultural south or between rural and urban 'cultures' or different social classes in the industrialized north) was potentially explosive in a situation where the great transformation from an agricultural to an industrial (and consumer) civilization was taking place. In other words, the OND was an innovative response to the extraordinarily *uneven* modernization of Italian society where the potential for social

Plate 1 Mussolini in his element. (*Source*: © Corbis/Underwood & Underwood.)

Plate 2 Mussolini in 1923. Soon to give up top-hat, smoking and democratic government. (*Source*: © Corbis/Bettmann.)

Plate 3 According to this postcard of the 1920s, Fascism saved Italy from the horrors of Bolshevism. (*Source:* © Mary Evans Picture Library/Weimar Archive.)

Plate 4 Contrasts in the Italy of the 1930s: peasant women and children and their house, near Terracina, about fifty kilometres from the capital (above); and the new Roman suburb of the E UR (below). (*Source*: © Alinari Archives Management, Florence/Bruni Archive (top) and Alamy Images/T S Corrigan (bottom).)

Plate 5 Making Italians Fascists: raw recruits and Fascist boy scouts. (*Source*: ©
Corbis/Lewis Wickes (top) and Alinari Archives Management/Luce Institute (bottom).)

Plate 6 Mussolini and fellow dictator in 1938. (*Source*: © akg-images Ltd.)

Plate 7 Hubris and nemesis of the Italian dictator: same city different pose.
Mussolini projected like an idol on Milan Cathedral in 1938 and the Duce's
(second from left) sordid end in a Milanese piazza in 1945. (*Source*: ©
Alinari Archives Management, Florence/Luce Institute (top) and Getty
Images/Hulton Archive (bottom).)

Plate 8 A cartoon reading puzzle from a children's comic of 1936 indicates what Fascism has supposedly achieved for the average Italian.

disintegration and class conflict was successfully checked by the ability of the Fascists 'to turn this apparent disadvantage toward the support of the Regime's claims to a superclass identity' (De Grazia, 1981: 151). The OND went some way in redistributing consumption in a society where the latter appeared as the most tangible sign of the Regime's success. Therefore the OND strove to provide for its members much that had hitherto been the province of elites: household goods such as clocks, radios or modern furniture; cheap holidays; subsidized entertainment in the form of theatre and cinema; access to sporting facilities; a warm room for playing cards or listening to football matches; swimming pools or skiing facilities; life or illness insurance policies; products for sale on hire-purchase (for example the *Necchi* sowing machine, or *Olivetti* typewriters).

Perhaps the story of how the radio first penetrated the life of Italians illustrates best the novel mixture of consumption, popular patriotism, and new forms of social interaction produced by the OND. The radio was a dictator's dream: consumers fell over each other to get their hands on the very piece of equipment that would make the dictatorship's imperatives known to and absorbed by all. Although invented by an Italian, Guglielmo Marconi (who was fêted by and gave his full support to Fascism), the fact that he had gone to Britain to commercialize radio rather than staying in Italy was an acute businessman's interpretation of Italy's low market potential. In Italy a national radio service had been set up by the mid-1920s but the diffusion of wireless was slow, with less than 30,000 sets sold by 1926. By 1939 a massive effort on the part of the government, which included subsidies to industry and radio consumers, meant that there were more than a million sets in operation throughout the country, although in Britain there were more than 9 million and in Germany more than 13 million (De Grazia, 1981: 463). Capturing the minds of Italy's rural population seemed much easier through the radio and so the Regime invested a considerable effort in 'introducing the sounds and rhythms of industrial society into the rural world, and of assuring a constant contact between the state and outlying rural areas' (De Grazia, 1981: 155). The OND was instrumental in making radio the success story that it turned out to be. The local section of the organization became the exclusive proprietor of a radio set and the collective listening to the major events of what was becoming the Fascist calendar was established as a new tradition.

The radio was, too, not just a megaphone for Mussolini's speeches but what transformed sporting events and Italy's successes in them into great celebratory events supposedly attesting to Italy's rebirth and modernization under the Fascist Regime. Sport as a gentleman's elite activity was transformed by organizations such as the OND into what became a permanent national obsession, at least as far as listening and then watching was concerned.

In the 1932 Los Angeles Olympics Italy won more medals than anybody except the hosts, and Italy's first two football World Cup triumphs came in the 1930s. The 1934 competition was hosted by Italy itself, with the players saluting their *Duce* in full view of the international public. The giant Primo Carnera won the world heavyweight boxing title in 1933, and Italian cycling became phenomenally popular and successful. At the 1936 Olympics in Berlin it was Ondina Valla, winner of the women's 80-metre hurdles, who filled Italian newspapers with stories of the new Fascist woman. Here was a new kind of Italian, not the cringing mandolin player, or organ grinder toadying for a dime, emigrating to shine shoes on the streets of New York, but proud, athletic, physically fit, competitive and utterly modern. Football became immensely popular in Fascist Italy and clubs such as *Juventus*, owned by the Turin Agnelli family of FIAT, or Fascist boss Leandro Arpinati's Bologna football club were the elite end of the safe and uplifting leisure sponsored by the OND in partnership with the corporate business world.

How far turning Italians into avid consumers of sport implied their 'fascis-tization' is debatable, and it is possible to imagine *azzurro* (the Italian team colour) becoming the most potent and apparently most permanent symbol of national identity with or without the Regime. Certainly, as De Grazia argues, Fascism's investment in making this type of leisure accessible to the masses (for example by sponsoring a vast stadium-building programme throughout Italy in the Fascist decades) at a time when imbalances in wealth would probably have left it in the hands of the rich or circumscribed it to certain regions, is convincing, but, as the passion for football in Argentina, Uruguay or Brazil might show, Fascism was hardly a requirement for the growth in the sport's popularity. The point is, though, that participation in, success at and a general interest in sport were imagined and interpreted as something to do with Fascism's transformation of life in Italy. The socialist peasants of Ravenna who had borne the brunt of Italo Balbo's squads in 1920–2 may have vehemently refused to have anything to do with the OND (Dogliani, 1999: 180) but there were many other Italians who were certainly prepared to play their card games under a portrait of Mussolini, or *bocce* in an OND-provided court than to forego playing at all. By doing this had they therefore bought into Fascism and really become proselytisers in Mussolini's new religion? Did Fascism, as Simonetta Falasca Zamponi put it, 'Burst open Italian society in order to mold it [and] exploded the humus of everyday life by imposing new practices' (Falasca-Zamponi, 1997: 14)?

There is no doubt that 'exploding the humus' of everyday life and creat-ing a Fascist 'new man' (Gentile, 1996: 96–9) may have been the dream of many thinkers of the Regime; indeed, after the Fascist 'revolution' and all its compromises, that Italy remained substantially the same, with its glaring inequalities, its backwardness, its priests, its diminutive monarch, its past glories and present mediocrity, was unacceptable and constantly risked making the Regime redundant. Whatever historians of Fascist culture might read into, say, the design of a new suburb on the outskirts of Rome, it was in fact always easier to erect a new suburb and develop a Fascist architectural style or to have a parade, to dedicate a monument, to make a speech, to change a rule, to mouth a slogan, than it was to reconstruct society with all the vested interests this would affect. Cultural revolution was easier than the real thing and much more likely to leave Mussolini ensconced in power. Change was effectively replaced by myth and the greatest myth of all was that of the *Duce* himself.

> The cult of Mussolini was the greatest resource for the construction of consensus. But at the same time it impeded the transformation of 'dictatorship' in 'regime'. The party found itself becoming more and more the resonating chamber for Mussolini.
>
> (Lyttelton, 1997: 205–6)

By the early 1930s Mussolini had become shorthand for Fascism, and obsequiousness to the *Duce* reached extravagant levels. But the zenith of his popularity was yet to come

THE ETHIOPIAN WAR

After Italy's conquest of Ethiopia in 1936 the *Duce* entitled himself 'founder of the Empire' and it was appended to his name thereafter to the exclusion of all else, as if to suggest that giving Italy a serious colony in Africa was by far the greatest achievement of his long career. As Renzo De Felice put it:

> The Ethiopian war was Mussolini's political masterpiece and his greatest success because he believed in it profoundly as in probably no other of his political ventures. He believed in it not just instrumentally, as serving his personal prestige . . . but intimately as something that corresponded to the raison d'être of his *historical role* because the war assumed for him the value of a *mission* whose aim was to make the (present and future) Nation recognise in his personal *vocation* its own *absolute duty*, and therefore to bring about the identification between *vox ducis* and *vox populi* that until that moment Fascism had been unable to really realise.
>
> (De Felice, 1974: 642)

The essential meaning of this is that the Ethiopian conquest produced the harmony between the Italian people and Mussolini that he had sought since 1922, and which justified the Fascist 'revolution'.

Had Italians really become Fascist in the way De Felice argued? The question is a pertinent one: the Regime had now had time to work on the people – it had eliminated, according to the Vittorio Veneter interpretation, all those political forces and their means of expression that sapped the determination of Italy to capitalize on the victory in the Great War, and to perform in the international arena; it had constructed an apparatus for forging a supposedly new 'Fascist' mentality and could now avail itself of a generation that had grown up under its aegis; it had built up the cult of the *Duce* through all methods available and had modernized the means of communication between state and people; on the destruction of the free running of liberal democracy it had come up with novel ways of suggesting representation through its highly original choreography, understood by many to be effective participation in the political arena. Italy had navigated the difficult early years of 1930s and the invasion and conquest of Ethiopia, brought to a felicitous conclusion, in the face of international hostility of the Great Powers, suggested an unprecedented coalescence between Fascism and society. Yet, like so many of the ingredients that made up the *minestrone* that was Fascism by the mid-1930s, a European conquest in Africa was neither new nor required the existence of a new 'Fascist' man. Can it not be argued that Italians merely gave their assent to 'their' country conquering itself a place in the sun in the way that the British and the French had done for their liberal democratic regimes since the scramble for Africa took off in the 1880s? 'Fascism' had nothing to do with it, or if it did, it was merely that it had ensured 'the adhesion of the masses to the [colonial] myth' (Del Boca, 1992a: 880). No mean feat to be sure, but not something that required the radical recasting of Italian culture and society either. So, what was the colonial myth in the Italian context and how Fascist was it?

Empire was linked specifically in Italy to the crushing heritage of ancient Rome. For many this 'legacy' meant more than managing Italy's Roman ruins for the benefit of tourists; rather, that past and the enormous prestige it was granted in European culture served to belittle the Italy of the present. Yet imperial Roman posturing had a pedigree that went back to the *Risorgimento* and in liberal Italy it had been a favourite theme that was always linked with colonial expansion.

By 1914 Italy's colonies consisted of three small territories (Eritrea, Somalia and Libya) plus a scattering of not very vital islands in the Mediterranean. The territories of Italy's liberal colonial empire were not of great strategic importance and lacked many of the means to make them viable without the kind of investments that Italy could not afford. Liberal Italy's Roman Empire was made up of the scraps left over after the choice pickings had gone to the other European powers. But even the securing of this not very significant booty had required of Italy a considerable, sometimes debilitating, investment of men and resources. In the 1880s and 1890s Eritrea was all that Italy kept after mounting one of the largest and most expensive colonial campaigns of the whole scramble for Africa. In 1896, having picked a fight with Ethiopia, Adowa saw the most crushing and unavenged defeat inflicted on a European power in the whole process of European expansion before 1914. But in Libya too, which had been seized with relative ease in 1911–12, resistance was so widespread that, during the First World War Italy lost control of the colony except for the bridgeheads of the coastal towns.

Despite all these difficulties and failures, colonial expansion in Africa remained an unsatisfied ambition for many. Adowa stained Italy's military reputation and for some was an unbearable humiliation that had to be avenged. That Ethiopia was the only truly independent territory left in Africa after the scramble was an irksome reminder of Italian failure. But it was not just national honour that was at stake, although a powerful message to the Great Powers of Europe that Italy would never accept a military setback as final and was no international lightweight, was imperative to the king, the Italian military and many a patriotic Italian. A more virile colonial policy also seemed to offer solutions to Italy's intractable population problem, as the millions who had departed for the New World and northern Europe to find a livelihood were being lost to the fatherland. Fascism made strenuous efforts to connect with Italian emigrants scattered through the world, but a much better solution would surely have been Italians opening up Italian territory rather than doing so for the greater glory of America, Britain, France, Brazil or Argentina. Fascism did not really change the basic premises of what fired Italian colonialism under the liberal regime. However, perhaps the link made with demography was emphasized to a greater degree and Fascism made it plain that, as usual, the liberal state had not done its homework and had failed vigorously to follow up what little it had achieved. Above all Fascism sold itself as acting truly on behalf of its people at large, unlike the sham populism of *Italietta* (a disparaging term denoting liberal Italy's unfulfilled expectations). In this discourse the demographic myth with regard to colonialism was fundamental. Mussolini characteristically linked the two in the catchy phrase 'the society of empty cots does not build empires'.

If Italy's decision to take on Ethiopia again after 40 years can be regarded as continuing where Crispi and Giolitti had left off, some new factors made 1935 more than a delayed episode in the scramble for Africa. Ethiopia as a member of the League of Nations had sat as a peer in the councils of European diplomacy – not usually the case in colonial conquest. Mussolini had benefited from a decade of political control and the opposition that had irked Crispi and Giolitti was gagged. Above all it was a test Mussolini set for 'his' Italy to compare with the one that he had loathed, first as a socialist and then as a Vittorio Veneter. This fact made success absolutely imperative, and in Africa, at last, Mussolini had a field of action in which there were no vested interests that had to be carefully dealt with, where there was no compromise or juggling required or alliances to be made that might taint or moderate the consequences of Fascist policies. Fascist ruthlessness, its manly 'couldn't give a damn' attitude, its camaraderie, its dare-devil bravado born in the trenches may have been restrained by tradition, other loci of power and identities at home, but in Africa it could run riot. Mussolini was not just engaging in the usual European colonial rhetoric when he said that, 'the new Italian, a far cry from the stereotypes of the past, would be born on the African frontier, the gymnasium of boldness, sacrifice and discipline' (Del Boca, 1996b: 421–2). According to Mussolini's son-in-law and foreign minister, **Galeazzo Ciano**, the *Duce* was convinced by the late 1930s that 'The revolution must start to affect the comportment of Italians. They must learn to be less tender-hearted, to become hard, implacable, hateful. That is to say, Masters' (in De Grand, 2004).

Galeazzo Ciano (1903–44): Wealthy son of Fascist minister, married Mussolini's daughter Edda in 1930 and made foreign minister in 1936. He wrote a useful and lucid diary while in office. He voted against his father-in-law in the Grand Council meeting of 24–5 July 1943 and for this he was executed in January 1944.

Even before taking on Ethiopia in 1935, this merciless rigour had already been on show in the 'reconquest' of Libya. Rebellion against Italian rule had been endemic since the 1911 occupation, and during First World War the pressure of fighting against Austro-Hungary in the Alps had removed Italian power beyond the walls of Libya's northern cities. In Cyrenaica the Islamic Senussi brotherhood under the leadership of Omar al Mukhtàr operated like fish in the sea of the indigenous peasantry and nomadic population's support. After Mussolini's rise to power, considerable military resources were diverted to the colony and the task of imposing Italian rule, with the vision of future Italian settlement, eventually became genocidal. Meeting with little success at first, the drastic measure of enclosing almost the entire population of Cyrenaica into concentration camps was adopted and the consequences for the local inhabitants proved disastrous. The population of the area dropped from almost a quarter of a million before the campaign to 142,000 in 1931 (Dogliani, 1999: 262). Mukhtàr was hanged in front of 20,000 of his own people in 1931 as the ultimate act of barbarity in a long list that, apart from the murder of women and children in the forcible incarceration of the indigenous people, included the gas bombing of Libyan villages. The behaviour of Italians in the Libyan reconquest was a sign of things to come in Ethiopia, but it should be stressed that Fascism was hardly a requirement for brutality in the colonial context. In the Italian case it was the determination to succeed, no matter the implications, that marked the Fascist phase of colonialism as compared to liberal. Most of the brutality was in fact carried out under the command of the Italian military, who it would be difficult to argue were acting more as Fascists than as soldiers of the Italian armed forces headed by the Italian king. The Italian commanders in charge of Italy's colonial campaigns in Libya and Ethiopia, Badoglio and **Rodolfo Graziani**, owed nothing to Mussolini for their successful military careers. Nevertheless, it was still possible for Badoglio to write to Graziani that 'by now the course has been set and we must carry it out to the end, even if the entire population of Cyrenaica must perish' (in De Grand, 2004).

Attacking Ethiopia was complicated because of its membership in the League of Nations. But a new factor had emerged that gave Mussolini a useful bargaining chip to offer France and Britain, on which the League depended. Hitler's coming to power in Germany in early 1933 transformed international relations in Europe. Although there was much talk of another Fascist 'revolution' having occurred, the reality was that Hitler's fulminations against the Versailles settlement were also directed at Italy, which had been present at the Paris peace conference, had incorporated German speakers in the South Tyrol within its borders, and looked on the reduction of Austria to a rump state in 1919 as one of the most tangible benefits of having won the Great War. With the emergence of a Germany determined to break the Versailles status quo, and possibly absorb Austria into a Germanic superstate, Mussolini had much to offer France and Britain, who assiduously sought his goodwill in the hope that a firm statement of united resolve might restrain Hitler.

There was friction between Nazi Germany and Italy to begin with. The Nazi assassination of the Austrian chancellor Engelbert Dollfuss in Vienna in July 1934 (when Mussolini's wife was entertaining his family in the Italian seaside resort of Riccione) and an attempted Nazi coup there prompted Italian troop deployments in the Alps. In exchange for his support of the status quo in Europe, Mussolini believed he would be left alone to do as he pleased in Africa, the League of Nations notwithstanding. Neither Britain nor France had vital interests at stake in Ethiopia and would happily have let the noisy Italian dictator have his little African triumph, even if this might mean the League losing face. At first they tried to buy Italy off by granting some kind of protectorate that would leave the Ethiopian emperor nominally in command, but Mussolini wanted more than this, and for obvious reasons: only the integration of Ethiopia into a new Italian empire would make the project worthwhile in terms of his and his Regime's prestige. And it was here that the first real problems began to emerge. In Britain public opinion placed its trust in a renewed League of Nations standing firm against a resurgent Germany, which had left the organization in 1933, and the humiliation of the League was not to be tolerated. When the latter voted that Italy was the 'aggressor', economic sanctions were imposed.

In Italy the League sanctions met with an extraordinary show of resolve that the Regime carefully orchestrated and to which the Italian people appear to have responded with enthusiasm. Autarky became the buzz-word, a

Rodolfo Graziani (1882–1955): Commander of the southern front in the Ethiopian War and governor of the colony. In the Second World War he was commander of the Italian forces in North Africa, where his army was defeated by the British. As RSI minister of war, he organized the repression of the partisans. He was found guilty of war crimes in 1948.

self-reliant Italy in a world in which the countries with the biggest colonial empires, France and Britain, castigated a young and dynamic underdog wanting nothing more than its own place in the sun. The Regime seems to have been successful in establishing widespread support among the Italian people. The wedding ring ceremonies of late 1935 were perhaps the most original way in which Fascism responded to the sanctions. The Regime called on women to bestow their gold wedding rings on the war effort and the response, however ambiguously 'spontaneous', was remarkably successful: tens of thousands of women (from the queen down) pledged themselves to the *Duce's* war with the donation of the symbolic marker of their status and identity. Autarky, economic self-reliance, took the form of a great mobilization of the Italian people to 'do their bit'. It involved such acts as the collection of metal bed frames and spare pots and pans, but what could be more emblematic than the great Sicilian playwright Luigi Pirandello ploughing into the national war effort that very icon of an international brotherhood of thought and progress (so emphatically undermined between 1914 and 1945), his gold Nobel prize medal? Sanctions did little to weaken Italy's war effort but rather had the effect of creating a kind of Italian 'finest hour'.

In Ethiopia, Mussolini's 'masterpiece' had dire consequences. The Regime's absolute imperative that this time nothing should, as in 1896, go awry, entailed a campaign on a vast scale with nothing left to chance and where the full force of a relatively modern industrial society was brought to bear on a still semi-feudal and agricultural one. Half a million Italian men made the trip to the Horn of Africa and vast quantities of up-to-date ordinance, including mustard gas bombs that had been banned by the Geneva Convention (signed by Fascist Italy in 1925), were shipped through the Suez canal the British left open, the latter anxious in the end that sanctions should not impede the *Duce* from having his little success, and throw him fully into Hitler's arms. The Italian military were effectively granted a blank cheque and were expected by Mussolini himself to forego all finickety rules of honourable behaviour in the pursuit of victory. The horrors that were to become standard on the European continent a few years later were meted out unhesitatingly by Italians throughout the campaign (see Del Boca, 1991), dispelling the cosy myth that Italians were inherently more humane than their future allies across the Alps. Apart from gassing villages (Del Boca, 1996) and, on many occasions, taking no prisoners, in Ethiopia solutions to logistical problems were solved with extreme violence. **Achille Starace**, who comes across as a weak-chinned toady in newsreels of him adulating Mussolini in Italy, had no qualms whatsoever in taking pleasure in severing prisoner's testicles before killing them in Ethiopia, or the murder of thousands of innocent Ethiopian passers-by in the streets of Addis Ababa after an attempted assassination of Italian governor Graziani in 1937 [**Doc. 27, p. 148**], or the

Achille Starace (1895–1945): Secretary of the Fascist Party between 1931 and 1939, and responsible for developing much of Fascism's style and choreography through the 1930s. He was removed from power by Mussolini in 1939, but executed by partisans in Milan in 1945.

premeditated liquidation of the Ethiopian clergy (De Grand, 2004). These were all part of what one young Tuscan on the spot, Indro Montanelli, probably Italy's most important postwar journalist and popularizing historian, called 'a lovely and long holiday given to us by our great Daddy for having spent thirteen long years at school behind a desk' (Del Boca, 1996: 29). To schoolboys who had missed out on the trenches, the war in Ethiopia embodied everything that had been promoted as the highest values of Fascist civilization: echoes of ancient Roman imperialism (although no ancient Roman remains were to be found in Ethiopia), the freeing of slaves, the opening up of territory for Italian workers, the civilizing of savages, accruing prestige to one's country, a moral purpose uniting a nation too long concerned with internal bickering. The thought of easy sex with native women, supposedly untrammelled by the moral constraints of their Italian counterparts, added to the potent brew.

Here was the classic European colonial *mélange* of uplifting ideals being carried through notwithstanding the unsavoury practicalities of their implementation. Italians concentrated on the former and closed their eyes to the latter, almost as if to say that this was the price to pay for greatness. In reality this was glory at a bargain price: the Italians involved could fight for the greater glory of their country without much risk of dying themselves [**Doc. 30, p. 150**]. The number of Italian casualties was so low that they actually had to be falsified upwards to make the war seem worthy of being won. Conquering Ethiopia's few and small cities was easy and achieved in a few months, but effectively controlling this massive and mountainous African territory always eluded Italy in its brief tenure at Addis Ababa.

For the Ethiopians who suffered at the hands of Italy, whether they did so because the latter was following 'traditional' and standard European colonial practice or rather because they were on the receiving end of the first 'Fascist' assault on the respectable morality that was to reach its high (or low) point on the eastern front between 1942 and 1945, may not have mattered much. Finding what is 'Fascist' in Italy's colonialism after 1935 as compared to what is 'normal' is an academic task that is extraordinarily fraught and is possibly one dictated by the incongruity of the Emperor Haile Selassie appealing to France and Britain, the biggest colonial powers, to stand by him in morally condemning Fascist, as opposed to liberal, imperialism.

On Italy's victory all this was irrelevant. In front of a truly 'oceanic' crowd on the 'fatal hills of Rome' the *Duce* 'refounded' the empire and proclaimed a victory for 'Fascism, peace, civilisation and humanity' (Bosworth, 2002: 309); few Italians disagreed. The tendency that Montanelli noticed, the *folie à deux* between Italian people and *Duce*, where what the rest of the world thought 'simply did not matter' (Del Boca, 1996: 29), meant that in spite of the expenditure of Italian resources in return for very little, in the middle of the great depression, when enthusiasm for Fascism may have been waning, Mussolini was suddenly able to lift its prestige into the stratosphere.

However there was a lingering and unpleasant aftertaste following the imperial banquet that all the gushing and hyperbole could not quite remove. The reality was that the benefits bestowed on Mussolini and his Regime by the victorious Ethiopian War would not have materialized had it not been for the spectre of Adolph Hitler. It is almost impossible to imagine Britain and France allowing themselves to be flouted as they had been in 1935–6 without Hitler's denigration of Versailles and the sickening prospect of yet another war with Germany, not Italy, staying their hand.

7

Mussolini and Hitler, 1936–8

THE DEAL WITH NAZISM

The historical debate on Italian foreign policy in the Fascist years has centred on the problem of how far Mussolini had a long-term vision whose central tenets remained stable even if his immediate tactics might have changed, or rather if the *Duce* simply made things up as he went along and stumbled from one crisis to the next without preconceptions, seeking always to capitalize for internal prestige purposes on the peculiar constellation of the moment. To a degree, the idea of a 'sawdust Caesar' strutting around in the international arena like an overdressed clown is as much a cliché as the other vision of Mussolini possessing an ideology that was a 'fanatical brand of imperialism' or an utterly 'rigid world-view' (Mallett, 2003: 225). In the latter conception Mussolini's 'good behaviour', his going along with the status quo and with the conventional rules of international diplomacy, were merely a time of preparation for the great assault on Britain and France for the Italianization of the Mediterranean and the conquest of an African super empire. Perhaps southern France and the Balkans including Greece, and, why not, bits of Turkey would also have recreated the story of the expansion of the ancient Roman Empire told in the sculpted maps that adorn the ex-*Via dell'Impero* in Rome [**Doc. 37, p. 155**]. Yet as Mack Smith already pointed out in 1975 and Bosworth has reiterated more recently, what must always be at the centre of analysis when dealing with Mussolini's foreign policy is a lucid capacity to distinguish between 'words and deeds' (Bosworth, 2002: 246), or to understand that a 'history of Mussolini's foreign policy has to be also, or even mainly, a history of propaganda' (Mack Smith, 1975: viii).

Like those pleasant but futile discussions on how nice it would be to win the national lottery, and to imagine to what use all those millions might be put, there is no doubt that the idea of a recreated Roman Empire, a new world in which a mighty Italy bestrode Europe, if not the globe, was an attractive proposition for the *Duce*. However, if one judges by Italian pre-paredness for war, how far the economy was geared towards it in the late 1930s, let alone Italy's actual will to fight, then it seems almost absurd to argue with MacGregor Knox that there was ever a serious intention to turn the pipe-dream into reality. In 1940–1 when Mussolini did assail heaven (i.e. took on Britain and France) it did look like a lot could be had with the minimum of expenditure, but the idea of a society bent on massive conquest, sculpted by the *Duce* into an ideologically motivated, fit and lithe, fanatical fighting machine, is obviously the way propaganda was bound to talk.

The most lasting consequence of Mussolini's 'masterpiece' was a realign-ment in Italian foreign policy that eventually led to a grand alliance with Nazi Germany and the intertwining of the fates of the Italian and German dicta-torships. The *Duce* backed the wrong horse in the end and effectively gave up all his achievements, 20 years of rule, the empire and his long career in a botched attempt to keep up with Hitler's plan for the recasting of Germany and of the world balance of power. Was this inevitable? Was the impetus behind the 'brutal friendship' (Deakin, 1966) a common ideology, deeply held beliefs that motivated the two Fascist tyrants? Did Hitler and Mussolini, as Macgregor Knox (2000) has argued, possess a 'common destiny' that issued from their need to employ war to carry through their respective stut-tering and compromise-ridden revolutions, and did both have an overriding master plan to overturn the status quo in their favour? It took Hitler a mere six years after his acquisition of power to challenge the established order of Europe with a military assailment of the Great Powers, Britain and France, whereas Mussolini, after almost two decades as *Duce*, had yet to assert Italy's supposed military prowess against any enemy that was more significant than Ethiopia or the republican government of Spain. This long period of 'good behaviour' on the Italian dictator's part would seem to suggest that a European war was not necessarily the logical outcome of an irreconcilable ideological fissure between those political regimes, liberal-democratic and/or communist on the one hand, Fascist on the other. There was no 'clash of civilizations', the outcome of which had to be a war of annihilation, and it is possible to conceive of a lingering Fascist dictatorship in Italy in a post-Hitlerian Europe, much as Francisco Franco's regime lived on into the 1970s.

Yet this last proposition needs to ignore, or at least to underplay, some of the most significant dynamics at work within the Italian dictatorship through the 1930s. Fascism disdained an 'easy life' and was anxious to be seen to espouse and achieve change. Mussolini could never simply rest on his laurels, as the eventual fizzling out of the Ethiopian War factor proved, and needed to find new reasons for both his personal 'historical role', and also for the whole and elephantine construction that was Fascism. As there was no going back, and standing still was not an option, *tireremo dritto* ('we will go forward', a slogan that responded to the League of Nations sanctions) was the only possible path to take. Whether this means that Italy's embroilment in the Second World War was what Knox has termed the 'polar opposite of social imperialism' (Knox, 1996: 114), that is war abroad to destroy rather than preserve the social order at home, is debatable in as far as the ultimate revolutionary impulse of Fascism, its desire to reconstruct Italian society, always trod an uneasy path between rhetoric and reality. However, what is certain is that with the coming to power of Hitler 'change' took on an altogether different meaning. Mussolini now had a rival, somebody else who claimed that his was a radical third way [**Doc. 31, p. 150**], and he led not a tin-pot dictatorship in a Europe in which they were now liberally scattered and all of which offered some sort of deference to the Italian model, but the great, powerful, industrialized German Reich. With Hitler in control north of the Alps, rhetoric, land reclamation, the *Balilla*, parades, military success against a poverty-stricken African country, or even winning the World Cup was simply not enough, and Mussolini's 'revolution' found itself very quickly having to keep up with the German pacemaker. The latter's tempo escalated towards the end of the 1930s, and when war began increased at such a dizzying rate that Italy simply fell out of the contest.

At first a lagging and overexerted *Duce* falling over to keep up with a dynamic *Führer* seemed a ridiculous proposition. In 1922, when Mussolini became prime minister, Hitler was unknown except to the Bavarian anti-semitic lunatic fringe, which hailed him as 'Germany's Mussolini' (Kershaw, 1998: 180). In 1923, as the construction of the Italian dictatorship began, Hitler shot briefly to fame with his botched 'Beerhall Putsch', a parody of the March on Rome, and his impact on history seemed to have been snuffed out almost before it began. Even when Nazism eventually became a mass movement, copied so many of Mussolini's innovations, from the brown as opposed to black shirts, the 'Roman' salute, to the title of *Führer* itself, and finally took power, Hitler needed Mussolini more than the other way round [**Doc. 33, p. 152**]. Yet there were signs that Hitler would foreshorten Mussolini's gradual fascistization and go for broke straight away. The Reichstag Fire Decree, the Enabling Act only a few weeks after Hitler's coming to power, and the 'Night of the Long Knives' of June 1934, especially the last, were greeted with some apprehension in Italy. Notwithstanding killings such as Matteotti's in 1924, the idea of simply emasculating the very movement that had contributed to Nazism's rise to power with over 200 cold-blooded murders was unthinkable; the equivalent in Italy would have been an elimination of many of the *rases*.

For Mussolini, Hitler's seriousness, his brutality on show during the 'Night of the Long Knives' was proof of his earnestness, although tempered by the *Führer*'s undoubted Italophilia and his obvious adulation of Mussolini as a figure of great historical standing. Hitler, always extremely vocal about his admiration for the *Duce*, differed from many German nationalists of his generation in his supposition that Italy, notwithstanding the Great War, was not a natural enemy of the Reich. Well before taking power, uniquely on the German right, he was prepared to ignore the problem of the German speakers of the South Tyrol in northern Italy who would have had full title to be included in visions of a racially defined new Germanic fatherland. In Hitler there was something of the northern European's romanticism about Italy's 'blue skies' and he definitely had a chocolate-box appreciation of Italian art, its cities and its history, which went with the Austrian small-town education that the *Führer* had received (*Mussolini e il Fascismo*, 2005) [**Doc. 33, p. 152**].

Seeing Italian Fascism's last phase as the effect of the related, but different, dynamic at work in the Third Reich does not mean that Mussolini simply became a puppet and Italy a client state of Germany. Rather, an uneasy alliance was eventually constructed in which the *Duce* attempted to parallel and capitalize on Hitler's successes while maintaining Italy's freedom of action both at home and abroad. Much of this was for internal consumption, constantly showing that Italy remained an independent and equal ally. The Ethiopian War had strengthened Mussolini in relation to Italy's elites. He had proven that 'his' Italy was superior to 'their' *Italietta* and the empire appeared to have a rosy future that would brush off on to the whole of Italy. Industrialists saw their profits surge as military contracts ballooned, the army's reputation had been enhanced with victory and the king took the crown of Ethiopia as his own. The Church looked on with pride and dreamed of bringing Coptic Christians 'back' into the Catholic fold. The Regime made sure that, whenever a ship, a piece of artillery, or an airplane departed for the Horn of Africa, a member of the clergy was present to make the sign of the cross and to spatter all with holy water. Mussolini's determination to bring Italy into a partnership with the Third Reich was the fruit of what seemed an impregnable position of prestige at home. The trump card of Ethiopia had been played to good effect and the shift from what can be termed traditional Italian foreign policy of friendship with Britain to one that rather saw in the latter the inhibitor of Italian aspirations was very much the result of Mussolini's self-confidence after 1936. It had now become possible for the *Duce* to do much as he liked, even to act against the wishes of the Italian establishment that had always been wary of Fascism's vociferous calls to revise the international order.

The sacrifice required for a rapprochement with Germany was the loss of Austria as an almost Italian client and buffer state. Yet allowing Hitler the great triumph of the *Anschluss* (the absorption of Austria) was pay-back for Ethiopia and the result of the shock of what seemed absolutely callous and perfidious indignation by the British and French at the Italian conquest.

Mussolini had had his triumph and it was only right that Hitler should be granted his. Although Austria was only absorbed into Germany in March 1938, in mid-1936 Mussolini had already more or less abandoned it to its massive Germanic neighbour at the same time as Hitler recognized Italy's conquest of Ethiopia as a legitimate one. Both dictators leaned on each other to make Versailles, the League of Nations and the whole status quo that emerged out of the Great War in Europe, a dead letter, and all without Britain and France lifting a finger. The real root of Anglo-French appeasement was that two parvenus from the provinces, Mussolini and Hitler, propped each other up at precisely the right moment from positions of extreme weakness had they been alone. Nazi Germany broke Versailles by reoccupying the Rhineland, initiating rearmament and occupying Austria, but it could hardly have done so if there had been a united front between Italy, France and Britain.

In mid-1936 the nature of the relationship between the two dictatorships was still not clearly defined. There was something personal, sentimental and enough ideological common ground to make it look like spiritual affinity, but it was essentially still one of convenience. There were significant differences that might resurface at any moment. Austria rankled, and who would emerge as paramount in the Balkans should French influence wane was also an issue. The South Tyrol festered, whatever Hitler might have said, and Mussolini had referred to Germans as barbarians on many occasions during the Great War – and sometimes afterwards, too. Germans were suffused with concepts of their own racial superiority over mere Latins, however much they delighted in visits to Venice, Rome or Florence, and a penchant for cowardice and fickleness was axiomatically held to be an Italian characteristic and had been confirmed respectively by Italy's abandonment of the Triple Alliance in 1914 and by Caporetto. Who would emerge as the junior partner, the lesser dictator, was still unclear, although the odds were stacked against the ruler of the much weaker Italy.

Still, for a while, the *Duce* came across as the mentor and it was characteristically the journalist Mussolini who picked up on a catchy name for his and Hitler's future combined orientation. The 'Axis', announced to the world in November 1936, was not a formal alliance, the latter term smacking too much of the old and tainted dealings of pre-war liberal diplomacy, but the delineation of an alternative locus of power as compared to the Anglo-French dominated League of Nations and Bolshevik Russia. Nothing much was actually agreed to, but it was made clear that in exchange for Germany's benevolent neutrality in the Ethiopian War and its recognition of the 'Empire of Rome', Italy passed over its claims to influence in Austria. Britain began a serious rearmament programme towards the beginning of 1937, being the last bastion of the spirit of Versailles and Geneva to fall.

The new spirit of cooperation between the dictators was symbolized by the appointment in 1936 of Mussolini's son-in-law, Galeazzo Ciano (at the remarkably young age of 33) as minister of foreign affairs. This young blood of the corporate state owed his career not to the trenches or the rise of Fascism but to his father's wealth and influence (he had been a minister in Mussolini governments) and his well-chosen bride Edda, the *Duce's* favourite offspring. Unlike any of the old *rases*, or even the men who emerged out of the prefectural bureaucracy to positions of influence in the Regime, Ciano has rightly been called 'Mussolini's shadow' (Moseley, 1999) in that his power depended wholly on his personal relationship with the *Duce*. Not averse to committing (in Ethiopia) the most horrific crimes and ordering in 1937 the murder of two prominent Italian anti-Fascists (Carlo and Nello Rosselli) residing in France, Ciano was at this stage in his career the very embodiment of the smart and unabashed young Italy looking for new friends and finding them in a vigorous Germany where the young bourgeois nobodies of the Nazi movement were landing high positions, and where the energy of a dynamic new generation appeared to be about to tear the crust off the lethargy and self-conscious snobbery of the old European diplomatic corps.

The consistency of the Axis relationship was first tested in Spain, and here what was revealed was that events, unlike in Ethiopia where nearly all had gone to plan, were always likely to dominate over long-term objectives and to develop a logic of their own. De Felice called Italian involvement a step into 'Spanish quicksand' (De Felice, 1981: 331), suggesting that it was not a well thought out strategy in 'pursuit of the keys to the western Mediterranean' (Knox, 2000: 144). The impetus for Italian involvement came from the Spanish rebels rather than from the *Duce*. In Spain the monarchy had been ousted in 1931 and a left-leaning republic had come into being, which had moved further to the left with the election in February 1936 of a Popular Front government that included communists and anarchists. First mooted in France and given the go-ahead by the Communist International in 1935, the Popular Front was essentially a response to the failure of the left in the face of both Mussolini's and Hitler's rise to power, and its main political plank consisted of the legitimization of communist parties to join national governments in defence of liberal freedoms, liquidated in Fascist Italy and Nazi Germany, that protected the right of parties of the left and the working-class movement, including the communists, to operate legally. With the communists at last willing to distinguish between Fascists and social democrats, whose labelling as Social Fascists in Germany before 1933 had contributed to Hitler's electoral success, the Popular Front proved a dangerous opponent for the right. The isolation and relative insignificance in international terms of the Popular Front victory in Spain was transformed with the election in May 1936 of another Popular Front government headed by the Jewish socialist, Léon Blum, this time in France. At the creation of the Axis (a few months after Blum's victory), Mussolini's words, 'It is not surprising that today we hoist the flag of anti-Bolshevism' (in Delzell, 1970: 202) were therefore referring not directly to the Soviet Union but to France and Spain. Spain itself teetered on the brink of civil war as the military, the Church, monarchists and a small Falangist Fascist party remained totally unreconciled to the Popular Front government, especially now that events in France seemed to favour its stabilization. A *pronunciamento* (military coup) was imminent. Why, then, did Italy become involved?

Clearly the continued existence of a Popular Front government in France (Blum refused to have anything to do with 'Matteotti's murderer') (Bosworth, 2002: 316) and Spain meant the creation of an anti-Fascist 'axis', a potential alternative to the normal 'bourgeois' languidness of European liberal democratic governments who had always been more likely to favour Fascism if the influence of communism threatened. Blum was perspicacious in drawing attention to the Matteotti crisis because the Popular Front was precisely a belated attempt, as Matteotti's had been, to drive a wedge between the far right and liberalism, the failure of which, with the Aventine Secession, had opened the door to Mussolini's dictatorship in Italy. As we know, it was exactly a 'Popular Front' writ large – the wartime alliance between the Soviet Union and the Anglo-Saxon liberal democracies, replicated in all of Europe's resistance movements as nationalists and communists fought together against Fascism – that did indeed spell the doom of both Fascism in Italy and Nazi Germany. Whatever the costs of involvement to Italy there was a realization that the destruction of the Popular Front in Spain would undermine, as indeed it eventually did, the forging of these kinds of anti-Fascist alliances throughout Europe (see Eley, 2002: ch. 17); only the horrors of the Nazi New Order after 1942 really resurrected them.

From this point of view, helping Francisco Franco, a Spanish general stationed in Morocco, to get his troops over into Spain to participate in a military *pronunciamento* was not part of a master plan for pushing the British out of the Mediterranean, or indeed the beginning of an anti-communist crusade. Rather it was a small favour granted to rebels who might topple the Popular Front and nip in the bud an anti-Fascist axis, as well as enhancing the young Ciano's prestige in foreign affairs. An airlift of Franco's troops quickly became a full-scale intervention with more than 50,000 soldiers deployed there and with a significant proportion of Italy's meagre supply of military equipment sinking without trace into the horror that was the Spanish quicksand. The promises of a rapid victory made by the future *Caudillo* to his Italian helpers proved elusive, and Spain settled down to a protracted civil war that was to last three years and was to see more than a million dead. Militarily the Italian 'volunteers' (many were in fact conscripted soldiers, but Italy had officially endorsed a non-intervention agreement with all the Great Powers) were probably not decisive in the conflict except at its very beginning, although at Guadalajara in March 1937 they were humiliatingly defeated. This last battle had pitted the Italian military against sections of the International Brigades, a collection of anti-Fascist volunteers hailing from outside Spain, among whom operated the Garibaldi brigade made up entirely of exiled Italians. The latter's slogan, 'today in Spain, tomorrow in Italy', was to prove prescient: Luigi Longo, an exiled leader of the Italian communists, fought in that battle for the republicans and was to be a major player in the Italian resistance to Nazi-Fascism after 1943, and was possibly involved in Mussolini's execution. For the *Duce*, Ciano and the Italian military who had at first merely dipped their toes into the conflict, Guadalajara meant that pulling out was unthinkable and more and more Italian energy was devoted to sustaining Franco's war effort.

In Spain, Fascist Italy and Nazi Germany for the first time found themselves fighting together and it made sense to agree on tactics, and in late 1936 a level of coordination was achieved. The Germans provided Franco with airplanes and pilots and in exchange were granted valuable mineral rights, whereas Mussolini was merely promised neutrality if Italy should enter a conflict with a third state, although it was he who sent tens of thousands of troops and really significant quantities of military equipment. In Italy intervention was supported strongly by the Catholic Church, for whom the Popular Front had in Spain been an unmitigated disaster, but the easy victory in Ethiopia (where fewer Italians had died than at Guadalajara) was not repeated and the 'ungratefulness' of the Spanish and Franco's persistence in never promising anything concrete to Italy sapped what kept the war going for Italy: anti-communism and preserving Italy's military prestige.

In September 1937 the *Duce* visited Germany and was treated to such an extraordinary show of appreciation by the German dictator that the bones of the Axis agreements appeared to be acquiring real flesh. The *Führer* even anxiously ordered a special plane to go and fetch some ripe pears to provide an adequate choice of fruit for Mussolini's table (Kershaw, 2000: 44), but it was the 800,000 people who (were) turned out to listen to Mussolini's speech that must have made the blacksmith's son from the Romagna believe that he was here getting into a serious relationship. In his speech, given in German, the *Duce* pointed out that this was not just an ordinary state visit 'which means I will be travelling somewhere else tomorrow', but rather that he was placing his 'revolution' in the same spiritual torrent as that of the Nazis. Their values were identical: anti-Bolshevik, the glorification of work, a spiritual faith in the nation, economic independence from the world market, the saving of 'western civilization' from the 'false and lying Gods of Geneva and Moscow'. If a war should ensue, he continued, 'Our two great nations – who together comprise an imposing, ever growing mass of 115 million people – stand together in a single, unshatterable determination' (in Delzell, 1970: 202–5). These were, of course, just words, but their context, their promises, the way in which the two dictators paraded to each other (in May 1938 Hitler's exchange visit to Italy was just as grandiose) were significant factors in shaping events that were to come. Hitler had courted Mussolini in an extravagant way and had largely succeeded in breaking any possibility of there being a united front against his own aggressive plans as Germany rearmed. Mussolini was truly dazzled by the flattery showered on him and, with the only price to pay being Austria, entered willingly into the embrace that would mean his downfall [Doc. 33, p. 152].

In November 1937 Italy acceded to the Anti-Comintern Pact that had been made a year before between Germany and Japan, promising mutual support in case of aggression from the Soviet Union. But it was, like the Axis, much more a statement of intent than a formal treaty and brought under the same umbrella the three powers who pledged no loyalty whatsoever to the order established at Versailles. Italy now quite definitely placed itself among the 'revisionists'. The 'Stresa front' agreed to (with France and Britain) before the Ethiopian war in April 1935, in which Italy had pledged itself to defend Austrian independence and to maintain Versailles intact, was dead and buried. Yet the Anti-Comintern Pact was directed against the USSR and did little except reiterate Italy's consistent stand against Bolshevism at home or in Spain, which was hardly about provoking the western powers into a fight; lambasting the reds was perfectly acceptable to men like Neville Chamberlain, now prime minister in Britain, and Léon Blum's Popular Front was on the verge of collapse. For Japan, encountering Russian power in Manchuria, and for Germany, a stone's throw from the red giant, the Soviet Union remained a threat and a rival; but for Italy it was but a distant enemy against which there was no dream of a 'final reckoning'. This divergence would become pronounced during the Second World War: Germany's aim after 1939 was to expand eastwards into the Soviet Union, leaving Italy to fight Britain in Africa and the Mediterranean, a theatre of war in which Hitler, in the end, was prepared to spend only small change.

THE APOTHEOSIS OF THE DICTATORSHIP

By the late 1930s the trajectory of Fascist Italy was being bent by the overwhelming gravitational field of Nazi Germany. This astronomical metaphor is appropriate because, apart from drawing attention to the differential in size and power between the two countries, it highlights the quality of their relationship. Until the German occupation of the peninsula in 1943, Italy controlled its internal and external policies, but it was nevertheless affected by the tidal surges produced by the existence and the development of the Third Reich. Fundamentally, the meaning of the Fascist 'revolution' was redefined once Hitler came to power. The Nazi dictatorship appeared to be free of all the compromises that Mussolini's Regime tolerated: there was no monarchy and Hitler was head of state, head of government and *Führer*; the Church had little influence; the army accepted Hitler as commander-in-chief; the SS police apparatus operated with ruthless efficiency; and Germany's network of detention camps made Italy's repressive apparatus look amateurish. The economy was roaring to success and the Third Reich's racial policies seemed to be turning the dream of the *Volksgemeinschaft* (racial community) into reality. By 1939, with threats alone, Hitler had brought into being a superstate that had absorbed all the German speakers of central Europe. In the face of this challenge Mussolini had three choices: (1) to stagnate as Fascist dictator; (2) to radicalize the Fascist 'revolution' at home and to search for success abroad, i.e. to 'keep up' with Hitler; or (3) to bask in the moral superiority of his version of a new civilization over that of Hitler's. All three options were fraught with difficulty. The first might reduce the *Duce* to a tin-pot and expendable dictatorlet. The second was a gamble that relied on Hitler's madness paying off. The third would only work if he could extricate Italy from Germany's embrace and at the same time prevent a reversion to some kind of liberal democracy. In the event, at different times and often simultaneously, Mussolini tried all these options but never made a firm decision as to which should take absolute priority and this uncertainty sapped his Regime's decisiveness and concurrently undermined his personal authority.

Before being forced to decide, it was possible to make it *look* like Fascism was entering a new and ultra-radical phase. This could be done by vigorous attacks on inconsequential elements in Italy. Rather than eliminate the monarchy Mussolini invented the title of 'First Marshall of the Empire' for himself (Bosworth, 2002: 347–8). In 1939 what was left of the old liberal Chamber of Deputies was abolished and replaced by the Chamber of the Fasces and Corporations, but the latter had the same members as before and the Senate was left intact. It was easier to run a campaign against the 'bourgeoisie', to deride its card games, its turns of phrase and gestures of greeting than it was to liquidate it as a social class. It was easier to fulminate against the Church than to test the loyalty of Italians to it by forcing them to choose between Fascism and the pope; it was easier to introduce the goosestep to the Italian army on parade than it was to tackle incompetence in its bloated upper echelons; it was easier to talk about '8 million bayonets' than to build the tens of thousands of tanks, pieces of artillery and airplanes required to engage in a major war in Europe. It was easier to eliminate English words from the Italian language, to rename football *Calcio* or change the supermarket Standard to *Standa* than it was to counter the all-pervasive influence of Hollywood. It was easier to denounce Jews and homosexuals than it was to take on industry or the banks. As the shock waves of the coming into existence of the Third Reich washed over Italy, the 'third wave' of Italy's fascistization took place.

The flagship of this renewed vigour in not allowing Italians to have an 'easy life' ('he that stands still is lost' ran a slogan coined in the late 1930s) was the Regime's decision in November 1938 to enact a series of laws based on a new concept of Italians as a distinct biological race. The main target was Jews. As Ciano had noted in his diary in late 1937, indeed, as Mussolini had himself suggested on many occasions before, 'I do not believe we should unleash in Italy an anti-semitic campaign. The problem just does not exist here' (Ciano, 1980: 336) yet not very long afterwards precisely this was done. Why? Mussolini was certainly not obeying some sort of directive from Berlin. In Germany there was as much surprise as in Italy that the Regime had taken this turn, particularly as it contrasted starkly with many of Mussolini's pubic utterances in the past. Not only had Italians been officially defined by him as 'not a race, nor a geographically defined region, but a people, historically perpetuating itself' (in Michaelis, 1978: 29), but Mussolini had in the early 1930s affirmed his own scepticism as far as theories of race were concerned (Michaelis, 1978: 28). Even on his visit to Germany in 1937, in the speech cited above, when he had talked about the spiritual affinity between Italian Fascism and Nazism, Mussolini had studiously not mentioned the question of race, although it would have presumably gone down well with his audience as well as with the *Führer*.

In the early 1930s Mussolini aimed at preventing Nazi Germany from encroaching on Austria, but the Ethiopian War and international isolation led him to change course and go down the path that led to the racial laws of 1938. Certainly the main justification for a 'new racial consciousness' on the part of the Regime was the conquest of empire (Preti, 1968: 214) but it is difficult not to see Mussolini's u-turn as anything more than opportunism in the climate of forging the Axis with Hitler. Yet there was no express demand by Nazi Germany for Italy to ape something like the Nuremberg racial laws of 1935. In reality Italy's anti-semitic legislation of 1938 must be seen as part of Mussolini's 'third wave' of fascistization that included the campaign against 'bourgeois' habits, the official adoption of corporativism, the establishment of a Ministry of Popular Culture (1937) and the further intensification of the *Duce*'s personality cult. This campaign was another leap in the direction of a 'revolution' without the need (and the grave dangers for the Regime) of actually having one. For Mussolini the move to an Italian version of a 'racial state' (Burleigh and Wippermann, 1991) was as much about the relationship with the Third Reich as it was with the need to make the Regime appear to be leading another great transformation.

The fewer than 60,000 Italian Jews were easy targets, and squeezing them out of society was a relatively painless way by which to produce the appearance of a radical reconstruction of the nation. Anti-semitism and Italy's new 'racial consciousness' was, like much of Fascism's 'third wave', a kind of 'virtual' revolution. Whereas in Nazi Germany anti-semitism was allied to a whole series of measures aiming at a radical 'genetic' restructuring of society where the separation (and then elimination) of the Jews was the spearhead of a process that involved, for example, the sterilization of those deemed to be social misfits, the killing of the disabled, homosexuals and Roma, the enslaving of Slavs and the selective dispensing of welfare according to interpretations of 'genetic worth', in Italy the campaign appeared like thunder from a blue sky. Some historians argue that the Third Reich was heading towards becoming a 'racial rather than a class society' (Burleigh and Wippermann, 1991: 306) and consider even the rush into full-scale international war as a vital part of the 'cleansing' process. In terms of racial policy, Fascism in Italy before 1938 had not envisaged anything like this and while it was easy for some, including Mussolini, to see in Social Darwinism a possible 'scientific' underpinning to their ultra-nationalism, there were significant factors militating against a full-scale adoption of biological racism as a defining characteristic of the Regime. The notion that international success would prove racial fitness excluded *Italietta* and, on most of the lists developed by Europe's racial theorists, Italians were low on the hierarchy. Within Italy too, the great socio-cultural divisions between north and south were often interpreted as racial ones. If anything, that the Fascist-sponsored Manifesto of Racial Scientists of July 1938 unequivocally stated that all Italians were a well-established and single 'Aryan' race [**Doc. 32, p. 151**] must have come as a relief. Mussolini, who contributed to the manifesto himself, surely enjoyed brushing aside Italy's great cultural cleavages and placing all Italians happily in one 'genetic' basket; an easy way of proving that Italians were already made. The exclusion of Jews from the 'racial' community was a small price to pay for lending credence to such an affirmation [**Doc. 32, p. 151**].

Although it is difficult to imagine that by defining Jews as belonging to a 'non-Italian' race, the Fascist Regime was taking the first step of what Raul Hilberg, the great historian of the Holocaust, has called the 'destruction process' (Hilberg, 1961), it is also unclear where Italy's racial anti-semitism would have led had not early defeats in the Second World War transformed the relationship with Nazi Germany. Notwithstanding Anthony Giddens' definition of Fascism as 'a set of political ideas, or an actual political system, based on notions of the superiority of some races over others' (Giddens, 1990: 740), it would be an oversimplification to see Italy's anti-semitic campaign as going down the road to the Holocaust. Before 1938 Jews were represented in the Fascist Party in the same proportion as they were in Italian society as a whole, and many had been prominent in the movement from its very earliest days. For this reason, when the Regime did turn to anti-semitism it was all the more painful, and comprehensible only in terms of craven kow-towing to Germany.

For Italian Jews, and the many foreign ones that had sought sanctuary in Italy from persecution in Germany, however 'virtual' the overall radicaliza-tion of the Regime might have been in the last three years of the 1930s, the impact of racial legislation was devastating. From the almost unique success story of integration (for example, there were 50 Jewish generals serving in the Italian army during the Great War), the members of the small commun-ity of Italian Jews were transformed into second-class citizens overnight. They were deprived of their livelihood, their social position, and eventually their property and equality before the law. However justified they were on biological precepts, the laws did not follow the guidelines of the Manifesto of Racial Scientists. On the one hand Jews who had converted to Christianity after September 1938 were liable to the sanctions of the law: i.e. they were 'biologically' defined as Jews; on the other, the state assumed the right of 'Aryanization', that is, a Jew could be declared not to be Jewish. This last clause obviously ridiculed the concept of biological racism as well as giving ample opportunity for mitigation by corruption.

The foreign Jews who had fled other anti-semitic regimes lost their citizen-ship and effectively became 'non-people'. Some Italian Jews emigrated, others lost their jobs or companies, although some were able to hand their concerns over to non-Jewish friends who could be trusted to give them back at an undefined future date. Jews were forbidden to go to school with Aryans and were barred from university (although those already attending were permitted to finish their degrees). The government pointed out that this was not per-secution, as in Germany, but 'discrimination', designed at separation. As has been suggested, the laws were contradictorily implemented (Zuccotti, 1987: 61). Nevertheless Jews, particularly foreign ones, were interned, and as the *Duce* brought Italy into the war, their numbers increased dramatically. Concentra-tion camps were set up at Ferramonti and Campagna, where conditions were harsh but, with barracks divided between kosher and non-kosher canteens, with camp-guards learning Yiddish, and with Jewish doctors from the camps providing clinics for local peasants, one historian has called Ferramonti 'the largest kibbutz on the European continent' (Steinberg, 2002: 229).

The ambiguousness of Fascism's racial laws pointed to a Regime that in the groundswell of the Third Reich's frenetic activity was losing a clear sense of direction. The whole barrage of the 'third wave' – including Italian regi-ments messing up the Prussian goosestep, the PNF's campaign against the handshake, the vituperation showered on vaguely defined 'bourgeois' values, and above all the Regime's new racial awareness – was not popular. Italy's economy stagnated. The war in Spain dragged on, claiming many Italian lives but offering few dividends. Franco's slow and excruciatingly cautious, if bloody, 'reconquest' of the country was not the sexy war Mussolini would have liked, but there was little to be done. The African empire had failed to absorb some of Italy's surplus population because the investment necessary was not available. Italian East Africa remained a heavy drain on Italy's finances. Rearmament was proceeding slowly.

If the empire, or indeed the still backward Italian economy, could not provide work for large swathes of Italy's poor, notwithstanding the campaign for autarky and the signs of European war on the horizon, Germany was entering a period of chronic labour shortage that would dog it throughout the war (and beyond). In 1937 Germany and Italy envisaged a worker-exchange programme, and in the next two years a large number of Italians, now unable to migrate to the Americas, were delivered to the Reich. Half a million Italians moved north by 1943, often thankful for higher wages and better conditions, but then regretting their choice as the Third Reich regarded them as much lower on the racial hierarchy than its own people. Whatever the vicissitudes of the Axis over the next years, these Italians were hostages in waiting whose presence in the Reich helped to steady Italian adherence to the German alliance. After the fall of Fascism in July 1943 the repressed bigotry of the Germans overflowed and 'worker exchange' became out-and-out forced labour, with the addition of 600,000 Italian prisoners of war. This was an ironic conclusion to Mussolini's trumpeted programme of granting workers to the Reich. The reality was that there was very little the German economy needed from Italy except labour and that Mussolini provided precisely this made a mockery of Fascism having done wonders for the 'proletarian nation'. Yet despite Fascist rhetoric, Italians were still prepared to emigrate for meagre wages and to accept bad working conditions, highlighting the still appalling economic underdevelopment in which much of the peninsula still found itself.

Mussolini's constraining choices, striving to keep up with the Third Reich, and accepting some form of subordination, were clearly tracks being followed simultaneously. It was at Munich in 1938 that for the last time the *Duce* posed as the conciliator, the 'good cop' in what was left of the European order that had emerged with the end of the Great War.

MUNICH: MUSSOLINI'S LAST PEACE

Czechoslovakia was a characteristic product of the Versailles settlement. The demise of the multi-national empire of the Habsburgs had created a number of small states that were meant to draw their legitimacy from neat national distinctions that were much more a product of the minds of the statesmen who reorganized Europe after the Great War than they were reflections of reality. Czechoslovakia, established in 1919, contained Czechs, Germans, Slovaks, Hungarians, Ukrainians, Jews, Poles, Roma and Croats. Without the mystique of the Habsburgs and the long tradition of compromise that had allowed the old Austrian Empire to function in an age of nationalism, Czechoslovakia's ethnic diversity was a volatile brew. At the same time, the catastrophic loss of prestige suffered by the German peoples in the empire and their fear of Slav domination led to growing demands that they be absorbed into Germany. After the *Anschluss* of March 1938 Germans throughout east central Europe clamoured to join the Third Reich, and those in Czechoslovakia, known as the Sudeten Germans, became the cause of an international crisis that threatened to plunge Europe into war.

As the atmosphere of the 'third wave' of fascistization permeated Italy it was Hitler that made the running on the international panorama. The *Duce* had accepted the *Anschluss* but it was more difficult to get Italians to do the same (government offices were bombarded with anonymous letters opposed to the rebirth of another Germanic colossus on Italy's border), and although in private Mussolini too was apprehensive, a long article penned by him for the *Il Popolo d'Italia* stated the plain truth that if Italy had stepped in to defend Austria 'resistance to our intervention would have come first and foremost from the Austrians themselves'. Mussolini could show off the *Anschluss* as 'putting the Axis into practice', but even he could not turn Hitler's 'Germanic' triumph into an Italian one. In this instance, as was to be the case for Czechoslovakia, he ended up using the peace ticket: 'this new equilibrium [produced by the *Anschluss*] will now finally permit the peaceful and fertile collaboration of all peoples', he wrote unconvincingly in *Il Popolo d'Italia* (OO XXIX: 70–1).

Once the *Führer* decided to take the Sudetenland he moved quickly, presenting the Czech government with an ultimatum that he knew to be unacceptable. His bold move immediately plunged Europe into crisis, but just as another European war began to seem inevitable, the almost-forgotten dictator of Italy emerged to save the day.

Had Mussolini been utterly bent on a war to prise the British out of the Mediterranean and to reclaim France's 'Italian' territories ('Corsica, Tunisia, Nice and Savoy' as carefully briefed hecklers in the Italian rubber-stamp parliament shouted on hearing a bellicose speech by Ciano), this would have surely been the most propitious moment to act. Although Mussolini assured Hitler that, if Czechoslovakia did mean war, he would stand by his Axis partner, it is by no means certain that the *Duce* was acting in good faith. According to Robert Mallet, frenetic plans were being made for 'a sudden, violent and, above all undeclared' war with Mussolini's 'hated foes' (Mallett, 2003: 192–3) in the Mediterranean, yet the *Duce* seems to have been relieved when his military chiefs assured him in no uncertain terms that Italy was still not ready for major military engagement. Bellicose blustering, being as tough and reckless as the German dictator, quickly changed when Mussolini was invited, or rather beseeched, by Chamberlain to somehow restrain the *Führer*.

The Munich conference of 29–30 September 1938 (only a few hours before the German army was meant to enter Czechoslovakia) was the result and, in it, Mussolini acted as conciliator, switching from the loose cannon of a few days before to penetrating and farsighted peacemaker. In reality the *Duce* had very little to do at Munich, as the deals were being struck between Hitler, Chamberlain and Daladier (for France), but who could take away from the fact that Italy was there, discussing the future of the globe (or so it seemed), with the big boys? Ciano noted in his diary, with great satisfaction, that the *Führer* and his entourage 'reserved' for the Italians at the conference 'a treatment of marked distinction' compared to the disdain for the British and French (Ciano, 1980: 187). What really mattered to Mussolini at this juncture was collecting a dividend by posing as peacemaker, but he also enjoyed the palpable unease felt by the British and French at the menacing presence of the two dictators. Not surprisingly, Mussolini had been in a very good mood on his way to the conference and on the way back he was even more jubilant. Hitler got everything he wanted without a war and, apart from the Czechs, Europeans breathed an enormous sigh of relief at a Mussolini-bestowed peace.

Crowds lined the railway line as the *Duce* and Ciano travelled back to Rome and there a multitude greeted them as the saviours of world peace. It was true that at Munich Italy had been granted a prominent space on the world stage; Mussolini had been loyal to Hitler and relatively approachable for France and Britain (thus keeping his options open), but there must have been some niggling doubts: those reports by the military that Italy was not ready for war; Hitler using the Italian dictator to make the democracies look silly; but, most of all, why were Italians, who Fascism had been turning into 'new men', whose greatest aspiration was to believe, to obey and to fight, so happy for a few more days to be sheep rather than to blow it all on one as a lion?

Yet with Hitler raising the stakes all the time it was now inconceivable to allow events to take their own course with Italy on the sidelines. As the Versailles order fell to pieces in front of everyone's eyes, concrete aims needed to be formulated and plans made. As Martin Clark puts it, 'in autumn 1938 Italian "foreign policy" became a frenetic search for quick returns' (Clark, 2005: 243). Malta, Suez, Egypt, Yugoslavia, Tunisia, East Africa, France, Albania, Greece were all potential targets. But fantastic reveries and the frenzies of desire always dashed themselves on one irksome imponderable: the Italian armed forces. Here was the crux of the travailed history of Fascism as it ran its course from 1938 to its collapse in 1943. The Regime's whole impetus, its justification, its legitimacy, its past achievements, its vision, its relationship to what the Vittorio Veneter spirit had had as its raison d'être after the Great War came to rest on this one shaky foundation stone. The latter to all intents and purposes cracked by March 1941 when a German invasion was required to bail Italy out of its botched attempt to conquer Greece. After this, for a while longer, the Italian Fascist Regime survived on the strength of the *Wehrmacht* but collapsed as the latter faltered.

Whatever plans were made after Munich, whatever Fascism's long-term goals might have been, war would eventually be necessary, and war that would inevitably have to be fought against France and Britain, not Ethiopia, the Spanish Republic, Albania or even Greece. It was Italy's extraordinary powerlessness to perform militarily, to do what Fascism had trumpeted was its very raison d'être, where the chasm between words and reality was so ludicrously vast as to reveal Mussolini's Regime to have all the qualities of the tin-pot dictatorship.

8

The Second World War and the End of Fascism, 1938–45

UNDERSTANDING ITALY'S PERFORMANCE IN THE SECOND WORLD WAR

Much historiographical controversy has raged over whether the ambitions of Italian Fascism should be taken seriously or if the Regime was just another of those Italian circus acts to which Europe and the USA had grown accustomed. Why did Italy fail so dramatically in waging war? Britain, without a 'new religion', without the hype, a mere liberal democracy, fought so much more efficiently and with so much more ideological conviction than did Italy. So too did the USA, without the need of a Ministry of Popular Culture or a dictator. What then had all the talk been about, what had been going on for more than 18 years? MacGregor Knox furnishes us with one answer: that war was the means by which 'total power' could be achieved, 'a barbarisation of Italian . . . society and the final taming or destruction of all institutions, from churches to officer corps, to the Italian monarchy, that blocked the Regime'[s path] at home' (Knox, 1996: 114). This is entirely different from Martin Clark's 'frenentic search for quick returns'. Two interrelated questions need to be considered when examining Italy's wartime experience: what was actually done in Italy to push forward Mussolini's 'revolution' and the 'barbarisation of Italian society', and why was its military effort so feeble?

Vincere, vincere, vincere (win, win, win) went one Fascist slogan of Caesarean memory, but it is hard to understand what the Regime did to put it into practice. In terms of its competitors, some statistics showing how far the Italian economy became geared for military engagement during the Second World War are enlightening: in 1941, at its peak, 23 per cent of the Italian GDP was dedicated to the war effort. Equivalent percentages for the much bigger economies of Germany, Britain and the USSR were respectively 64, 52 and 61 (Bosworth, 2005: 466). The figure for Italy therefore beggars belief. *Italietta* in the First World War was able to allocate almost 40 per cent of its GDP for war. In terms of state expenditure the comparison between Mussolini's Italy and the liberal period is even more stark: 20 compared to 76 per cent (Rochat and Massobrio, 1978: 267). One other statistic is also instructive: in 1942 the USA was building more airplanes in a week than Italian industry could turn out in a year (Bosworth, 2002: 372).

These numbers lead to two conclusions. First, as far as Italian resources invested during the Second World War are concerned, Italy could only be a third-rate power, whatever its ambitions or its rhetoric. Second, but more important and more surprising, is a fact that Rochat emphasizes: '[during the Second World War]', he argues, 'the Regime was unable and unwilling to put into effect a general mobilisation of national energy that was even remotely comparable to what had been achieved by liberal Italy during the First' (Rochat and Massobrio, 1978: 267). For a Regime that was a product of the spirit of Vittorio Veneto this is perplexing, but the evidence suggests that Rochat's summary is accurate. Italy's disastrous war was not just a reflection of relative economic weakness (although this would probably have been determinant in the long run anyway) but, as Mussolini might have put it, it was also a problem that was 'quintessentially political'. In other words, Italy's appalling performance was the fruit of the inability and unwillingness of the *Duce* to put to the test through war the equilibriums that his Regime had constructed since 1922. Far from the flight into war being a means by which it would be possible to continue and to radicalize Fascism's 'revolution', to topple what was left of the establishment to increase his own power, what Mussolini tried to do was to fight a major European war *without* in any way altering the balance of forces that had been the product of his long period in government. Most telling in this regard is the extraordinary story of Aldo Vidussoni.

Towards the end of 1941 Italy had already been severely bruised in Greece and was in the thick of a war dictated by the military successes of the Third Reich. Operation Barbarossa was already underway (with some Italian participation) and in December Italy had declared war on the USA, adding this formidable enemy to both the British Empire and the USSR. With all the world's super-powers now counted amongst Italy's adversaries (and with Germany a relatively unhelpful ally in terms of resource sharing) and a long and bloody war of attrition in prospect, the time had surely come to gather together the Regime's most loyal and trusted talent in a massive mobilization of the Italian people, to brush aside opposition, and forge a new consensus for the huge sacrifices required by the war effort. The instrument to do this was already at hand in the Fascist Party and its huge network of organizations throughout the country. Yet, at this critical juncture, Mussolini appointed a 28-year-old nonentity to head the PNF: Aldo Vidussoni's only credentials for this job were having lost an arm and an eye as a Fascist volunteer in Italy's war in Spain, and a couple of months at the head of the Fascist University Student Union. Youth and ardour were insufficient to deal with what Ciano called 'that ambience of old whores which is the Party' (Ciano, 1980: 572). The 'old whores' did not take too well to seeing this child, who had been born when they were about to start digging trenches in the Alps, being suddenly elevated to command them. Vidussoni was young, and it is probable that Mussolini appointed him on the vague idea that Italy's salvation might be found in the generation that had grown up under the Fascist Regime. But surely what was really required to put Italy on a radical war footing was a caucus of trusted party men, much as those Hitler trusted to pursue Germany's own war effort, to which the levers of power required for the mobilization of the Italian people could be given. Vidussoni's appointment was proof that Mussolini had no intention of carrying through a war-induced radicalization of Fascism. The divide and rule, the juggling and balancing that had been sufficient to keep his dictatorship going over the last two decades was to continue. Business as usual was all Mussolini had to offer in the face of the biggest war humanity had ever engaged in. Now, almost 60 years old, the *Duce* had finally run out of ideas or, more accurately, had worked himself into a dead-end.

By early 1942 Mussolini's political system depended on the alliance with Germany for its survival. While Germany transformed itself into a total-war society, Mussolini was unwilling to jeopardize the complicated equilibrium created in Italy since 1920. So used had he become at playing this game that it was too late to do anything about it by 1941. Persecuting Jews, as the centrepiece of Fascism's 'third wave', could be passed off as a radical reconstruction of society without affecting the tacitly accepted rules of how society really worked, but when it came to fighting a war against serious enemies, as was the case when building an airplane, two and two could simply not equal five. The only hope was that a comprehensive victory by the Third Reich would assign to Italy a worthy place in which Mussolini's own prestige would be enhanced and in which *then* he might be able to tackle some of his Regime's compromises with the past.

In April 1943, a few weeks before the fall of Fascism, Vidussoni, having achieved nothing except perhaps to make the *Duce* remember, as Ciano had before him, how nice it was to be young, was replaced by Carlo Scorza, who promised to at last swing the party into an absolute and total drive behind the war effort. But it was already about three years too late.

Before the collapse of Fascism in July 1943, Italy's Second World War can be divided into three distinct phases that were, in different ways, products of Italy's weakness relative to Germany. First was the period of 'non-belligerence', from the outbreak of war on 1 September 1939 to Italy's entry in June 1940; the second, often referred to as Mussolini's Mediterranean 'parallel' war, saw Italy pitted against Britain in North Africa and involved the opening of a new theatre in the Balkans with the Italian invasion of Greece on 28 October 1940; the third saw this parallel war collapse with unexpected defeat on all fronts and, with Germany's shoring up of the Italian war effort (from the spring of 1941), Italy was effectively reduced to a German satellite. For two years after this Italy fought on in North Africa, in the Balkans and in Russia, but always now under German military command. In early 1943 the war became a defensive one and time began to run out for Italy, which was unable and unwilling to transform the war effort into a mass mobilization of the Italian people. As Fascism approached its doom, it is pertinent to ask why no Vittorio Veneto followed the Caporetto that was Fascist Italy's Second World War.

THE COLLAPSE OF FASCISM

On 18 February 1943 Joseph Goebbels, the propaganda minister of the Third Reich, made a speech in the *Sportpalast*, Berlin, inciting the German people to raise its efforts in pursuing what looked like a war that was now heading for defeat. Yet Goebbels was able to argue convincingly that there was no alternative to continuing to fight. Beyond the threshold of defeat lay a future that was wholly unimaginable except in terms of a catastrophic annihilation of what Goebbels referred to as 'European Civilization' (Goebbels, 1943). The eradication of the possibility of imagining futures that were different from that depicted and elaborated by the Regime was a major aspiration of Nazism and Italian Fascism. Indeed, the extent to which any society is 'totalitarian' can be measured by how far it is able to confine ideas of the future to its own. The difference between what Goebbels talked about in his speech, and which was generally accepted by his listeners, and what occurred in Italy, was that for both the elite and the people a future without Mussolini and without Fascism became imaginable and indeed desirable. Had Italy faced the possibility of a Soviet invasion rather than one by the liberal democracies, things would probably have been different; as in Germany, the red menace would have concentrated minds wonderfully and the alliance between elites and Regime would surely have lasted longer. Notwithstanding more than 20 years of Fascist rule, the 'mental attitude' of Italy's elites, and of its people, proved not to be of the stern stuff required by totalitarianism. Why?

The answer lies in Italy's failure to capitalize on Germany's successes after June 1940. Mussolini had decided on 'non-belligerence' because he and his military advisors realized that Italy was in no state to fight both France and Britain in the autumn of 1939. However much it may have tortured the man who had advocated intervention in 1914 to keep Italy out of a conflict that was deciding the fate of Europe, Mussolini recognized the advantage of waiting to see who would come out on top in the war. His hope was that both sides would balance each other out and that Italy would come in as the extra weight required for a German victory. With Hitler's extraordinary successes in the invasion of France in the spring of 1940 Mussolini breathed a sigh of relief that he had at least chosen the right side. But understanding that no Italian help was required for Germany's triumph to be assured was harder to swallow. With France on the verge of surrender and Britain having withdrawn to its island fortress, Italy, as justifiably the French were wont to say afterwards, stabbed the prone body of *La Grande Nation* in the back. Yet even the few days of fighting in the Alps that were what Italy got before the French capitulation, had left many question marks. Italy's little offensive had been badly organized and showed all the signs of the problems that were to come. But for the moment it did not matter, Hitler marched through Paris and the Axis and the Pact of Steel appeared to have been the right choice. Yet, while Hitler continuously pointed out to Ciano that Italy was free to do as it saw fit in the Mediterranean (Rochat and Massobrio, 1978: 273), the meagre loot he passed on at France's fall did nothing to help. Hitler's policy of pacifying France by allowing it a rump government and to keep its colonies meant that Tunisia, which would have been extraordinarily useful to Italy against Britain in the Mediterranean, remained off-limits. Even Corsica was left to the new French puppet government rather than being handed over to Mussolini, as might have been anticipated by the island's ethnicity.

The critical turning point for Italy was the downgrading by Hitler of the war effort against Britain. The English Channel prevented another German blitzkrieg and by the beginning of 1941 Hitler turned his attention to the east. For Italy, Hitler's decision to concentrate on attacking the Soviet Union (of which Italy knew nothing) without having either defeated or brought Britain to the negotiating table had catastrophic implications. Britain itself could do little against Germany, secure as it was in continental Europe and far from the reach of the Royal Navy, but Italy was an altogether different story. It was extremely vulnerable and it took little time for British military superiority to show. An Italian offensive into Egypt came to nothing and in one night, 11–12 November 1940, Italy's naval capacity was reduced by half as the Royal Navy launched a devastating air bombing raid on the port of Taranto. In March 1941 the Italian navy was decisively defeated at Matapan, where ominously the Italian flagship, with a name so significant for Italy's history over the last two decades, the *Vittorio Veneto*, also suffered damage. By the spring of 1941 Italy had lost even that empire whose conquest had been so important for the Regime back in what must have seemed the good old days of the mid-1930s. Haile Selassie re-entered the Ethiopian capital of Addis Ababa in May to reclaim the throne that he had lost for only five years.

Italy's role in the first year of its Second World War was probably most significant for the way it kept the British, unable to get at Nazi Germany, buoyant with some anti-Axis successes. Italy's failures and Germany's triumphs made the Pact of Steel into a difficult alliance [**Doc. 35, p. 154**]. In some ways, Italy's war was fought as much *against* Germany as it was Britain in the sense that Germany's continental hegemony after the defeat of France meant that Italy had to seek to readdress the enormous imbalance that was emerging in the relationship between the two partners. Not being able to inflict defeats on Britain (Malta, a British possession just a stone's throw from Sicily, was, for example, never conquered), Italy's 'parallel war' turned on Greece but foundered there in the extraordinary debacle of late 1940 and early 1941. Had German arms not intervened in both the Balkans and North Africa in the middle of 1941, Italy would already have lost the war and then quickly risked a British invasion of the Italian peninsula. This last scenario worried the Germans. Italy, as a weak underbelly to Germany's continental empire, threatened to allow the British back on to the European mainland from which they had been ejected at Dunkirk in May–June 1940. Germany therefore ploughed as much energy as it could spare to sustain the Italian war effort and thereby the Regime. The failed invasion of Greece and the discrepancy between British and Italian power in the Mediterranean had turned Italy into a German satellite. Hitler now had a major stake in preserving Mussolini's grip on power, as it was becoming unlikely that anybody else could actually keep Italy in the war. The Axis partnership had now become an embrace from which escape for Italy would have to be via an ejection of Mussolini's Regime; yet the latter eventuality risked provoking a German (as opposed to British) invasion, the consequences of which nobody was as yet prepared to imagine. In the event Italy was invaded by both.

Although Hitler may have been a lover of all things Italian, his patience was beginning to dry up (Bosworth, 2002: 379) and to many Germans Italy's appalling performance on the battlefield was a symptom of what they had known all along: that in spite of Italy's great Roman past, contemporary Italians were a lesser, degenerate people. In 1942 reports circulated in the Italian capital of Alsatian dogs being used to control Italian workers in Germany and even Mussolini could not bear the thought that, as he put it, 'the sons of a race that has given humanity Caesar, Dante and Michelangelo are being set upon by dogs belonging to Huns' (Ciano, 1980: 538–9). Something must be done, said Mussolini, but the man who was now referred to viciously in Germany as *Gauleiter* (the boss of a Nazi Party territorial section) of Italy (Salvatorelli and Mira, 1964: 1028) did nothing. Italian workers in the Reich now became virtual hostages, and their treatment increasingly resembled that of the coerced workers being forcibly brought to Germany from the Nazi empire in the east.

Symptomatic of the Italian war being squeezed oppressively between enemy and partner was a catastrophic lethargy that affected both government and the economy. Unlike the other Great Powers participating in the war, Italy was unable or unwilling to raise production significantly (Milward, 1977: 97). Even taking into account Italy's lack of raw materials (it was totally reliant on Germany for coal and oil throughout the war), the explanation for its woeful economic performance must be attributed to the weaknesses of its government, political system and society. Caught as it was between wishing Germany to win – but not to win too easily or too decisively – and at the same time appalled by the idea of having to engage in all-out war against Britain and the USA, the Regime was simply unable to react effectively [Doc. 36, p. 154]. In Japan, Germany, the USA, Britain and the Soviet Union there was a will to fight that in Italy was missing.

Yet this inertia becomes explicable as a logical outcome of the peculiar way in which Fascism had introduced itself into Italian society. In other words, if Italy's ruling elites had been divided on Italy's entry into the Great War in 1915 but pulled together during that conflict, in 1939–43 it was precisely because Italy was 'Fascist' that they were unable to do so again. The much easier alternative to fighting was, as Mussolini had fretted about on many occasions, to jettison Fascism. However, there were three significant risks in doing this: the first, and perhaps the most obvious, was that Hitler would turn against his betrayers with the ferocity for which he was now famous; the second was that Mussolini might appeal to the people and that their love of the *Duce* would prove to be deeper than anticipated, provoking a possible civil war; the third was that a divided ruling class would mean that the subversives might return triumphantly to Italian politics. In the event all these scenarios occurred to varying degrees, but before 1943 (and the removal of Mussolini from power) indecision over what direction to take resulted in a political and economic paralysis that made fighting a major European war at the level of a Great Power well-nigh impossible.

On the ground Italians themselves continued to fight and orders were generally obeyed, but a future without Fascism was now being imagined. One story that brings this out is that of the way Jews were dealt with in Italy and in those territories that were granted to Italy in the Nazi new order. As has been said, Mussolini had by the failure to take Greece more or less sacrificed control over foreign policy for maintenance of his rule in Italy. Naturally this involved the relationship with the Jews. The original logic in Italy's anti-semitic laws of 1938 had served to demonstrate the Regime's 'revolutionary' impetus and to eliminate discrepancies in the myth of Axis unity. But as this unity had turned rapidly into subservience, the way Italy dealt with the Jews became shot through with the desires of many, including at times Mussolini himself, to distinguish their Regime from Hitler's. Up to a point, the *Duce* was prepared to limit the persecution of Jews in practice, if not on paper, as a measure of political independence on the home front. In August 1942 the German government, as part of its sweep of all occupied Europe aiming at the 'final solution' of the Jewish question, asked Italy to hand over all Jews of non-Italian nationality under Italian jurisdiction. Although Mussolini gave the go-ahead himself, there was a serious attempt on the part of the Italian army to obstruct Jews being handed over to the German authorities. It was so successful that, 'until the sudden armistice on 8 September 1943 ended the Axis partnership, no Jew under Italian protection of the Italian forces was ever surrendered to the Germans' (Steinberg, 2002: 4). The Italian army's murderous behaviour in Ethiopia and in Yugoslavia contradicts the facile idea of Italians being 'nice' people, but the circumstances of the Axis relationship after 1941 and the catastrophic collapse of the Italian army's reputation led Italians to reconsider their future. Not sharing in the Nazi killing process might at least salvage something in the face of military debacle and humiliation.

As Italy's war lurched from one crisis to the next, the gap between the Regime's ambitions and its capabilities became more and more gaping, and so too did that between the Regime and the elites that had permitted its installation in the first place. Mussolini was well aware that he had, after 20 years in power, still failed to construct the totalitarianism of which he had so often talked. The king was still there, as he had been long ago in October 1922. The Church had supported the Regime but always demanded its own pound of flesh. The alliance with Hitler had strained the relationship, and military defeat had caused the Church to begin to make plans for a future without Mussolini. The business world, too, was disconsolate with what was happening. Notwithstanding the strains Italy was under in the First World War, industry had continued to have access to raw materials and money markets through its partnerships with Britain and the USA. The situation now was entirely different. Starved of raw materials, except what was grudgingly passed on by the Germans, production did not increase significantly, despite the requirements of war. The privations of the war, the constant bad news from the front, and the bombs that began to rain down on Italy's industrial cities broke what spell Fascism might have had over the Italian people. Food shortages became ever more serious as the war progressed, and by the beginning of 1943 the biggest concern for most people was finding enough to eat. In some cities food riots broke out and, more importantly, for the first time since the early 1920s, workers downed their tools and struck in some areas of the industrial triangle in 1942. The Regime could provide no solutions to these problems – and by the summer of 1943 it no longer tried.

On the evening of 24 July 1943, as the Allies landed in Sicily and with Rome still under shock from a bombing that had destroyed the historic basilica of San Lorenzo and some surrounding buildings, the Fascist Grand Council, which had last met before the outbreak of war, convened. What brought it together on this occasion was a series of exchanges between many of the Fascist leaders of the old generation who were still council members but who were, on the whole, bereft of power, as they had long since been abandoned in Mussolini's many ministerial reshuffles. Scorza suggested sending some of the Fascist old guard around Italy to rally the people behind the war effort. Farinacci, who still believed in the war, pleaded with Mussolini to hold a meeting of the Grand Council where the *Duce* would make it clear to all why Italy should continue to fight.

Many of the Council's members were disgruntled and had been privately discussing in what way Italy might extricate itself from the conflict that Mussolini had decided on without consulting them. Even Ciano had been downgraded, moved from the Foreign Ministry to a job as ambassador to the Vatican in February 1943. Bottai, too, had just lost the Ministry of Education; people like **Dino Grandi** had been more or less mothballed by the *Duce* over the years; a nice job as ambassador to Britain and later president of the Chamber of Deputies did not mean he was making policy. Emilio De Bono had long since ceased to have a close relationship with Mussolini. Cesare Maria De Vecchi had become progressively more of a monarchist and was distrusted by the *Duce*. Perhaps Vidussoni's appointment as party secretary had been the last straw for many an old Fascist leader.

Hoping to exonerate himself from responsibility for Italy's woes (this is what he talked about at the meeting) among his old party comrades, Mussolini agreed to the Council sitting going ahead. By 2.00 a.m. on 25 July, after a long discussion, Grandi's motion that control of the nation's armed forces should return to the king was carried, with even Ciano giving it his support. Mussolini failed to react. The grenades Grandi and Bottai carried in their pockets proved superfluous. For Mussolini there was perhaps something reminiscent in this Council meeting of his ejection from the Socialist Party way back in 1914 when had said to his 'betrayers', 'you hate me now because you love me'. But he had been 31 years old then and ideas had not been lacking; now he was 60 and he had only succeeded, as the king was to tell him the day after the Grand Council meeting, in becoming 'the most hated man in Italy' (Bosworth, 2002: 401). The Grand Council 'decision' (in reality it had no power to decide anything) was perhaps not intended, even by those who voted for Grandi's motion, to provoke Mussolini's downfall but more probably to counter the paralysis in government with regard to the war

Dino Grandi (1895–1988): Became a Fascist in 1920 and was involved in squadism in the Emilia Romagna region. A moderate throughout the Regime, he favoured a conciliatory attitude to Britain, where he was Italian ambassador 1932–9. Mussolini's alliance with Hitler led him to favour a monarchical dictatorship, and he was instrumental in Mussolini's fall.

effort, that is to begin to seek a way out of the consequences of military defeat. Mussolini might have reacted by calling out the Fascist militia. Its head, Enzo Galbiati, who voted against Grandi's motion, had suggested contacting SS leader Heinrich Himmler, and Scorza might have been able to mobilize some sections of the party in the *Duce's* defence; but Mussolini asked for nothing. Before leaving for the meeting his wife had told him to arrest the entire Council but either Mussolini did not have the political acumen of his wife, or he felt he could ignore any 'decision' made by his crusty old party comrades and rely on the king, as he had done at crucial moments in 1922 and 1925. Yet it must have been clear to the *Duce* by now that only in a victorious Italy could he continue to exist. There was still a glimmer of a chance, as Mussolini had pleaded with Hitler the last time they had met, that Germany would somehow stop fighting in the east and turn its attention to Italy's enemies in the west.

Perhaps on this slim hope, the day after the Council meeting, Mussolini kept an appointment he had with the king. Nervously, the monarch informed him that he was no longer the right man to head the government and that for his own safety he was being placed under arrest. What the king had given to the young Romagnol provincial more than two decades before was being taken back. In all the years of the dictatorship this sword of Damocles had never fallen, as Mussolini had always had something to offer that was more palatable to the king than any alternative; the *Duce* now had nothing and that small part of the old liberal constitution – that the power of the prime minister was held on the authority of the king – that Fascism had never succeeded in overturning proved to be the *Duce's* undoing [**Doc. 38, p. 156**].

THE DEATH OF A NATION: ITALY BETWEEN 1943 AND 1945

Mussolini's arrest and whisking away to imprisonment proved easy. Over all those years in power he had failed to create for himself (as Hitler had done so effectively) a *Duce*-dependent bodyguard such as the SS. As the war turned there had been no appeal to the people in the Goebbels manner, but only a radical loss of self-confidence in all who had been associated closely with his rule. The king's decision had been taken because the unthinkable was happening and bombs were falling on Rome as though it was just another city of the Axis empire. No one lifted a finger to save the man who had been adulated like a god or a Roman emperor for a generation. Again and again the news was transmitted over the radio that Mussolini had fallen from power and that Badoglio had been asked by the king to form a new government. The bulletin also stated that Italy would continue to fight along-side Germany, but no one believed that this was really the case. Italy's piaz-zas filled with jubilant crowds celebrating what they believed was the end of the war – perhaps rather more than Mussolini's fall. But the *Duce* and the humiliating, costly and useless war had become synonymous.

But a more prosaic reality was apparent to Badoglio and the king. Italy's comic-opera behaviour had a serious side that could not simply be forgotten in all the jubilation. Churchill's famous speech that 'one man alone' had been responsible for pitting Italy against Britain was being taken rather too liter-ally. Both the Anglo-Americans (especially the British who had been fighting Hitler's ally for some considerable time) and the Germans themselves under-standably wanted to use Italy to the full to pursue their greater war effort against each other and it was this desire that spoiled the Italian party; the king hoped against hope that having made a mess of the war Italy could now pretend it had not happened, and an authoritarian government, shorn of Mussolini and under the guidance of his faithful army generals, would be left alone to get its own house in order.

And the Italian people? Would they simply accept the king's actions as final and agree that all their woes were the responsibility of 'one man alone'? It was better not to wait for an answer. The Italian army might have been indecisive against its external enemies but it had a surprising clarity of vision when it came to dealing with its own people. On 27 July General Roatta issued a circular to all military commands on the Italian mainland that they were not to allow the jubilation at Mussolini's fall to transform itself into an anti-authoritarian challenge. At least 83 people were killed, 308 wounded and 1,500 arrested in the army's taking control of the celebration of Mussolini's downfall (Rochat and Massobrio, 1978: 297–8).

But events moved faster than anybody had anticipated. In Germany, an Italian defection from the Axis was expected and preparations had been made for a possible occupation of the peninsula well before July 1943. The Italian army, with hundreds of thousands of troops in the Balkans, in Russia and in France, as well as in Italy, was ordered by Badoglio to carry on fight-ing alongside Germany, but this command was only a desperate attempt to buy time for some kind of arrangement to be reached with the Allies with-out immediate German reaction. When the news was finally made public that Italy had surrendered to the Allies and was now fighting *against* the Germans the catastrophe remembered in Italy as '8 September' took its con-fused and tragic course.

If the desire to put Italy (and its monarch) under the protection of the Allies inspired Badoglio's negotiations, the side with effective power in the peninsula was much more likely to be the Germans. As Nazi armoured divisions sped into Italy, the king, Badoglio and the top ranking generals of the Italian army fled for their lives. The crush of stripes, medals, stars and emblazoned epaulettes trying to scramble on to the ship heading for Brindisi, a city in Allied hands deep in the south, was such that *carabinieri* (the Italian police) were required to control the panicking officers (Rochat and Massobrio, 1978: 305). Bereft of a command structure and without orders, tens of thousands of troops stationed across the peninsula interpreted events as leave to return home. Soldiers stationed abroad were simply left to fend for themselves; the majority fell into German hands, those who resisted were butchered (as happened on the Greek island of Kefalonia) and yet others joined Greek, Yugoslav or Albanian partisans. The Italian army that had always been regarded as the 'school of the nation', that had held the Piave after Caporetto and won at Vittorio Veneto, that had been the embodiment of everything that Fascism held most dearly, melted away like snow on a warm spring morning.

Some historians have labelled this moment in Italy's history as 'the death of the nation' (Galli Della Loggia, 1996). In the face of the advancing Germans, Italy's ruling class abdicated command and at the same time its people, as represented by the thousands of troops who either went AWOL or, with a handful of exceptions, let themselves be taken prisoner without offering resistance, regarded 'their' fatherland as one would regard a corpse. Foreign armies were again fighting on Italian soil for control of its future as the Italian people looked on. So runs the argument – and at one level it is unchallengeable. Yet such a view presupposes a very specific understanding of nationhood. The Italy that had passed through Fascism, that had participated in an ignominiously lost and unpopular war, that had been abandoned so shamefully by its ruling class was indeed not worth defending and it was shrugged off and left unceremoniously to be fought over by others. But there were many alternative 'Italies', other identities that rested on the peasant world, on Catholicism, the family, the locality or on social class, which found themselves reacquiring a locus for expression as the vacuum produced by the Fascist state's renunciation became apparent; in any case they had never in any meaningful sense disappeared, except in Fascist rhetoric.

On Mussolini's downfall, as has been said, what was celebrated was peace, but from 8 September 1943 war returned with a vengeance to the peninsula and did not go away again for almost two years. The Allies landed in Italy's south but were unable to prevent the German army from taking control of the peninsula below Rome. As Italian military power dissipated in the extraordinary events of 8 September, Italy became the battleground between the Allies slowly moving northward and the Germans attempting to hold them as far away from the borders of the Reich for as long as possible. It took until April 1945 for the Allies to come out on top, although the Germans remained on the defensive throughout the campaign, but for longish periods of time stable 'borders' were established. Badoglio's 'government', with no authority except that granted by the Allies, was ensconced within Allied-held territory in the south, but Badoglio and the king's past links to Fascism prevented it from becoming universally recognized as the basis of a future Italian state. Although the Allies recognized Badoglio and his entourage as Italy's legitimate government the Italian resistance movement, which began to grow in confidence and power in the Nazi-occupied zones and to claim a role in reforming a government in those freed by the Allies, felt no obligation to do the same.

Italy's history moved at breakneck speed, but on 25 July 1943 it seemed that at last it was to be sundered from the one man who had played so great a part in it from well before the First World War. After his arrest Mussolini was shuttled from prison to prison by the *carabinieri* and they finally settled on a ski resort 2,000 metres up in the Apennines. Notwithstanding the improbability of such a hideout, the Germans got to know where the ex-*Duce* was being held. On 12 September, in what must be one of the most amazing episodes of the entire war, Mussolini was 'rescued' by a group of German SS commandoes, who delivered him safe and sound at the court of Hitler in Munich only a few hours later. Apart from Hitler's genuine personal affection for the Italian ex-dictator, rescuing Mussolini was part of a German plan to establish a puppet German 'Fascist' government behind the front line in German-occupied Italy, with Mussolini as its legitimizing head. This was proposed to the ex-*Duce* and, after some hesitation, he accepted.

Why he did so is a matter of debate. That he was a Fascist and therefore bound to continue the ideologically driven struggle along with his 'Nazi-Fascist' partner against the forces of freedom was the view put forward by those who took up arms against his new political administration. But there had been enough discrepancy between his and Hitler's vision as well as the obvious hopelessness of the German war effort to mean that accepting Hitler's offer was by no means a foregone conclusion. Championed by De Felice, this view has gone further and suggested that Mussolini took the opportunity offered by Hitler reluctantly and only when he understood that it was the best way to mitigate the ferocity of a Nazi occupation of Italy. The ex-*Duce*, De Felice wrote,

> accepted Hitler's project because he was motivated by patriotism . . . [He] returned to power to place himself at the service of his country because only by doing this could he prevent Hitler from transforming Italy into a new Poland and to therefore ensure that the Regime of occupation would be less heavy and less tragic.

(De Felice, 1995: 114–15)

Mussolini here appears as a bright shield trying to fend off Nazi barbarism, almost a saint taking up the heavy burden of martyrdom for a thankless people. Yet De Felice admits that the price of Mussolini's choice was a very high one. Without the blessing his assent to Hitler's plan gave the Nazi occupation, the resistance would have been a straightforward struggle for national liberation, headed perhaps by some Italian general, if not the king. With Mussolini's choice, however, the left was able to take control of the resistance movement and thus allow Stalinist communism to make of Italy its most significant bridgehead in the west in the postwar years.

De Felice's argument is a subtle one and implicitly suggests that the Italian Communist Party was as much a danger to Italy as the Nazis were. But perhaps it would be correct to argue that Mussolini's motivations were simpler. According to Bosworth, despite everything he had gone through, Mussolini had not lost his passion for power and a sense of personal loyalty to Hitler in the face of the betrayals in his homeland. In any case the only options were to go into hiding, to end his own life or to face a trial by the Allies and certain execution (Bosworth, 2002: 404). Like most people, Mussolini chose to carry on living and see what the future might bring. The Hitler-inspired Italian Social Republic (*RSI – Repubblica Sociale Italiana*) walked the thin line between tragedy and farce but for Mussolini a few more weeks as dictator of even a rump Italy were always going to be more attractive than death.

So, within ten days of 8 September Mussolini proclaimed to the Italian people, who did not know what had happened to him after 25 July, that a new republican Fascist state had been born and that the war against the Allies was to continue alongside Germany. Badoglio and the king were traitors, in cahoots with the enemy, selling Italy to the plutocratic democracies.

The subordination of the Italian to the German dictatorship, which had begun even before the outbreak of war, was now complete. Without German support the RSI would have collapsed immediately. Yet it would be a mistake to imagine that it was simply imposed on Italy without a connection being made with sentiments in which some Italians still believed. The betrayal of the Germans and the dissolving of the Italian army had shocked many, and the RSI offered a chance to redeem Italy's honour [**Doc. 39, p. 156**]. Added to this, as the resistance movement picked up in late 1943 and the Italian Communist Party became prominent in its organization, anti-communism became the mainstay of what consensus the RSI was able to muster. Men who had been compromised with the old Fascist Regime were found to staff the RSI administration, although many of the big guns of old Fascism were regarded as traitors after the Grand Council vote. Those who did not manage to elude capture, including Ciano and De Bono (one of the leaders of the March on Rome), were executed after a trial held in Verona in early 1944.

Graziani, who had lost the race to Addis Ababa back in 1936 to no other than the hated Badoglio, joined the RSI as minister of defence and Giovanni Gentile gave his intellectual blessing to the new Regime also. Renato Ricci of the old *Opera Nazionale Balilla* headed the RSI militia and Alessandro Pavolini, who had been a minor intellectual of the old Regime, took up responsibilities for the party and the Ministry of Popular Culture. Farinacci once again did not get a job, as he had been too avid in courting the Germans in the hope that he might head a new republican Fascism rather than his old *Duce*.

While it was true that in the RSI nothing could be done without German approval, here, at least on paper, was a chance for some of Fascism's radical old programme to be implemented (or imagined) without the compromises that had been required for Mussolini to stay in power before. The single most important statement of policy issued by the RSI, known as the Verona Manifesto, appeared in November 1943. Having little to do with Mussolini (who did not contribute to its drafting but checked it after it was written), the Manifesto stated that a new constitutional assembly would derive its power from the people and not the traitorous king. It would 'choose' the 'head of the Republic' every five years. The RSI was to be officially Catholic and in time of war Jews were to be considered as belonging 'to an enemy nation'. On social issues a kind of radical corporativism with enhanced worker power was proposed as the 'third way' that old Italian Fascism had never become (Schnapp, 2000: 198–204) and was not to become yet again. The programme was a set of principles that would take time to implement, and if it was true that there was now no need to hold to the compromises of the past, there were new ones that were just as pressing and even more constraining. The first was the requirements of the German war effort, which took priority over anything the RSI might have hoped to achieve. Wages, production and any envisaged social experimentation were blocked by the need to provide men and materiel for the *Wehrmacht*. Captured Italian prisoners of war (more than half a million) were never released by Hitler to form some kind of separate RSI armed force, but were used as cheap labour in Germany.

By 1944, the RSI was plagued by the internal enemy of the resistance movement to which it had to dedicate much of its attention. By the winter of that year, outside the main cities, a full-scale civil war was in the offing. German anxiety over letting the RSI have its own army was eventually assuaged by chronic manpower shortages, but the army had to be trained in Germany and its political reliability ensured. Most importantly, though, the RSI was undermined by the Allied front as it moved slowly but inexorably up the peninsula. Everything about Mussolini's new Regime was temporary, made wafer-thin by the certainty of a final Allied victory. It was the German occupation forces who refused to consider the possibility of the latter and made believing differently extremely dangerous.

It was during the RSI period that the clemency of Italians to the Jews in many cases dried up. Their separation from the rest of the people under the old Fascist Regime made the deportation of over half of them to Auschwitz comparatively easy. One of the reasons for what appeal the RSI had, and certainly one that its propaganda emphasized, was that the Allies were attempting to conquer Italy with a 'racially degenerate' mix of American blacks and French and British colonial troops. One poster dating to the RSI shows a racist caricature of an African-American soldier selling that icon of classical civilization, the *Venus de Milo*, for two dollars, another by the same artist depicting the sacking of a church (Centro Furio Jesi, 1994: 201–2).

What the creation of the RSI showed most cogently was that Italians were still as bitterly divided as ever. 'Consensus' in old Fascism's vision of things meant little more than the removal of platforms through which opposition could find a voice. The underlying problems that had been present in the *biennio rosso*, which had expressed themselves in the difficult political vicissitudes of liberal Italy, remained. After 25 July 1943 the space granted to an opposition became progressively broader, notwithstanding draconian measures of repression used by the RSI and the German Occupation forces.

Between 1943 and 1945 Italians were offered a variety of allegiances: to the Badoglio government, which promised a conservative return to the status quo ante 1922; to the moderate resistance, which offered a modernized and democratic Italy; to the radical resistance, which might use the occasion of the anti-Nazi struggle to bring about a socialist revolution [**Doc. 39, p. 156**]. Then there were the Allies telling Italians 'you, too, can be like us', promising the American dream (with which Italians were familiar through emigration and through Hollywood) to all. Then there was the Nazi-Fascism of the RSI, which offered a specific vision of patriotism: it claimed to be defending Italy from Stalin and argued that only by sticking with Germany would Italy redeem its honour after the betrayal of 8 September and would Italy be preserved from the clutches of 'Judeo-plutocratic-Bolshevism'.

But the Germans themselves, as had been the case throughout the Nazi New Order in Europe, were unwilling to trust their allies. The Reich absorbed those territories Italy had made its own in the Great War. Trent and Trieste now became part of what seemed a new Hapsburg Empire and the South Tyrol, that province of German speakers that Hitler had promised Mussolini would never get in the way of an Italian alliance, became part of Germany also. It was strange that Mussolini himself, who had done so much to turn Cesare Battistsi (hanged by the Austrians in 1916), his old colleague from his socialist and interventionist days, into the greatest hero of Italy's First World War, should have been responsible for the 'deal' that gave his city,

Trent, back to a German Reich. The Vittorio Veneter consensus, at the heart of the rise and stabilization of Fascism in the early 1920s, was shattered. All that was left was anti-communism, a thirst for revenge on old colleagues, a politically undefined and intellectually unelaborated racism, and the *Wehrmacht* and the SS.

In the end, the might of the Anglo-American military prevailed and for Mussolini the logic of having chosen and rechosen Hitler reached its grisly conclusion. In April 1945 German power in northern Italy collapsed. The Allies had broken into the Po Valley and all Italy's northern cities were free for the taking. An organized armed insurrection and a partisan movement that now numbered perhaps 100,000 or more (Ginsborg, 2000: 70) took control of those northern cities in which Fascism had been born so many years before, and handed them over to the advancing Allies. In March 1944 Togliatti, on orders from Stalin, recognized Badoglio's as a legitimate wartime government, thus deradicalizing the resistance and subsuming it in overall Allied imperatives, but he had also ensured that the resistance itself did not (as he had witnessed in Spain) descend into a miasma of bloody squabbles. In stopping the resistance movement short of social revolution, the aspirations of many of Italy's poor, its peasants and its workers, were not met, yet it would be going too far to argue with Paul Ginsborg that 'the forces fighting for change in the years 1943–5 did not succeed in making [a] profound break with the past' (Ginsborg, 2000: 71). From the political (but not economic) point of view, the Italy of post-1945 fell into the hands of the 'real' Italy, and it was precisely the 'subversives', Italians of the left and Catholics, whose attempt to edge out the liberals in the years following the First World War had been so critical in the rise of Fascism, that were enfranchised fully for the first time. What choices they made after 1945 were their own.

Mussolini, in the end, joined the list of prominent members of his Regime that paid for Fascism with their lives. As the German army retreated over the Alps in disorder, the ex-*Duce* appears to have been confused as to what to do. A first idea to sell his life dearly with a detachment of Fascist die-hards in an Alpine valley was characteristically abandoned and, on 27 April, a small convoy (containing Mussolini, some RSI ministers as well as Mussolini's mistress Claretta Petacci) headed northward from Como a few miles above Milan into the mountains. Switzerland was nearby and it is possible the *Duce* wanted to make his escape there. At some point along the way two trucks of retreating German airforce men joined the convoy. As the valley ahead was patrolled by partisans Mussolini was given a German army coat and helmet. He put these on and waited. A few miles further on the convoy was halted by partisans and, after a short battle, it was agreed that the Germans could proceed, but any Italians on the trucks had to be handed over. So familiar were all Italians with the face of the *Duce* that he was quickly recognized and it was a twist of historical fate that at the critical moment of his capture he should have been wearing the uniform of the country with which his own Regime's destiny had become so inexorably caught up. He was taken off the truck and imprisoned in a nearby farmhouse. The next day, communist hatchet men, on party orders, were sent up from Milan for the actual execution. Riddled with bullet wounds, Mussolini's misshapen body and that of Petacci and some leaders of the RSI were brought to Piazzale Loreto in Milan where a few months earlier the Nazis had carried out some bloody reprisals. There, their bodies were hung upside down and exhibited to the crowds in a moment of extraordinary cathartic release. The city where Mussolini had edited *Avanti!* and *Il Popolo d'Italia*, where Fascism had been born in 1919 and which in so many ways represented what was most modern and most European in Italian society, was, appropriately, where Mussolini made his final and perhaps most dramatic public appearance.

Part 3

CONCLUSION

9

The Place of Italian Fascism in European history

Two days after Mussolini's death the other dictator in the Pact of Steel took his own life in the smouldering ruins of Berlin. Mussolini had come to power 11 years before Hitler but the German dictator and the Italian succumbed quite appropriately within a few hours of each other. Together, the two corporals who had experienced the trenches, who both hailed from small provincial towns far from their respective capital cities, had attempted and failed to find a role for the two countries whose unification disrupted and warped the old and established European states system of the nineteenth century. Both Hitler and Mussolini were products of the trauma that was the First World War. The peculiar psychosis born in that terrible experience provoked the even greater cataclysm that was the Second World War. Mussolini and Hitler left behind them millions of deaths, bereavements, displacements and further traumas; each case a tragedy that deserves to be remembered and to be told over and over again. So too must the horror of a world in which so many were called to kill and to kill again.

It is sometimes difficult to imagine that the generation of Europeans who matured between 1914 and 1945 were of the same stuff as us. They killed or threw away their lives, or bore the unbearable deaths of innumerable loved ones in a way and for causes that seem altogether alien and remote to us today. But on close inspection the inhabitants of Mussolini's Italy were not significantly different from those of today. What they desired was a life in which they felt at ease with the world. But it was the gap between expectations and reality that made the difference. Fascist Italy belonged to a very peculiar era. The Italy that pre-dated Fascism was a restless construction that cannot be defined as a democracy and that, like much of Europe before 1945, was balanced precariously on a volatile mix of pressing dissatisfactions. Poverty was still the lot of the majority of its inhabitants and the search for a better future, one that would provide enough food, warmth, shelter and clothing, remained an unsolved imperative. That so many millions left their continent and home to attain something better was just the most visible symptom of a Europe where many things were amiss.

Three years after Mussolini's birth the following inscription was placed at the mighty foot of the Statue of Liberty in New York harbour:

> 'Keep, ancient lands, your storied pomp!' cries she
> With silent lips. 'Give me your tired, your poor,
> Your huddled masses yearning to breathe free,
> The wretched refuse of your teeming shore,
> Send these, the homeless, tempest-tossed to me,
> I lift my lamp beside the golden door!'

No description of Italy, although it was a message to all of Europe, could have been more appropriate and instructive than that which greeted the hundreds of thousands of emigrants passing that gigantic silhouette. All Italy's 'storied pomp' was as chaff for these sweepings of the old continent. Yet the tantalizing expectations of a world free from want somewhere in the not too distant future were apparent to all through the extraordinary achievements of industrial civilization. Fascism's love of the airplane, with the *Duce* taking command in the cockpit whenever he could, his son being pushed to be a pilot, and the adulation meted out to the hero of the skies Italo Balbo, was no coincidence. In Mussolini's lifetime humanity had taken to the skies for the first time, yet the world below kept so many tied to the miseries and frustrations of everyday life.

The myth of progress and the hope in a betterment of the human condition imbued even the peripheral village in which the young Benito grew up. Nothing can be more telling than the names he received: socialist heroes famous in Mexico, Paris and Italy itself. It was no coincidence that within Mussolini's life trajectory socialism and Fascism were inextricably bound up. These political antagonists issued from the same stable in that they both stood against seeing in liberalism the 'final unalterable verdict of civilisation' (Delzell, 1970: 102). Why? For the simple reason that liberalism would, as Mussolini and Gentile put it when defining Fascism, 'lead to certain ruin'. After 1918 who could deny what, again, was set down in 'the Doctrine of Fascism'?

> The era of Liberalism, after having accumulated an infinity of Gordian knots, tried to untie them in the slaughter of the World War – and never has any religion demanded of its votaries such a monstrous sacrifice. Perhaps the Liberal Gods were athirst for Blood?
>
> (in Delzell, 1970: 102)

What united Mussolini the 'revolutionary' and Mussolini the '*Duce*' was a feeling that liberalism had played out its historical usefulness and that its unfulfilled promises demanded a response. His abandonment of revolutionary socialism was an attempt to claim liberalism's Great War for a new vision of what Italy should now be. For so many Europeans of the trench generation it was intolerable that things should imply return to normality after satisfying the 'Liberal Gods' thirst for blood'. Hence the descent of the continent after 1918 into what Michael Burleigh has called 'apocalyptic times' (Burleigh, 2001: 812). The conditions for those models of society that rejected liberalism – for Fascism and Bolshevism existed in spirit long before 1917 – were produced by the upheavals of war, which turned small splinter groups into viable political alternatives with very broad blueprints for their implementation.

Italians proved themselves unable to cope with what liberalism had expected of them in fighting that Great War, and, facing the challenge of the 'real' Italy's political assault in the post-war years, the liberal state itself abdicated and gave power to what was after all only a vociferous minority, if perhaps the most characteristic product, of the spirit of the Vittorio Veneters. These circumstances were significant in shaping what the Fascist Regime eventually became and also what it was unable to become. Fascism, as has been argued throughout this book, was invented as it went along. Mussolini's insistence that his political outlook was based on 'action' and 'will' rather than on a political philosophy comparable to Marxism or to liberalism was really nothing more than an understanding that the foundations on which his power rested were above all dictated by compromise with what had gone before. Part of the deal was naturally that Fascism was never actually complete, and that there was always something else that had to be done to bring about the true Fascist 'dawn', whose sunrise would be perpetually relegated to the not-too-distant future. That day did not arrive in 1922 with the March on Rome, it did not arrive with the establishment of the dictatorship in 1925, it did not arrive with the conciliation with the Church, nor with the conquest of Ethiopia, nor with the alliance with Nazi Germany, or indeed with Italians being defined as a biologically distinct and 'Aryan' race. And it certainly did not arrive with Italy's Second World War or the RSI.

Fascism's one absolutely rock-solid achievement was to have crushed the subversive threat to the Italian social order in the years after the Great War. But, it must be stressed, this was accomplished in partnership with the liberal state and, barring a few dissenting and isolated voices among liberals themselves, with the full approval of the institutions that were at the liberal state's very foundations: the monarchy, the army, Italian industry and business, agriculture, parliament, local government, the ministerial bureaucracies, the diplomatic service, the police force, the law courts and the legal system (and the list could go on) – all fully consented to form an Axis with Fascism in the removal of the loci in which subversive Italy had a voice, and, increasingly after 1918, some muscle too. The Fascist Regime was payback for a job well done and for ensuring that the subversives remained permanently excluded from the Italian political system.

It should come as no surprise that Fascism's demise (the result of the contingencies of the international order) heralded the return to the political arena of those forces that had been blotted out during its rise, almost as if the *Duce's* dictatorship had never been. In Bernardo Bertolucci's 1976 film *Novecento* this return to the political struggle of the *biennio rosso* is dramatically symbolized by the socialist peasants of the Po Valley in the spring of 1945 digging up the red flags they had carefully hidden during Fascism's ascendancy. According to this version of the story, the basic premises that had given rise to the political struggles of the period after the First World War were still there and Fascism had done nothing whatsoever to remove them. It had merely been capable, for little more than two decades, to clamp a lid on the seething cauldron. In 1945 Italy was still a poor agricultural country whose people, in spite of everything Fascism had tried to do, remained painstakingly ill-at-ease with themselves.

Yet the upshot of the resistance, the 'return' of Italy to democracy and the new state's guaranteeing of liberal freedoms, proved neither to be a recipe for some form of socialist revolution nor for another Fascism. Here, once again, it was the era in which Italy was immersed that mattered. In the decades that followed the Second World War capitalism succeeded in transforming Italy in a way that made Fascism's 'achievements' seem paltry indeed. After 1945 liberal capitalism in Italy was guaranteed by an American-dominated international order to which the ruling Christian Democrats fully subscribed and to which the Italian people in general also acquiesced. According to the way that the world had been seen by the Vittorio Veneters, this might have been interpreted as the 'death of the nation' in this abdication to the superpowers that dominated the Cold War world. But times had changed. In part, Mussolini had been blinkered by a vision of things from which all Europeans of his generation only rarely escaped – a vision that consisted of a fantasy landscape where the Roman Empire really had ruled the 'world', where history was one long catalogue of national achievements, where all that mattered happened in one small continent (and nearly always in the western half of it at that). That Mussolini and Hitler could nonchalantly declare war on the USA without first defeating the USSR and the British Empire was the result of a miserably provincial worldview. The internecine rivalry of Europe's tiny fatherlands brought that continent's moment of hegemony to a close. It was strange that in the 1930s Britain, France, Germany and Italy, four countries that bordered each other, neighbours in a small smudge on the globe, should have held the future of the world (or so they thought) in their hands. In reality they were dwarves disputing in the shadow of waking giants.

American dollars, a full plate, a car, a warm flat and a holiday once a year, in other words a real rise in the standard of living and the chance for most Italians to become modern consumers in a consumer-orientated world, removed the venom from the Italian political situation in the same way it was removed from all western Europe. To all intents and purposes, liberalism as the 'final, unalterable verdict of civilization', was able, as Mussolini always deep down knew it would, to reduce Fascism to dust because those very freedoms that were repressed by the dictatorship – the vote, a free press, debate, political organizations, trade unions – were associated in post-1945 Italy with the right and the possibility to consume. The consensus built on this formidable alliance made Mussolini's cult, the OND, the PNF, the 'return of Empire to the fatal hills of Rome', or all the other paraphernalia of the 'sacralized politics' that was Fascism, seem nothing more than a strange dead-end down which Italy had been brought by a man who was a prisoner to, and represented so extraordinarily well, the hubris of the unique generation that made Europe the 'Dark Continent' (Mazower, 1998) of the world's twentieth century.

Part 4

DOCUMENTS

Document 1   PATRIOTISM IN NEWLY UNIFIED ITALY

De Amicis' Cuore was Italy's best-selling book throughout the liberal and Fascist period. It can be regarded as one of the foremost texts in the 'national-ization' of the Italian people. The following was intended as a model of beha-viour and of desire for boys growing up in liberal Italy, and mixed concepts of social progress, national conciliation with almost mystical patriotism; it was meant to be recited as a prayer.

Italy, my country, dear and noble land where my father and mother were born and will be buried, where I hope to live and die; beautiful Italy, great and glorious for many centuries, united and free now for some years; you have shed such divine light on the world, and for you so many valiant men have died on the battlefield and so many heroes on the scaffold; august mother of three hundred towns and thirty million sons and daughters . . . I love you my sacred homeland! I swear to you that I shall love all your chil-dren as brothers; that your great and good sons living and dead will always have an honoured place in my heart; that I shall be an honest and industri-ous citizen, intent always on improving myself to make myself worthy of you, so that I may use my modest powers to work for a day when poverty, ignorance, injustice and crime may be banished from your borders and you will be able to live and expand, calm in the majesty of your right and strength. I swear that I shall serve you as best I can, with head, hands and heart, humbly and boldly; and that if a day comes when I must give my blood and my life for you, I shall give my blood and I shall die crying to the heavens your holy name and offering my last kiss to your blessed flag.

Source: 'Prayer to Italy', in Edmondo De Amicis, *Cuore: The Heart of a Boy* (London: Owen/Unesco, 1986), p. 229 (first published 1886).

————◄●►————

Document 2   CRITICISM OF LIBERAL ITALY

Written in 1871 by Italy's most famous poet, Carducci, these verses express the idea that liberal Italy (Italietta) was unable or unwilling to live up to the glori-ous inheritance of ancient Rome. The poem refers to a Roman legend that the city was once saved by the squawking of geese, awoken at night by invading Gauls. Italy is here pictured as an invader and the geese must be told to hush as they do not recognize in the new Italian nation the legitimate master of the Eternal City. The second verse quoted here sees the final end of Italy sold off by Italian finance minister Quintino Sella to foreign curiosity seekers.

Quiet, quiet! What is this din
Heard by the light of the moon?

Geese of the Capitol, quiet! For I am
Italy, united and great

. . .

Until Sella, one day at the end of the month,
Noticing the coffers were empty,
Sold to an English Lord, archeologist
My august carcass.

Source: Canto dell'Italia che va in Campidoglio (Song of Italy that goes to the Capitol),
in Josue Carducci, *Poesie di Giosue Carducci* (Bologna: Zanichelli, 1908), p. 471.

————◀●▶————

THE FUTURIST MANIFESTO   **Document 3**

*The Futurist Manifesto, published initially in Paris, Europe's cultural and
avant-gard capital, was original in that it associated war, a radical conception
of modernity and patriotism in a boiling cauldron of ideas that seemed particularly apt in the atmosphere engendered a few years later in the trenches
and battlefields of the First World War. Highly influential in the origins of the
Fascist movement, Futurism was able to formulate for many young intellectuals, an alternative to both socialism and the traditional right. Mussolini's eventual compromises with the Italian monarchy, the liberal state and the Church,
and in general the forces of order, distanced Futurism from Fascism, but it
nevertheless remained within the pale of Fascist culture through the Regime.*

We will glorify war – the world's only hygiene – militarism, patriotism, the
destructive gesture of freedom-bringers, beautiful ideas worth dying for, and
scorn for woman.

We will destroy the museums, libraries, academies of every kind, will fight
moralism, feminism, every opportunistic or utilitarian cowardice.

We will sing of great crowds excited by work, by pleasure, and by riot; we
will sing of the multicoloured, polyphonic tides of revolution in the modern
capitals; we will sing of the vibrant nightly fervour of arsenals and shipyards
blazing with violent electric moons; greedy railway stations that devour
smoke-plumed serpents; factories hung on clouds by the crooked lines of
their smoke; bridges that stride the rivers like giant gymnasts, flashing in the
sun with a glitter of knives; adventurous steamers that sniff the horizon;
deep-chested locomotives whose wheels paw the tracks like the hooves of
enormous steel horses bridled by tubing; and the sleek flight of planes whose
propellers chatter in the wind like banners and seem to cheer like an enthusiastic crowd.

It is in Italy that we are issuing this manifesto of ruinous and incendiary violence, by which we today are founding Futurism, because we want to deliver Italy from its gangrene of professors, archaeologists, tourist guides and antiquaries. Italy has been too long the great second-hand market. We want to get rid of the innumerable museums which cover it with innumerable cemeteries. Museums, cemeteries! Truly identical in their sinister juxtaposition of bodies that do not know each other. Public dormitories where you sleep side-by-side forever with beings you hate or do not know. Reciprocal ferocity of the painters and sculptors who murder each other in the same museum with blows of line and colour.

Source: Filippo Marinetti, 'Futurist Manifesto', *Le Figaro*, 20 February 1909 (available at http://en.wikisource.org/w/index.php?title=Futurist_Manifesto&oldid=248202).

Document 4   THE PROLETARIAN NATION

The most tangible sign of liberal Italy's failings was the number of Italians prepared to leave the peninsula. In the years between unification and the outbreak of the First World War, more than 10 million Italians emigrated to northern Europe and the Americas, posing difficult questions for a country that considered itself a modernizing Great Power. Giovanni Pascoli, poet and disciple of Carducci, picks up on Nationalist Association's founder Enrico Corradini's idea of Italy as the 'proletarian nation' in a speech delivered in 1911 at Barga, a small town in a region that was being depopulated by emigration. Pascoli, in the fiftieth anniversary of the foundation of the Italian state, celebrates the Italian invasion of Libya as the way forward for a nation that, like the proletariat, has nothing to lose but its chains. Pascoli's speech is also therefore a call for the Italian workers to place their loyalty not in subversive parties wanting class war but in a renewed nation looking after their interests.

The Great Proletarian Nation has stirred . . .

The world set Italians to work and at the same time paid them a pittance and labelled them as Carcamanos! Gringos! Cincali! Degos!

In all but name they had become Negroes. In America, the citizens of the country of the man who had discovered it, were placed outside the law and outside of humanity: they are subject to lynchings for the simple fact that they were Italians . . .[Yet] They cut isthmuses, tunnelled through mountains, lifted up embankments, constructed ports, dug for coal, cut forests, put virgin land to the plough, built monuments and gave life to factories . . . they built roads where there had been none, they built cities in virgin forests, where there were deserts they laid orchards, orange groves, vineyards.

Now Italy, the great martyr of the nations, after only fifty years of new life, has answered the call of duty in contributing to the civilisation of the world; in her right to not be suffocated and blocked in her own seas; in her maternal office of providing for her sons what they most desire: work. This, the Third Italy has taken up its solemn task [to not be] lesser than the first two.

Source: Giovanni Pascoli, 'The great proletarian has stirred', *La Tribuna*, 27 November 1911.

THE YOUNG MUSSOLINI CONDEMNS ITALY'S WAR IN LIBYA, 1   **Document 5**

The young socialist firebrand Benito Mussolini, about to rise to fame as editor of Italy's most important socialist newspaper, Avanti!, *here condemns Italy's imperial war for the conquest of Libya and talks of the justice of inter-class over inter-national war. In an article in the same newspaper the following month, Mussolini argues that Italy's war in Libya serves to distract Italian workers from really pressing issues. From a different perspective to the Futurists or the nationalists, Mussolini too challenges the legitimacy of the liberal state.*

If the Fatherland, which is itself a fictitious invention that has no future, demands sacrifices of blood and money, the proletariat that follows the orders of the Socialists, will respond with a general strike. War between nations will therefore become war between classes.

Source: *La Lotta di Classe*, 23 September 1911; in Renzo De Felice, *Mussolini il Rivoluzionario* (Turin: Einaudi, 1965), p. 105.

THE YOUNG MUSSOLINI CONDEMNS ITALY'S WAR IN LIBYA, 2   **Document 6**

The Libyan adventure was meant to be for many a diversion to distract the country from posing and solving its complex and very grave internal problems . . . in the eventuality of an Italian occupation the Italian proletariat must keep itself ready for enacting a general strike.

Source: *La Lotta di Classe*, 5 August 1911, in Renzo De Felice, *Mussolini il Rivoluzionario* (Turin: Einaudi, 1965), p. 104.

Document 7 LEFT-WING INTERVENTIONISM

Like Mussolini, Filippo Corridoni was a man of the left (veteran of countless strikes and agitations for which he had been arrested on more than 30 occasions) and tortured by what stance to adopt in relation to the Great War that erupted throughout Europe in late 1914. While Italy remained neutral, a movement grew calling for Italian intervention. The logic of why left-wingers such as Mussolini became involved in this movement to push Italy into war is summed up neatly by the following article published by Corridoni in a left-wing revolutionary newspaper, Avanguardia, *in December 1914.*

The problem of war is too much for proletarian brains. The worker can only see in war murder, poverty and hunger, (murder, poverty and hunger that he has to bear) and he is therefore against war. What does he care if in ten, twenty years the sacrifices of today will bring incalculable benefits? What does he care if the current war can open the way to social revolution, eliminating the last survivals of feudal domination, and striking a mortal blow to the monarchist principle . . . ?

Bread, yes, but ideas and education matter. Of course physical needs matter, but so do the spiritual and the cultural. The proletariat is not a class until it has acquired class consciousness, and this will only happen when the organization broadens its outlook to other struggles that go beyond wages and work-hours. We eat to live, not live to eat.

Source: *Avanguardia*, December 1914, in Renzo De Felice, *Mussolini il Rivoluzionario* (Turin: Einaudi, 1965), p. 293.

Document 8 THE DEFEAT OF CAPORETTO

The crushing defeat of Caporetto in October 1917 was taken by many to be a sign that there was something disastrously wrong in Italian politics and society and that a root and branch renewal of the fatherland was in future required. The following is a description and commentary of what happened on that day by an Italian officer, taken from his diary.

24 October

I will try to sum up what has happened and what I have seen although it defies belief; I cannot picture it all, all the events that have overwhelmed me and that are overwhelming the fortunes and the honour of Italy. By three o'clock the Austrians had already won the biggest battle in history . . .

At Caporetto I found our head of military command who ordered me to halt the great torrent of fleeing people and soldiers that was out of control.

We tried to stop those carrying a rifle, letting through those who had none to clear the way . . . but further up, they had understood what was going on, and threw their rifles away . . . Ah! We all live making a pact with cowardice. Now even procreation is cowardly. There are a few elect, born of violence, the children of men. The legality of love has made of life a coward . . .

I find an officer who shouts:

'Run or they'll get us!'

'And the others?'

'Run, run, get away, go!'

We jump in our vehicle . . . around the car, a pressing cowardly humanity screams savagely:

'Run! Run!'

Run. Honour too has taken to its heels.

Source: Attilio Frescura, *Diario di un'imboscato* (Milan: Mursia, 1981), pp. 248–50.

———————◀●▶———————

THE *ARDITI* **Document 9**

The Arditi (burning ones) were specially trained commandos developed for close-quarter fighting and hair-raising missions in the latter part of the war. Privileged compared to the average soldier, they developed a strong sense of loyalty to their units and were prepared to take startling risks for the love of danger and country. They became the comic-book heroes of Italy's Great War and the painful return to civilian life after 1918 led many into violent and dissident political groupings, such as Gabriele D'Annunzio's legionaries (who forcibly occupied the city of Fiume in disputed Yugoslav-Italian territories in 1919) and Mussolini's Fascist squads. The following is an extract from a book of memoires of an Ardito.

We would go into battle as none had done in the past, because for us war was a party [*festa*], the purpose of our dreams, the point at which all our hopes and desires converged, the agonisingly yearned for object of our love. We went to battle . . . as do all peoples born and bred for war, shouting with joy at the top of our voices, shooting and making music. Around us we left a blaze of enthusiasm.

Source: Paolo Giudici, *Reparti d'Assalto* (Milan: Alpes, 1928), p. 39, in Giorgio Rochat, *Gli Arditi della Grande Guerra* (Milan: Feltrinelli, 1981), p. 36.

———————◀●▶———————

Document 10   THE IDEAL SOLDIER

Pietro Jahier, officer in the Great War and minor writer in postwar Italy, pub-lished this description of the ideal soldier in a trench magazine a few months after Caporetto. The idea of the trenches as the forge of a classless and truly compact society of men dedicated body and soul to the fatherland is a typical example of the myth constructed by the Vittorio Veneters, so influential in the rise of Fascism.

The soldier
is the man who has triumphed over the needs of the flesh and its misery: hunger, thirst, sloth and struggle.

The soldier
is the man who knows how to obey; who obeys at all costs; who never makes excuses.

For this
he has the surest and strongest character; the only character that will know how to command.

The soldier
is the truest man; be he rich or poor, his identical uniform permits none to distinguish. The soldier can only be distinguished by his heart.

The soldier
is the most unselfish man.
The civilian works for his home and his children; but the soldier for all homes and all children . . .

The soldier
is the representative of the whole fatherland: the civilian represents one constituency, one city, one region; the soldier represents all the fatherland . . .

Source: 'What is a soldier?', in Pietro Jahier, *L'Astico, Giornale delle Trincee* (Vicenza, 1918); in Mario Stern, *1915–1918 La guerra sugli altopiani* (Vicenza: Neri Pozza, 2000), pp. 494–5.

Document 11   THE LEGEND OF THE PIAVE

E.A. Mario's The Legend of the Piave (La leggenda del Piave) was one of Italy's most popular songs after the Great War. It fully encapsulates the Vittorio Veneter myth. It refers to the moment after Caporetto when Italy rallied at the

Piave river and went on to win the war. The song suggests that the river swelled and flooded its banks in order to stop the advance of the German-Austrian troops, in a supposed moment of mystical connection between Italians and their sacred territory.

The Piave murmured calm and placid at the crossing
of the first infantry troops on 24 May;
the army marched to the frontier
to make a barrier against the enemy.

. . .

From the beloved river we heard
gentle and low the sound of the waves.

. . .

The Piave murmured: 'the foreigner shall not pass!'

But a sad night we heard of a terrible happening
and the Piave heard . . .
Ah, how many people it saw coming, leaving their homes;
because the enemy broke through at Caporetto.

. . .

the Piave murmured: 'the foreigner returns!'

We saw the Piave raising its waters
the waves fought as one with the soldiers
Red with the blood of the arrogant foe,
the Piave commanded: 'foreigner go back!'

Source: E.A. Mario, *The Legend of the Piave*, 1918, in Giovanni Di Capua, *Faccetta Nera, canti dell'ebbrezza fascista* (Scipioni: Valentano, 2000), p. 46.

————◄●►————

FASCIST SQUADISM   **Document 12**

This Fascist squad song parodies and transforms the meaning of La leggenda del Piave. *The war in the trenches, glorified by E.A. Mario, is here transposed to the streets of Italy. The enemy, however, are the 'Bolsheviks' and the Piave river the Fascist squads.*

Italy murmured disconsolate at the passing
Of the red rags every May Day.
Bolshevism marched to break all barriers
To take from the Fatherland all frontiers;

They want to sow hunger and dishonour
To abandon Italy to the oppressor

It was a language false and black
Italy murmured – 'they are worse than foreigners'

But salvation is at hand, its wings outstretched
It took the piazzas back
The Fascio commanded – 'the beasts back to their lairs'

Source: La leggenda del Fascio, 1920, in Giovanni Di Capua, Faccetta Nera, canti dell'ebbrezza fascista (Scipioni: Valentano, 2000), p. 52.

———————◀◉▶———————

Document 13   EARLY FASCIST PROGRAMMES

It is notoriously difficult to find in the Fascist movement's early programmes a coherent set of policies. However, some basic themes remain as core principles in early Italian Fascism, although other issues may have varied quite radically. Some of the former are illustrated here, picked out of Mussolini's speeches and programme documents at the launching of the Fasci di Combattimento *(Combat Groups) in Milan in March 1919.*

We don't need to place ourselves programmatically on a revolutionary footing because, in a historic sense, we already did so in 1915 . . .

We declare war against socialism, not because it is socialism but because it is opposed to nationalism . . . we intend to be an active minority, to attract the proletariat away from the official Socialist party. But if the middle class think that we are going to be lightning rods, they are mistaken. We must go halfway towards meeting the workers . . .

If the present regime is to be superseded we must be ready to take its place. For this reason we are establishing the Fasci as organs of creativity and agitation that will be able to rush into the piazzas and cry out, 'The right to the political succession belongs to us because we were the ones who pushed the country into the war and led it to victory.'

We are against all dictatorship, whether they be of the sabre or the cocked hat, of wealth or numbers. The only dictatorship we acknowledge is that of the will and intelligence.

Source: Il Popolo d'Italia, 24 March 1919, in Charles Delzell (ed.) *Mediterranean Fascism* (New York: Walker & Company, 1970), pp. 8–11.

———————◀◉▶———————

THE 1919 ELECTIONS **Document 14**

Data on the national elections of 1919 shows that the 'subversive' parties (the Socialist Party and the Catholic PPI) held by far the most seats in parliament. The liberals and allied groupings, which had controlled the Italian parliament since unification, had lost their majority. The political crisis of liberal Italy after the First World War is plainly visible here, in the sense that granting power to the subversive parties (as the electorate demanded) was not considered to be a realistic option for Italy's elites, always traditionally represented by liberal parliamentary groupings. In this situation parliament and effective government was hamstrung. In the 1921 election liberals had to ally with right-wing Vittorio Veneter forces (for example the Fascists) in order to maintain a respectable number of seats in parliament. By 1924, with Mussolini in power, the 'national lists' included a coalition of all 'anti-subversive' groupings in which the Fascist party predominated. The 60 per cent gained by the national list secured Mussolini a large majority but it was still dependent on the support of liberal and other groupings and a pall of illegality hung over the election results. The socialist Giacomo Matteotti and many others did not consider the 1924 election results to be legitimate due to government intimidation of voters. By 1924 the Italian Communist Party, which split off from the Socialist Party in 1921, was fairly well established.

Party or parliamentary grouping	1919 election		1921 election		1924 elections	
	%	Seats	%	Seats	%	Seats
Liberal groupings/national lists (in 1921 and 1924 including Fascists)	36.5	197	37	216	60.1	355
Catholic Popular Party (PPI)	20.5	100	20.4	108	9	39
Socialist Party (PSI)	32.3	156	24.7	123	10.9	44
Communist Party	–	–	4.6	15	3.7	19

Source: Giovanni Sabbatucci and Vittorio Vidotto V. (eds), *Storia d'Italia. Guerre e Fascismo* (Rome-Bari: Laterza, 1997), pp. 748–9.

————◆————

LANDLORDS DEFEND THEMSELVES **Document 15**

In the face of the growing challenge from socialist and Catholic peasant trade unions and what was seen as an abdication by the state to defend landlordly power, spontaneous anti-peasant associations of landlords created the terrain in which Fascist squads found their most characteristic role. Naturally, the landlords suggested that the Fascist squads were not just defending them but civilization, the nation and all good citizens. The following is an extract from a landlord-owned newspaper published in a small agricultural town near Florence, Borgo San Lorenzo, at the height of the biennio rosso.

A war to the death has been declared against the bourgeoisie, to whom the world owes all its scientific, technical and political progress, and in the pro-gramme against this bourgeoisie there figures organised violence, collective and individual, of thought and action . . .

The government, unable to defend the state, allows the nation to suffer the blows of the trade union movement, and subjugates it [the nation] before the ills of a policy at once anti-national and harmful to the state.

It is this system of yielding and surrendering rights, duties and power . . . which has promoted the organised violence of classes and parties.

From this observation of fact, and from this sense that the government is abandoning the most vital interests and rights of society, has arisen the idea of citizens' defence force.

Source: Messaggero del Mugello, 8 February 1920, in Frank Snowden, *The Fascist Revolution in Tuscany* (Cambridge: Cambridge University Press, 1989), pp. 60–1.

Document 16   MUSSOLINI'S FIRST SPEECH TO PARLIAMENT

After the March on Rome, in his first speech as prime minister, Mussolini faced up to the problem of how the Fascist movement fitted into the constitutional framework of liberal Italy. The Duce of Fascism here adopts the carrot and stick approach, which serves to deflate concern over the semi-legal way in which Mussolini had come to power. The 'carrot' is Mussolini's promise to abide by the constitution and to share power; the 'stick' is the threat that the Fascist squads might be unleashed at any time.

Gentlemen! What I am doing now in this hall is an act of formal deference to you, for which I ask no special gratitude. To the melancholy zealots of super-constitutionalism I shall leave the task of making their more or less pitiful lamentations about recent events . . .

I could have abused my victory, but I refused to do so. I imposed limits on myself. I told myself that the better wisdom is that which does not lose control of itself after victory. With 300,000 youths, armed to the teeth, fully determined and almost mystically ready to act on any command of mine, I could have punished all those who defamed and tried to sully Fascism. I

could have transformed this drab, silent hall into a bivouac for my squads
. . . I could have barred the doors of parliament and formed a government
exclusively of Fascists. I could have done so; but I chose not to, at least for
the present.

Source: Mussolini's first speech in parliament as prime minister, 16 November 1922,
in Charles Delzell (ed.), *Mediterranean Fascism* (New York: Walker & Company,
1970), pp. 45–6.

GIOLITTI SUPPORTS MUSSOLINI'S FIRST GOVERNMENT   **Document 17**

*Why did the liberals go along with Fascism? Giovanni Giolitti, many times
Italian prime minister and impeccable liberal, suggests why he was not against
Mussolini being invited to form a government in 1922. Here, in 1924, he is
ready to form an electoral pact with the Fascists, whom he assumes will stick
to the constitution after the elections. Giolitti's support of Mussolini's early
governments was absolutely vital for the establishment of Fascism, which
still only had a small electoral mandate. On the whole the reasons why many
non-subversive forces were prepared to ally with Fascism are outlined here: the
desire for stable government and an end to the paralysis caused by the irrup-
tion of the subversive parties into parliament (and more broadly in Italian
society) after 1918.*

Electors! . . .

    After having ascertained the impotence to which parliament had been
reduced in its inability to form and to sustain a government, is it really all
that surprising that another government emerged outside of the parliamentary orbit? Of this deviation from the parliamentary regime have the leaders
of the socialist and popular party reason to complain, as it was precisely them
that made a parliamentary government an absolute impossibility? Could the
country be without a government?

    When the ministry presided over by Mussolini presented itself to the
Chamber, obviously in a rather unusual way, I judged, together with my
friends, that it was our duty to give Mussolini our support so that it would
be possible for his ministry to rule with parliament and therefore to eliminate
all irregularities . . . If Mussolini's ministry was not parliamentary it was most
certainly constitutional, nominated by the king.

Source: Speech by Giovanni Giolitti to his electors at Dronero, 16 March 1924, in
Discorsi Parlamentari di Giovanni Giolitti, IV (Rome: Tipografia della camera dei
deputati, 1956), p. 1899.

Document 18   MATTEOTTI'S SPEECH TO THE CHAMBER OF DEPUTIES

The well-known reformist socialist Giacomo Matteotti reacted to the large
government majority in the 1924 elections, which had (to a degree) been won
through coercion, with a speech that was essentially a call to more moderate
forces in the government coalition to ditch Mussolini and the Fascist move-
ment's methods. A regrouping of Mussolini's coalition, which included liberals,
after the 1924 elections, might well have been fatal to Mussolini's premiership.
The subversive parties' failure to recognize the legitimacy of the 1924 parlia-
ment explains not only the murder of Matteotti shortly after the speech, but
also, in part, why only dictatorship could ensure Mussolini's continuing hold
on power. The alternative envisaged by Matteotti in this speech was that a
broad democratic coalition of moderate socialists, liberals and other forces
should return Italy to a path of normality, eschewing the use of force in main-
taining governmental power.

You declare every day that you want to re-establish the authority of the state
and the force of law. Do it, if there is still time; otherwise you will really ruin
what is the intimate essence, the moral right of the Nation. Do not continue
further to keep the nation divided between masters and subjects, because
this system certainly provokes licence and rebellion. If freedom is granted, it
is true, there may be mistakes, momentary excesses, but the Italian people,
as all others, has demonstrated that it knows how to correct itself. [Inter-
ruptions from the Right.] We deplore rather that you want to show that
only our people in the world cannot stand on its own two feet and must be
governed by force. Yet our population was educating and raising itself up,
including through our efforts. You want to push everything back again. We
defend the free sovereignty of the Italian people, to whom we send our most
heart-felt greetings, and we demand that it reacquire its dignity by annulling
these elections marred by the violence of the governmental junta. [Applause
from the far left.]

Source: Speech of Giacomo Matteotti to the Italian Chamber of Deputies, 30 May
1924 (available in Italian at www.romacivica.net/anpiroma/antifascismo/
antifascismo1b.html).

Document 19   MUSSOLINI'S 'CLARIFICATION' SPEECH

Mussolini's speech to the Italian parliament on 3 January 1925 marks the
beginning of the slide from what was essentially a Mussolini-dominated coali-
tion and constitutional government to outright dictatorship. In the wake of the
Matteotti crisis and the emptying of parliament of the subversives through the

Aventine Secession, Mussolini here draws a line and challenges his coalition partners (and the king) to oust him from power and suffer the consequences if they do so. They chose not to, and the restructuring of the Italian political system (the outlawing of all political parties barring the PNF, the ending of local democracy by appointing local councils, the modification of the electoral law making all prospective parliamentary candidates subject to the approval of the Fascist Grand Council, a rigid control of the press, the enhancing of police powers) followed fairly rapidly.

Gentlemen, the speech I am about to deliver should not perhaps be classified, strictly speaking, as a parliamentary address . . . A speech of this sort may or may not lead to a vote on policy . . . I have had too many of them. Article 47 of the Constitution says: 'The Chamber of Deputies has the right to impeach the king's ministers and to bring them before the High Court of Justice [the Senate].' I ask formally whether there is anyone, either in or out of this Chamber, who wants to avail himself of Article 47?

My speech therefore will be very clear and such as to bring about absolute clarification . . .

They said that Fascism is a horde of barbarians encamped in the country, a movement of bandits and marauders! They raised a moral question . . . Very well, I now declare before this assembly that I assume, I alone, full political, moral, and historical responsibility for all that has happened . . .

When two irreducible elements are locked in struggle, the solution is force. In history there never has been any other solution, and there never will be . . . You may be sure that in the next forty-eight hours after this speech, the situation will be clarified in every field.

Source: Mussolini's 'clarification' speech, 3 January 1925, in Charles Delzell (ed.), *Mediterranean Fascism* (New York: Walker & Company, 1970), pp. 57–9.

THE LATERAN PACTS **Document 20**

The relationship between the Fascist Regime and the Catholic Church was in the nature of 'you scratch my back, I scratch yours'. In return for Italian recognition of the Church's jurisdictional rights over the Vatican and its full sovereign statehood, as well as Italian schools being given the task of teaching Catholic doctrine, the Church granted full legitimacy to the Fascist Regime, notwithstanding, for example, the recent elimination of independent Catholic political parties. The following are extracts from the Lateran Pacts of 1929 in which, for the first time, the Italian state and the Church recognize each other's

right to exist on Italian territory. We have here two examples of the recipro-
cally beneficial deal that in general marked the relationship between Fascism
and the Church.

Art. 20. All bishops, before taking possession of their diocese, will take the oath of fealty to the Head of State, according to following formula: 'Before God and His Holy Gospel I swear and promise as is fitting in a Bishop, fealty to the Italian State. I swear and promise to respect, and to make respected by my clergy the King and Government established according to the constitutional law of the State. Further, I swear and promise not to take part in any agreement, nor to be present at any meeting, which might injure the Italian State and public order, and that I will not permit my clergy to do so. Desirous of promoting the welfare and the interests of the Italian State I will seek to avoid any course that may injure it.' . . .

Art. 36. Italy considers the teaching of Christian doctrine in accordance with Catholic tradition, as both the basis and the crown of public education. It therefore agrees that the religious teaching now given in the public elementary schools shall be extended to the secondary schools, in accordance with a programme to be drawn up between the Holy See and the State. Such teaching shall be given by masters and professors, whether priests or religious, approved by ecclesiastical authority, and even by lay masters and professors, who, for this purpose, shall be provided with certificates of capacity by the Ordinary of the diocese. The revocation of such certificate by the Ordinary forthwith deprives the teacher of his right to teach. For such religious instruction in public schools text books may only be used that have been approved by ecclesiastical authority.

Source: The Lateran Pacts of 1929: the Concordat, in John Pollard, *The Vatican and Italian Fascism 1929–32* (Cambidge: Cambridge University Press, 1985), pp. 208–31.

Document 21   THE FASCIST CONCEPTION OF THE STATE

The relationship between Fascism and the Italian state was a complex one.
In Fascism's conception, heavily influenced by Nationalist thinking, the state
was to be renewed and made more efficient and totalitarian, rather than side-
stepped or even replaced by new Fascist Party organizations. On the whole,
whatever has been said and written, Mussolini tended to exert his power
through the normal channels of the state as inherited from the liberal period.

Fascist politics turns entirely on the concept of the national State . . . Both Nationalism and Fascism place the State at the foundation of every individual value and right. For both, the State is not a consequence, but a beginning.

The relationship between the individual and the State proposed by Nationalism was the direct antithesis of that advanced by individualistic liberalism and socialism. For liberals and socialists, on the other hand, the individual is understood to be something that precedes the State, who finds in the State something external, something that limits and controls, that suppresses liberty, and that condemns him to those circumstances in which he is born, circumstances within which he must live and die. For Fascism, on the other hand, the 'State' and the 'individual' are terms that are inseparable in a necessary synthesis.

Source: Giovanni Gentile, *Origins and Doctrine of Fascism* (New Brunswick: Transaction Publishers, 2002), p. 25; originally published as *Origini e Dottrina del Fascismo* (Rome: Libreria del Littorio, 1929).

RESPECT FOR STATE AUTHORITY   **Document 22**

In practical terms the above often meant working through the already created institutions of the liberal state. The following is a directive issued by Mussolini in 1927 stating categorically that the Fascist movement itself was subject to the power of state authority (in this instance the prefecture), defined here as 'Regime'.

I reaffirm that the Prefect is the highest State authority in each province. He is the direct representative of central government. All citizens, and especially those who have the privilege and honour to be Fascist party members, owe respect and obedience to the highest political representative of the Fascist regime.

Source: Quoted in M. Clark, *Modern Italy 1871–1982* (London: Longman, 1996), p. 235.

ACHIEVEMENTS OF FASCISM   **Document 23**

Plate 8 shows a cartoon reading puzzle from a children's comic of 1936, indicating what Fascism had supposedly achieved for the average Italian. Translated and with the puzzles solved, it reads as follows:

Few isolated houses, a lonely church, and as far as the eye could see marshes and quagmires . . . Poverty and sadness reigned. Man's work was badly compensated by an imprisoned nature; a meagre crust of bread unable to feed all hungry mouths. Antonio had a lot of children to feed but bread was hard to come by. He therefore decided to seek his fortune in America. With his heart aching, and having embraced his children, he decided to leave the land he loved. It is a hard life to wander in distant lands overseas, looking for work and bread. In this good man's heart each day that passed brought him no luck. It was better for the poor man to return to his own country rather than working among strangers, and to enrich with the work of his own hands, heartless speculators. The poor man returned to his county more miserable than ever. 'But my God' he exclaimed, rubbing his eyes, 'this is not my country!' Down there in the sunlit plain, a lovely town, full of life seemed to be beckoning to him. Poverty had disappeared, no more stagnant water, but waving fields of wheat and trees heavy with delicious fruit: 'Oh my house? Surely not; that isn't my house but a small palace', he whispered taken aback. He knocked on the door; a woman surrounded by four children dressed as Fascist Boy Scouts came to open: 'was this really my own house, with my children and my good wife? I had gone to America, whereas fortune was here at hand all along', exclaimed the good man crying like a child. 'Tell me that I am really awake, that the things I see with my own eyes, that I touch with my own hands are not a vision but reality! Who is responsible for this fabulous gift?' 'We owe it all to our beloved DUCE', answered the little choir made up of his children and his wife.

Source: Il Balilla, 1 November 1936, p. 12.

Document 24   THE SPIRIT OF FASCISM

Italian foreign minister and son-in-law of the Duce, Ciano, an airforce pilot, sums up perfectly here the spirit of the Fascist 'new man'; chilling nonchalance at bombing of innocent civilians appears to be just one more engagement in this young yuppie's hectic schedule.

1 November 1940
At last the sun is shining. I take advantage of it to carry out a bombardment of Sallonica with cherries on top.

    On my way back I am attacked by Greek fighter planes: all goes well and two of theirs go down. But I must confess – it was the first time I had a fighter on my tail – it is a nasty sensation. From Tirana I head for Taranto to confer with the *Duce*, from Taranto to Rome and then off I go to Germany.

Source: Galeazzo Ciano, Diario 1937–1943 (Milan: Rizzoli, 1980), p. 475.

FASCIST MANHOOD   **Document 25**

*Ciano is here referring to a letter of complaint he has personally received from
a certain Professor Faccini. It is February 1941 and the Italian invasion of
Greece has proved an unedifying fiasco. The diary entry refers to an 18-year-
old, therefore to a young man born in 1923, who would have had the full
opportunity of being socialized, via all the liminal paths constructed in two
decades of Fascism, to Fascist manhood.*

23 January 1941
I gave the *Duce* a serious and hard letter written by Prof. Faccini of Leghorn.
His eighteen-year-old son, called up on January 17, was sent that very day to
Albania. He didn't even know what a firearm was. This explains so many
things.

Source: Galeazzo Ciano, *Diario 1937–1943* (Milan: Rizzoli, 1980), p. 502.

LIMITED EFFECTS OF FASCISM   **Document 26**

Carlo Levi, artist and doctor from Turin, was sent to confino *(internal exile)
in a mountain village deep in the south of Italy in the 1930s for anti-Fascist
activity. According to him, however hard Fascism tried to inculcate the Italian
people with its ideas and values, the peasantry he encountered remained essentially unreachable, distrustful and cut off from what the Regime believed in.
The following is Levi's description of the way the peasantry of Gagliano
greeted the news that Italy was going to war in Ethiopia.*

There were a great number of speeches at this time and Don Luigi was zeal-
ous in calling public meetings. It was October and our troops had crossed
the Mareb; the war with Abyssinia had begun. Italians, arise! . . .

 The peasants were not interested in the war. The radio thundered and
Don Luigi spent all hours of the school day . . . haranguing the children so
loudly that he could be heard all over the village and teaching them to sing
'Little Black Face' [a song celebrating Italy's invasion of Ethiopia]. Holding
forth in the square he announced that Marconi had invented a secret weapon
that would cause the entire British navy to explode. He and the other Great
Schoolmaster and Radio Speaker in Rome went around saying that war was
made in order to benefit the peasants of Gagliano, who would soon have
all the land they wanted . . . Unfortunately the two schoolteachers talked so
much of the grandeur of Rome that the peasants had no confidence in anything they said; they simply shook their heads in silent and mistrustful resignation. So the 'fellows in Rome' wanted war and left it to the peasants to do

the fighting . . . It seemed that the schoolchildren and their teachers, Fascist Scouts, Red Cross ladies, the widows and mothers of Milanese veterans, women of fashion in Florence, grocers, shopkeepers, pensioners, journalists, policemen and government employees in Rome, in short all those generally grouped together as the 'Italian people', were swept off their feet by a wave of glory and enthusiasm. Here in Gagliano I could see nothing . . . It soon became clear that not only the purpose of the war but the way it was being conducted as well was the business of that other Italy beyond the mountains and had little to do with the peasants.

Source: Carlo Levi, trans. Frances Frenaye, *Christ Stopped at Eboli* (Harmondsworth: Penguin, 1984), pp. 130–1.

Document 27   THE CONQUEST OF ETHIOPIA

The conquest of Ethiopia in 1935–6 was portrayed as the fulfilment of many aspects of the Fascist raison d'être. Here we have a typical example of how this notion was spelled out and disseminated. The text is taken from a history school textbook for 14-year-olds, published in 1937.

The rapid flowering of the Italian nation through the efforts of Fascism and the Duce; the growth of the population, to whom the Italian peninsula, with its lack of raw material for its advanced industries, was not sufficient; Italy's small number of colonies. The consciousness of Italy's power, acquired with great sacrifices and Roman virtue and with the discipline imposed by the Fascist Regime; the profound sense of injustice with which, after the Great War, the Allies had distributed the fruits of victory. All these reasons pushed Italy towards the desire for more territory and to the conquest of a broader area in which to live and work . . .

   The Italian people, grown in number and in power, victorious in every field of human activity, emboldened by ten years of stern Fascist discipline, was now mature to compete with the Great Nations of Europe and the world and to conquer that primacy which made it the worthy inheritor of the tradition of Rome, the heroic effort of the Great War and the spiritual rebirth that is Fascism. What did the Italian people ask? Nothing more than its due.

Source: A. Severino and G. Vergano, *Corso di storia per l'avviamento al lavoro*, II (Turin: Ciantore, 1937), pp. 121–2.

THE EXPECTED ROLE OF WOMEN **Document 28**

In the following text, taken from an educational guide dealing with colonial issues for Fascist Party women's organizations, the role Fascism assigned to women is made abundantly clear.

The problem does not consist in simply satisfying the sexual instincts of men. If this was the case the solution would not be too difficult to organise. But in Africa even more than elsewhere . . . womankind has the social function of being, above all, companion to man in the highest and most noble sense of the term. Until in our overseas territories the family unit (superb foundation and upholder of Latin society) as it is be found in Italy is not faithfully reproduced in the colonies, our colonisation can be said to have only been partially successful. We must deplore the habit of many officers and civil servants who, even if they are taking up long-term residence in Addis Ababa or in one of the more comfortable centres of the Empire, leave their wife and children in Italy.

In any case women can, in a certain order of job, find fruitful employment in Africa as copy typists, telephone operators, teachers, office workers, etc.

Source: Istituto Coloniale Fascista, *Nozioni coloniali per le organizzazioni femminili del partito nazionale fascista* (Colonial principles for female organizations of the Fascist Party) (Rome: Castaldi, 1938), p. 115.

TERRORIZING ADDIS ABABA, 1 **Document 29**

Like all European imperialisms Italian colonial expansion meant depriving the local peoples of their territory. Although Ethiopia was conquered easily enough in 1935–6, rebellion remained endemic. After an assassination attempt on Italian Viceroy Rodolfo Graziani by Ethiopian partisans in February 1937, the city of Addis Ababa was put to the torch by Italian soldiers, Fascist militiamen and settlers in an orgy of bloodshed. The scenes that were to become familiar in Europe (including Italy under Nazi occupation) a few years later were presaged in the brutal killings of innocent Ethiopian civilians by ordinary Italians in the days that followed the failed assassination attempt. Both these accounts are related by Italian eyewitnesses.

All the civilians that happened to be in Addis Ababa took on the task of wreaking vengeance with lightning speed and in the true spirit of Fascist squadism. Armed with clubs and iron bars, they went round the city killing whoever was still out in the streets . . . I saw a lorry driver who, after having knocked down an old Negro with blows from a stick, shoved a bayonet right through his head from ear to ear. It goes without saying that the victims were all innocent and unaware of what was going on.

Source: Ciro Poggiali, *Diario AOI* (Milan: Longanesi, 1971), p. 182.

Document 30   TERRORIZING ADDIS ABABA, 2

In the late afternoon . . . a few hundred squads made up of blackshirts, drivers and Libyan Ascaris went into the native-quarters of the city and began a rabid man-hunt . . . In general they would set fire to a Tucul [Ethiopian house] with petrol and then throw hand grenades at the people trying to get out. I heard one man bragging that he had 'done ten Tuculs' with only one jerry can of petrol. Another complained how tired his right arm was with all the grenades he had thrown. I knew a lot of these men personally. They were shopkeepers, businessmen, drivers, and office workers; people who I considered to be completely respectable; people who hadn't fired a single shot during the war and that were now full of rancour and capable of unsuspected violence. The fact is that they could do what they liked without risk of punishment. The only risk was being awarded a medal.

Source: Interview conducted with T. Dordini by Angelo Del Boca in Addis Ababa, 26 March 1965, quoted in Angelo Del Boca, *Gli italiani in Africa orientale*, III: *La caduta dell'impero* (Milan: Mondadori, 1992), pp. 84–5.

Document 31   NAZISM AND ITALIAN FASCISM

The relationship between Nazism and Italian Fascism was a complex one. In the following article, Mussolini (writing anonymously and fresh from his first trip to Nazi Germany in September 1937) suggests that there is a spiritual affinity between all those countries possessing regimes that stand against liberalism and Bolshevism (including, for example, Japan). The temptation to claim Italian spiritual pre-eminence over the inexorable European decline in democracy and liberal certitudes often overrode differences in historical development, ideology, etc. The year 1937 (i.e. before the general European war began) was a moment of great friendship between Germany and Italy.

Europe and Fascism

The affirmation made by Mussolini in Berlin . . . that the Europe of tomorrow will be Fascist not so much because of propaganda but because of the logic of events, has given rise to comment and debates.

This does not surprise us. The opposite would have. It is clear that all those who at the moment represent conservation and reaction – capitalism, parliamentary democracy, socialism, communism, liberalism and a certain kind of spineless Catholicism with which we will one day deal with in our own style – are against us who represent the twentieth century, while they represent the nineteenth . . .

Every nation will have 'its own' Fascism; that is a Fascism adapted to the peculiarities of a given people: there has never been and there will never be a standardised Fascism to export, but there is a complex of doctrines, methods, experience, achievements, above all achievements, that little by little . . . are penetrating all the states of the European community and represent everything that is 'new' in the history of civilised man . . .

The two peoples who carry this new kind of civilisation are hardly the last in terms of their contribution to philosophy and spiritual creativity . . . The contribution of the German and Italian people to the civilisation of the human race was and is formidable.

Source: *Il Popolo d'Italia*, 6 October 1937, in E. Susmel and D. Susmel (eds), *Opera Ommia di Benito Mussolini* (Florence: La Fenice, 1951–62): XIX, pp. 1–2.

THE MANIFESTO OF RACIAL SCIENTISTS **Document 32**

The Manifesto of Racial Scientists was part of Mussolini's attempt to put his and Hitler's Regime on an equal spiritual footing as well as to cultivate an 'imperial' attitude after the conquest of Ethiopia. It declared straightforwardly that Italians were a ready-made Nordic Aryan race and introduced anti-semitism to an Italian society undergoing the 'third wave' of fascistization and as a prelude to the racial laws that followed the issuing of the Manifesto by a few months. The Manifesto was authored by a minor academic, Dr Guido Landra, but much of the document was inspired by Mussolini himself, who more or less told Landra what to include in it. A series of prominent scientists legitimized the Manifesto with their signature after it had been approved by the Duce, although there was much consternation in the Italian academic community (and beyond) at its release.

The population of Italy today is of Aryan origin and its civilization is Aryan. This Aryan people has inhabited Italy for several thousand years; little remains of the civilization of the pre-Aryan people. The origin of the Italians today comes essentially from the elements of those same races that constitute and will constitute the permanent living fabric of Europe . . . There exists today a pure 'Italian Race'. This announcement is not based on the confusion of the biological concept of race with the historic linguistic concept of people and nation, but on the very pure blood relationship that unites the Italians of today to the generations that for thousands of years have inhabited Italy. This ancient purity of blood is the grandest title of nobility of the Italian nation . . .

The Jews do not belong to the Italian race. Of the Semites that have landed in the course of the centuries on the sacred soil of our Fatherland nothing in general remains . . . The Jews represent the only population that never assimilated in Italy because they are composed of non-European racial elements, different in an absolute sense from those elements that gave rise to the Italians.

The purely European physical and psychological characteristics of the Italians must not be altered in any way.

Source: Manifesto of Racial Scientists, *Il Giornale d'Italia*, 14 July 1938; this translation from Aaron Gillette, 'The origins of the "Manifesto of Racial Scientists"', *Journal of Modern Italian Studies* 6, 3 (2001), pp. 318–20.

Document 33   HITLER'S VIEW OF MUSSOLINI AND ITALY

Hitler's personal admiration of Mussolini was unflagging. Here the German dictator ruminates on what Italy, Italian Fascism and the Duce mean to him.

Night of 21–22 July 1941

I must say, I always enjoy meeting the Duce. He's a great personality. It's curious to think that, at the same period as myself, he was working in the building trade in Germany. Our programme was worked out in 1919 and at that time I knew nothing about him. Our doctrines are based on the foundations proper to each of them but . . . don't suppose that events in Italy had no influence on us. The March on Rome in 1922 was one of the turning-points in history . . .

If Mussolini had been outdistanced by Marxism, I don't know if we would have succeeded in holding out. At that time National Socialism was a very fragile growth . . .

As I walked with him in the garden of the Villa Borghese, I could easily compare his profile with that of the Roman busts, and I realised he was one of the Caesars. There's no doubt at all that Mussolini is the heir of the great men of that period . . .

Italy is the country where intelligence created the notion of the State. The Roman Empire is a great political creation, the greatest of all . . . The Renaissance was the dawn of a new era, in which Aryan man found himself anew. There's our own past on Italian soil. A man who is indifferent to history is a man without hearing, without sight . . .

The magic of Florence and Rome, of Ravenna, Siena, Perugia! Tuscany and Umbria, how lovely they are!

Source: Adolf Hitler, *Hitler's Table Talk* (London: Weidenfeld & Nicolson, 1973), pp. 9–10.

GERMAN SUCCESS EMBITTERS MUSSOLINI   **Document 34**

Mussolini was flabbergasted and awed by Hitler's military successes in the early years of the Second World War, but Italy's weak performance in the conflict made the power gap between the two dictatorships so gaping that the alliance with Germany quickly became from Italy's point of view an uneasy and constraining one. If in public the Regime trumpeted Axis unity, in private Mussolini often lived his role as 'Germany's ignoble second' (in Ciano's words, and echoing the relationship between Austria-Hungary and Germany in the First World War) with anguish and a sense of bitter resentment. In the following excerpt from Ciano's diary, German success in Yugoslavia (as compared to Italian failure there) is bitterly contested by the Duce.

10 June 1941

Mussolini took the occasion of growing German encroachment in Croatia to pronounce the most anti-German diatribe I had ever heard. It was the polemical Mussolini, therefore Mussolini at his best. 'It is not important', he said, 'that the Germans recognise our rights in Croatia on paper, when in practice they take everything for themselves and leave us a pile of bones. They are untrustworthy scoundrels and things cannot go on like this for much longer . . . I am utterly sick of the Germans since List made an armistice with Greece behind our backs and the infantry of the Casale division – all men from Forlí who detest Germany – found at the Perati bridge a Germanic soldier standing legs wide who barred their way, thus giving Germany the fruits of victory. And personally I have had enough of Hitler and his way of behaving. These discussions preceded by a bell ring are detestable. You call a waiter with a bell. But what kind of discussions are they anyway? For five hours I have to withstand a useless and tedious monologue. He [Hitler] talked for hours and hours about Hess, the *Bismarck*, things appertaining generally to the war, but without making an order for the day, without getting to the sinews of a problem, without making a decision. In the meantime, I will continue to fortify our Alpine border. It will all come in handy one day. But, for the moment there isn't much we can do; we have to grit our teeth and bear it . . .'

Source: Galeazzo Ciano, *Diario 1937–1943* (Milan: Rizzoli, 1980), pp. 523–4.

Document 35   THE PACT OF STEEL

Italy's friendly relationship with a belligerent Germany eventually brought the country into a war for which it was hopelessly unprepared. The Pact of Steel (signed 22 May 1939) presumed an ideological closeness between Nazism and Italian Fascism, but for Mussolini, it was not meant to be a prelude to war with the western Democracies, at least in the short term. The Pact effectively gave the direction of the relationship between the two dictatorships to the most aggressive and reckless partner.

Firmly united by the inner affinity between their ideologies and the comprehensive solidarity of their interests, the German and Italian nations are resolved in future also to act side by side and with united forces to secure their living space and to maintain the peace.

Following this path, marked out for them by history, Germany and Italy intend, in the midst of a world of unrest and disintegration, to serve the task of safeguarding the foundations of European civilization . . .

Art. 3 If, contrary to the wishes and hopes of the High Contracting Parties, it should happen that one of them became involved in warlike complications with another Power or Powers, the other High Contracting Party would immediately come to its assistance as an ally and support it with all its military forces on land, at sea and in the air . . .

Art. 5 The High Contracting Parties undertake even now that in the event of war waged jointly, they will conclude an armistice and peace only in full agreement with each other.

Source: Pact of Steel between Italy and Germany, 22 May 1939, in Charles Delzell (ed.), *Mediterranean Fascism* (New York: Walker & Company, 1970), pp. 208–9.

Document 36   ITALIAN LACK OF MILITARY PREPAREDNESS

Hitler's preparation for an invasion of Poland in September 1939 (which potentially meant war against Britain and France) meant that the Pact of Steel was likely to drag in Italy also. But a war against Britain and France was a sobering prospect for an Italy that had, for all the bluster, so far only tested its strength against Ethiopia. A lack of materiel was in the end the excuse Italy used to stay out of the conflict. On being told this by the Italians, Hitler asked Mussolini for a list of what was required, and in Rome a flurry of activity led to the drawing up of a list that the Germans could not possibly satisfy. The following describes the episode from Ciano's point of view and testifies to the amazing amateurishness of Italian military preparedness.

26 August – In Berlin they want the list of our requirements in a hurry. For this reason we meet up at 10 at Palazzo Venezia with the military Chiefs of Staff . . . Before going into the Duce's room I recall to these comrades their sense of responsibility: they must tell the truth on the state of our supplies, and should not – as often happens – be criminally overoptimistic . . . Our requirements are huge because our stockpiles are non-existent. We draw up a list that could kill a bull if it could read. Afterwards, on my own with the *Duce* we prepare a message for Hitler; we explain why our need for materiel is huge and without it, we conclude, we cannot possibly go to war . . . Attolico [Italian ambassador in Berlin], in forwarding the request acts on a misunderstanding. (In a meeting I had with him later he told me it wasn't a misunderstanding, rather that he got things wrong on purpose in order to discourage the Germans from meeting our demands.) He asks for immediate delivery of all the materiel: something utterly impossible because we are dealing with 170,000,000 Tonnes that need 17,000 trains.

Source: Galeazzo Ciano, *Diario 1937–1943* (Milan: Rizzoli, Milan, 1980), pp. 334–5.

--------◀●▶--------

DECLARATION OF WAR   **Document 37**

The Fascist Regime's terror at the thought of war with Britain and France in September 1939 was assuaged by Hitler's brilliant military successes of early 1940. With France about to collapse and Britain very much on the defensive Mussolini made the decision to intervene alongside the Germans. The following is taken from the Duce's *speech (10 June 1940) announcing Italy's decla-ration of war. The idea of the 'proletarian nation' (see Doc. 4) constrained by the monopoly held by Britain of the world's resources finally breaking out is central to Mussolini's justification for declaring war.*

An hour that has been marked out by destiny is sounding in the sky above our fatherland! The hour of irrevocable decisions! The declaration of war has already been handed to the ambassadors of Great Britain and France. We are going onto the battlefield against the plutocratic and reactionary democracies of the West who at every stage have hindered the march and have often threatened the very existence of the Italian people . . .

After having solved the problem of our land frontiers, we are taking up arms in order to establish our maritime frontiers. We want to break the territorial and military chains that are strangling us in our own sea. A nation of 45 million souls is not truly free unless it has free access to the ocean.

The gigantic struggle is only one phase of the logical development of our revolution; it is the struggle of people who though poor are rich in workers versus exploiters who cling fiercely to their monopoly of all the earth's wealth and gold; it is the struggle of young and fertile peoples against sterile ones who stand on the verge of decline; it is the struggle between two centuries and two ideas . . .

People of Italy! Rush to arms, and show your tenacity, your courage, your valour!

Source: Mussolini's speech declaring war, 10 June 1940, in Charles Delzell (ed.), *Mediterranean Fascism* (New York: Walker & Company, 1970), pp. 213–15.

Document 38   THE GRANDI MOTION

The Grandi motion of the Grand Council meeting, which was passed on 24 July 1943, was the catalyst for Mussolini's fall. It confirms that it was failure in the war that destroyed confidence in the Duce. The continued existence of the monarchy as an alternative constitutional compass point throughout the Fascist Regime here becomes determinant. The Grandi motion also appears to suggest that the Fascist parenthesis has come to a close and Italy will return to its Risorgimento inheritance.

Having examined the internal and international situation and the political and military conduct of the war,

[The Grand Council] proclaims the sacred duty of all Italians to defend at whatever cost the unity, independence, and liberty of our fatherland, the fruits of the sacrifices and efforts of four generations, embracing the period from the Risorgimento to the present day . . .

It invites the Head of Government to request His Majesty the King – towards whom the heart of the nation turns with loyalty and confidence – to assume, for the honour of the fatherland, not only the effective command of the Armed Forces . . . but also that supreme power of decision which our laws ascribe to him, and which, throughout the nation's history, has ever been the glorious heritage of our august dynasty of Savoy.

Source: Grandi motion, 24 July 1943, in Charles Delzell (ed.), *Mediterranean Fascism*, (New York: Walker & Company, 1970), p. 222.

Document 39   DEATH OF THE NATION?

In September 2003, on the sixtieth anniversary of the 'death of the nation', the Italian newspaper La Stampa *organized a discussion between two men whose*

*lives took a very different course on that day six decades before. Mirko
Tremaglia, minister in Silvio Berlusconi's right-wing government and long-
time militant of the Italian neo-Fascist political party (the* Movimento
Sociale Italiano *or MSI) was 17 years old in 1943 and recalled the events
of that long gone fateful day, as did Alessandro Curzi, a little younger than
Tremaglia, who had become a communist in the resistance movement and in
2003 was editor of the Communist Party newspaper* Liberazione. *They both
recall the same day 60 years before with very different feelings.*

[Tremaglia, who fought for the RSI]: I heard the news of the armistice on the
radio. It was much worse than the 25 July . . . We had believed in the lie that
Badoglio would continue to fight alongside the Germans. This was the end
of everything . . . The betrayal, the shame. I was a war orphan; my Father
was buried at Asmara [in Eritrea]. Outside I saw a flag being waved in joy as
if this was a day to celebrate. I felt physically sick.

[Curzi, who joined the communist resistance]: Flags had a similar but opposite effect. We waved the Italian flag with a hole in the middle: we had torn
out the badge of the Savoys [the Italian royal family]. We felt we were Italy.
We felt that a chapter of history had closed and the moment of our
liberation had arrived . . . It wasn't just Fascism or the monarchy that had
fallen but an entire ruling class that had collapsed.

Source: *La Stampa*, 8 September 2003.

———————◀●▶———————

Further Reading

Primary sources

As one might expect from a dictator, Mussolini enjoyed the sound of his own voice but he was also a prolific journalist. Consequently his collected works, spanning a four-decade-long career, run to 36 volumes. The **Opera Omnia di Benito Mussolini** edited by Edoardo and Duilio Susmel (Florence: La Fenice, 1951–62; referred to in the main text as OO), is of course in Italian but there is a significant amount of the *Duce's* writing available in English: Charles Delzell (ed.), **Mediterranean Fascism, 1919–1945** (New York: Walker & Company, 1970) has now been joined by John Pollard, **The Fascist Experience in Italy** (London: Routledge, 1998) and Jeffrey Schnapp (ed.), **A Primer of Italian Fascism** (Lincoln: University of Nebraska Press, 2000) which all provide material that goes well beyond Mussolini's utterances. Documents can also be found in Samuel Halperin, **Mussolini and Italian Fascism** (New York: Van Nostrand Reinhold, 1964) and John Whittam, **Fascist Italy** (Manchester: Manchester University Press, 1995). Mussolini's reminiscences, written in the last two years of his life, have been translated with an earlier autobiography and can be found in Benito Mussolini, **My Rise and Fall** (New York: Da Capo Press, 1998). Along with Mussolini's 1932 interviews with the journalist Emil Ludwig, published as **Talks with Mussolini** (London: G. Allen & Unwin, 1932), these sources are useful to understand how the *Duce* wanted to portray himself and the Regime to the world at different junctures.

The official definition of Fascism penned for Mussolini by philosopher Giovanni Gentile can be found in Giovanni Gentile, **Origins and Doctrine of Fascism: With Selections from Other Works** (New Brunswick: Transaction, 2002). Galeazzo Ciano's **Diary** (London: Weidenfeld & Nicolson, 2002) is an invaluable document for understanding the mentality of the Fascist elite as well as the vicissitudes of Italian foreign policy in the years up to and including the Second World War.

Suggestive novels and memoirs published in English translation include such classics as Emilio Lussu, **The Sardinian Brigade** (London: Prion Press, 2000) on the Italian First World War; Carlo Levi, **Christ Stopped at Eboli**, (Harmondsworth: Penguin, 1984) on a *confinato's* experience of Italy's deep south; the semi-autobiographical novels of (contradictory) anti-Fascist Ignazio Silone: **Fontamara** and **Bread and Wine**, published in the **Abruzzo Trilogy** (South Royalton: Steerforth Press, 2000); and Giorgio Bassani, **The Garden of the Finzi-Continis** (London: Quartet, 1997), which recounts the vicissitudes of a Jewish family in Ferrara during the Regime.

To get a visual feel of what Fascist Italy was like, or at least what it wanted people to believe it was like, even though some difficulty may be encountered in initially navigating this Italian website, the *Istituto Luce* in Rome has placed tens of thousands of Fascist newsreels online. These can be accessed freely at www.archivioluce.it

Historiography

The trajectories that histories of Italian Fascism have taken since 1945 (and even before) are helpfully extrapolated in R.J.B. Bosworth, **The Italian Dictatorship: Problems and Perspectives in the Interpretation of Mussolini and Fascism** (New York: Arnold, 1998). Articles by John Davis – 'Remapping Italy's path to the twentieth century', *Journal of Modern History*, 66, 2 (1994), pp. 291–320, and 'Modern Italy – historical perspectives since 1945' in M. Bentley (ed.), **Companion to Historiography** (London: Routledge, 1997) – do not concentrate exclusively on Fascism but are useful in a not overcrowded field. The following reviews also stand out: John Whittam, 'Fascism and Anti-Fascism in Italy: history, memory and culture', *Journal of Contemporary History*, 36, 1 (2001), pp. 163–71; Saverio Battente, 'Nation and state building in Italy: recent historiographical interpretations (1989–1997), II, from Fascism to the Republic', *Journal of Modern Italian Studies*, 6, 1 (2001), pp. 94–105; Paul Corner, 'Italian Fascism: whatever happened to dictatorship?' *Journal of Modern History*, 74 (June 2002), pp. 325–51; Anthony Cardoza, 'Recasting the Duce for the new century: recent scholarship on Mussolini and Italian Fascism', *Journal of Modern History*, 77 (September 2005), pp. 722–37; R.J.B. Bosworth, 'The Italian *Novecento* and its historians', *The Historical Journal*, 49, 1 (2006), pp. 317–29. Two books of collected essays, not exclusively on historiography but very useful for getting to grips with some of the key debates, are John A. Davis (ed.), **Gramsci and Italy's Passive Revolution** (London: Croom Helm, 1979) and David Forgacs (ed.), **Rethinking Italian Fascism: Capitalism, Populism and Culture** (London: Lawrence & Wishart, 1986).

Patrizia Dogliani and R.J.B. Bosworth (eds), *Italian Fascism: History, Memory and Representation* (Basingstoke: Macmillan, 1999) is a lucid depiction of how Italian society has engaged with its Fascist past after 1945.

The historical dictionaries, Philip Cannistraro, *Historical Dictionary of Fascist Italy* (Westport, Conn.: Greenwood Press, 1982) and Frank Coppa, *Dictionary of Modern Italian History* (Westport, Conn.: Greenwood Press, 1985) are not strong on historiography but are good as steering and reference tools.

General books on modern Italian history

There is a broad range of survey histories of modern Italy in which Fascism obviously plays a significant part. Martin Clark, *Modern Italy, 1871–1995* (London: Longman, 1996) has established itself rightly as the standard text and although it is still challenged by the much older (first published in 1956) Denis Mack Smith, *Modern Italy: A Political History* (Ann Arbor: University of Michigan Press, 1997), which has been periodically updated, it worthily continues in the British tradition of always failing to take Italians seriously. Edward Tannenbaum and Emiliana Noether, *Modern Italy: A Topical History since 1861* (New York: New York University Press, 1974) is a solid, if ageing, text and Christopher Seton-Watson, *Italy from Liberalism to Fascism, 1870–1925* (London: Methuen, 1967) is often worth returning to. Harry Hearder, *Italy: A Short History* (Cambridge: Cambridge University Press, 1990) and Christopher Duggan, *A Concise History of Italy* (Cambridge: Cambridge University Press, 1994) are useful, and the vast time span covered by both does not take away from the incisiveness of two authors who specialize in Italy's nineteenth and twentieth centuries. Spencer Di Scala, *Italy: From Revolution to Republic, 1700 to the Present* (Boulder: Westview Press, 2006) is now into its third edition, testifying to the book's user-friendliness. A new overview, Jonathan Dunnage, *Twentieth Century Italy, a Social History* (Harlow: Pearson Education, 2002), handles the contradictory nature of Italian history with skill and has an excellent bibliography. Nicholas Doumanis, *Italy: Inventing the Nation* (London: Arnold, 2001) is an exploration of the contradictory nature of Italy as national construction over a long time-scale.

Overviews of Italian Fascism and Mussolini biographies

Early overviews of Italian Fascism, apart from the eulogies sponsored by the Regime, of which the most important was Gioacchino Volpe, *History of the*

Fascist Movement (Rome: Soc. An. Poligrafica Italiana, 1934), were penned by the cluster of anti-Fascist academics and political activists who fled Italy in the 1920s. The most important of these was Gaetano Salvemini, whose *Under the Axe of Fascism* (New York: Citadel, 1971) was first published in 1936 but remained popular well after 1945, and Angelo Tasca's *The Rise of Italian Fascism 1918–1922* (London: Methuen, 1938), famous for its setting the agenda that 'to understand Fascism we must write its history', by which he meant that Marxist interpretations of Fascism needed to be slotted into the idiosyncrasies, chance and personalities of history. Some of Antonio Gramsci's writings on Italian Fascism, penned while he was in prison rather than exile in the 1930s, can be found in David Forgacs (ed.), *A Gramsci Reader: Selected Writings 1916–1935* (New York: New York University Press, 2000). Early liberal-British writers concerned with Fascism are best represented by Herman Finer (although he was a Romanian émigré), in his study *Mussolini's Italy* (London: Gollancz, 1935) and an example of American writers is Gilbert Seldes, *Sawdust Caesar: The Untold Story of Mussolini and Fascism* (New York: Harper & Brothers, 1935).

In post-war years, as the horrors of Nazi crimes became apparent and with the exigencies of the Cold War pressing, much writing on Italian Fascism tended to highlight its shoddiness and Mussolini's unworthiness to hold a place among the truly totalitarian dictators. Christopher Hibbert, *Benito Mussolini: A Biography* (London: Longmans, 1962) set the scene and was bolstered by such studies as Ivone Kirkpatrick, *Mussolini, a Study in Power* (New York: Hawthorn books, 1964). By the mid 1960s the first volume of Renzo De Felice's Mussolini biography had come out, and it was to be followed by a further seven over the next 30 years as *Mussolini* (Turin: Einaudi, 1965–1997), becoming progressively more controversial but claiming a pre-eminence over the field. No translation of this huge work has yet been attempted but De Felice's overall thesis can be found in his and Michael Ledeen's *Fascism: An Informal Introduction to its Theory and Practice* (New Brunswick, NJ: Transaction Books, 1976). By the 1970s a clutch of overview histories testified to a now mature and defined subject area of interest in Anglo-Saxon academia: Alan Cassels, *Fascist Italy* (London: Routledge & Kegan Paul, 1969), Elizabeth Wiskemann, *Fascism in Italy: Its Development and Influence* (London: Macmillan, 1970) and the still unsurpassed Adrian Lyttelton, *The Seizure of Power: Fascism in Italy, 1919–1929* (London: Weidenfeld & Nicolson, 1973). Other examples include Edward R. Tannenbaum, *Fascism in Italy: Society and Culture, 1922–1945* (London: Allen Lane, 1973) and Roland Sarti, *The Ax Within: Italian Fascism in Action* (New York: New Viewpoints, 1974).

Denis Mack Smith, *Mussolini* (London: Weidenfeld & Nicolson, 1981) was written as a rebuttal to De Felice, painting a picture of the *Duce* not as in tune with the hopes and desires of the Italian people, a figure emerging now in De Felice's biography, but as the cruel and petty tyrant that squared with the traditional view from across the Channel and the Atlantic. Mack Smith's biography set the standard until Richard Bosworth's **Mussolini** (London: Arnold, 2002); if this penetrating biography is taken in conjunction with **Mussolini's Italy: Life under the Dictatorship 1915–1945** (London: Perguin, 2005) by the same author, a comprehensive and weighty political-social history of Fascist Italy has at last become available. It is difficult to see these two books being superseded for a long time to come. After the two empty decades that separate it from Mack Smith's, Bosworth's biography came out at a particularly busy time for rewriting the *Duce's* story: Nicholas Farrell, **Mussolini: A New Life** (London: Weidenfeld & Nicolson, 2003) favours the De Felician quasi hero who is passed off as 'new', and Martin Clark, **Mussolini** (Harlow: Pearson, 2005) promises far less but in fact delivers more (Clark's verve is as compulsive as ever). A very short but candid profile of Mussolini is Anthony Cardoza, **Benito Mussolini: The First Fascist** (New York: Pearson Longman, 2006), and Peter Neville, **Mussolini** (London: Routledge, 2004) is a good introductory text.

If no major scholarly Mussolini biographies in English came out between 1981 and 2002, a number of survey histories of Italian Fascism did: a short but well-argued introduction, Alexander J. De Grand, **Italian Fascism: Its Origins and Development** (Lincoln: University of Nebraska Press, 1982) has become a must for undergraduates writing on Fascism for the first time, and a succinct but useful introduction by Martin Blinkhorn, **Mussolini and Fascist Italy** (London: Routledge, 2006) first appeared in 1984 and is now in its third edition. Philip Morgan's **Italian Fascism, 1915–1945** (Basingstoke: Palgrave, 2004) which first appeared in 1994, is the best introductory book available and John Whittam, **Fascist Italy** (Manchester: Manchester University Press, 1995) is shorter but of similar quality.

Fascisms?

Much interest in Italian Fascism has been focused not so much on seeking to understand it in and for itself but as an obligatory stop on the way to finding the holy grail of a generic international fascism (with a small 'f') or its interpretative rival, totalitarianism. Those interested in constructing such models have tended to cull the Italian experience for what international scholarship, for obvious reasons, considers the more pressing task of understanding Nazi Germany. Notwithstanding the way this has often skewed research agendas, much light has been shed on Italian Fascism by the endeavours of political scientists and historians trying to make sense of the horrors of the Third Reich or indeed Stalin's Russia. These studies have in turn produced books summing up historiographical debate, possibly with the proposal of a new theory, apart from an obligatory assessment of what has gone before. However, the idea of fascism being a political genre rather than a one-off experience confined to Italy was first mooted by socialists and communists in the immediate years after Mussolini's seizure of power, gaining momentum after Hitler claimed Germany in 1933. Leon Trotsky, in **The Struggle against Fascism in Germany** (New York: Pathfinder Press, 1971) saw in fascism a temporary salvation for a capitalism that was inevitably headed for socialist revolution, and Daniel Guerin, **Fascism and Big Business** (New York: Monad Press, 1973), first published in 1936, remains a classic of this approach. An up-to-date version is Dave Renton, **Fascism: Theory and Practice** (London: Pluto Press, 1999), which provides an overview of older Marxist theorizing on fascism, as do Renzo De Felice, **Interpretations of Fascism** (Cambridge: Harvard University Press, 1977) and Chapter 9 of Richard Bosworth, **The Italian Dictatorship: Problems and Perspectives in the Interpretation of Mussolini and Fascism** (New York: Arnold, 1998).

If Marxists suggested fascism was a sibling of capitalist liberalism and focused on convergences between Mussolini's Regime and the Third Reich, totalitarianism preferred to see connections between the latter and the Soviet Union, with Italy somewhat left out in the cold. The classic works in this approach are Hannah Arendt, **The Origins of Totalitarianism** (London: Allen & Unwin, 1967) and Carl Friedrich and Zbigniew Brzezinski, **Totalitarian Dictatorship and Autocracy** (New York: Praeger, 1965), published originally in the decade after the Second World War. After a 20-year fall from favour, totalitarianism has returned renewed and more liable at least to take Italian Fascism into consideration than of old. James A. Gregor, **The Faces of Janus: Marxism and Fascism in the Twentieth Century** (Yale: Yale University Press, 2000) and David Roberts, **The Totalitarian Experiment in Twentieth-Century Europe: Understanding the Poverty of Great Politics** (London: Routledge, 2006) are recent examples written by Italianists. As a means of putting Italian Fascism, Nazism and communism in the same basket, the concept of political religion is becoming ever more popular. For Italy the doyen of this approach is Emilio Gentile, **The Sacralization of Politics in Fascist Italy** (Cambridge, Mass.: Harvard University Press, 1996) but for a more comparative view and a more riveting read see some sections in Michael Burleigh, **Sacred Causes: The Clash of Religion and Politics, from the Great War to the War on Terror** (London: HarperCollins Publishers, 2007).

According to Roger Griffin, **International Fascism: Theories, Causes and the New Consensus** (London: Arnold, 1998) the interpretative 'triad' of Fascism, totalitarianism and (political) religion (see 'Introduction: God's counterfeiters?', **Totalitarian Movements and Political Religions**, 5, 3 (Winter 2004), pp. 291–325) can inject new life into the idea of fascism as genre as long as scholars realize that Marxist and class-based interpretations have now been superseded. If one takes Roger Eatwell, *Fascism: A History* (London: Chatto & Windus, 1995), Robert Paxton, *The Anatomy of Fascism* (New York: Knopf, 2004), as well as Michael Mann, *Fascists* (Cambridge: Cambridge University Press, 2004), Roger Griffin is right in perceiving a 'new consensus' that gives primacy to ideas and that allows fascism a revolutionary impulse in its own right. Much of this work beats the path first taken by George Mosse in the 1960s and 1970s, the thrust of which can be found in, for example, *The Fascist Revolution: Toward a General Theory of Fascism* (New York: H. Fertig, 1999). Less willingly recognized as a precursor is the fascinating but flawed Ernst Nolte, *Three Faces of Fascism: Action Française, Italian Fascism, National Socialism* (London: Weidenfeld & Nicolson, 1965). The argument that fascisms shared a common revolutionary ideology born in the seething and rich political debate of the French Third Republic is to be found in the seminal Zeev Sternhell, *Neither Right nor Left: Fascist Ideology in France* (Berkeley: University of California Press, 1986).

For introductions to understanding the great debates on fascism as genre, Richard Griffiths, *An Intelligent Person's Guide to Fascism* (London: Duckworth, 2000) is a good place to start, as might be Richard Thurlow, *Fascism* (Cambridge: Cambridge University Press, 1999). Kevin Passmore, *Fascism: A Very Short Introduction* (Oxford: Oxford University Press, 2002) packs a remarkable amount into a brief text, and Peter Davies and Derek Lynch, *The Routledge Companion to Fascism and the Far Right* (London: Routledge, 2002) goes some way to being what its title suggests. Stuart Woolf (ed.), *Fascism in Europe* (London: Methuen, 1981) was an early attempt (first published in 1968) to find areas of comparison between Europe's varieties of fascism, and now Aristotle Kallis, *The Fascism Reader* (London: Routledge, 2003) brings into one volume much that has been significant in writing on Europe's fascisms since 1945. Martin Blinkhorn, *Fascism and the Right in Europe, 1919–1945* (Harlow: Longman, 2000) is more than an appraisal of other theoreticians and offers a lucid and unruffled comparative analysis, and in so doing shows how far the Longman *Seminar Studies* series format can go. Philip Morgan, *Fascism in Europe, 1919–1945* (London and New York: Routledge, 2003) is an excellent survey and refreshingly and self-consciously avoids the temptation of a new explanatory synthesis, something to which Stanley Payne unhelpfully succumbs in *A History of Fascism, 1914–1945* (Madison: University of Wisconsin Press, 1995), which is otherwise a sterling piece of scholarship. Books directly comparing Nazi Germany and Fascist Italy include Alexander J. De Grand, *Fascist Italy and Nazi Germany: The 'Fascist' Style of Rule* (New York: Routledge, 1996), and Richard Bessel, *Fascist Italy and Nazi Germany: Comparisons and Contrasts* (New

York: Cambridge University Press, 1996). On the way the notion of totalitarianism is developed by Abbott Gleason in *Totalitarianism: The Inner History of the Cold War* (New York: Oxford University Press, 1995).

Select monographic studies on aspects of Italian Fascism

Excepting foreign policy and Mussolini's relationship with fellow-dictator Hitler – which produced, for example, the still towering F. W. Deakin, *The Brutal Friendship: Mussolini, Hitler and the Fall of Italian Fascism* (London: Weidenfeld & Nicolson, 1962) – monographic studies, or the social and cultural history of aspects of Italian Fascism, only took off in the late 1960s. Study of Resistance to Fascism, for example, Roberto Battaglia, *The Story of the Italian Resistance* (London: Odhams, 1957) and Charles F. Delzell, *Mussolini's Enemies: The Italian Anti-Fascist Resistance* (Princeton, NJ: Princeton University Press, 1961), was an exception, but it was the rise of Fascism in Italy's disparate localities that at first most interested social historians, often working within a loose Marxist paradigm. These studies tended to see Fascism's origins in the crisis caused by the working-class or peasant challenge to the social order in the immediate post-war years. As a movement Fascism was 'reaction'; with little or no ideology or impetus of its own, its raison d'être was what it stood against.

As monographs accumulated, different aspects of a similar story were revealed: Paul Corner, *Fascism in Ferrara, 1915–1925* (Oxford: Oxford University Press, 1975); Anthony Cardoza, *Agrarian Elites and Italian Fascism: The Province of Bologna, 1901–1926* (Princeton, NJ: Princeton University Press, 1982); Frank Snowden, *Violence and Great Estates in the South of Italy: Apulia, 1900–1922* (Cambridge: Cambridge University Press, 1986); Alice A. Kelikian, *Town and Country under Fascism: The Transformation of Brescia, 1915–1926* (Oxford : Oxford University Press, 1986); Frank Snowden, *The Fascist Revolution in Tuscany, 1919–1922* (Cambridge: Cambridge University Press, 1989). Countering these, David D. Roberts, *The Syndicalist Tradition and Italian Fascism* (Manchester: Manchester University Press, 1979) and A. James Gregor, *Italian Fascism and Developmental Dictatorship* (Princeton, NJ: Princeton University Press, 1979), argued that Fascism had a positive agenda of its own. A. James Gregor, in, for example, *The Young Mussolini and the Intellectual Origins of Fascism* (Berkeley: University of California Press, 1979) and *Mussolini's Intellectuals: Fascist Social and Political Thought* (Princeton, NJ: Princeton University Press, 2005) has made this approach a distinctive feature of his research. The relationship between liberal Italy's institutions or civil society and the rise of

Fascism have been probed by such books as Jonathan Morris, *The Political Economy of Shopkeeping in Milan, 1886–1922* (Cambridge: Cambridge University Press, 1993), or Jonathan Dunnage, *The Italian Police and the Rise of Fascism: A Case Study of the Province of Bologna, 1897–1925* (Westport, Conn.: Praeger, 1997).

These last two books are excellent representatives of the mushrooming interest in all aspects of the Italian Fascist experience since the early 1980s. Topics as diverse as cinema, youth associations, colonial culture, gender, race and more have been added to a renewed exploration of the older staples of foreign policy, politics and resistance, although studies on social class and the rise of Fascism have tended to be more unusual. Here some of the major works in this ever-expanding torrent are highlighted but the choice is selective rather than comprehensive. On women and Italian Fascism the seminal Victoria De Grazia, *How Fascism Ruled Women: Italy, 1922–1945* (Berkeley: University of California Press, 1992) opened up a field that is now very rich: Robin Pickering-Iazzi, *Mothers of Invention: Women, Italian Fascism, and Culture* (Minneapolis: University of Minnesota Press, 1995); David G. Horn, *Social Bodies: Science, Reproduction, and Italian Modernity* (Princeton: Princeton University Press, 1994); and Perry R. Willson, *Peasant Women and Politics in Fascist Italy: The Massaie Rurali* (New York: Routledge, 2002). This last volume is a study of what Fascism would have liked to label its 'social engineering' institutions. On this see also Victoria De Grazia, *The Culture of Consent: Mass Organization of Leisure in Fascist Italy* (Cambridge: Cambridge University Press, 1981), whose interpretative acuteness is still impressive. Tracy H. Koon, *Believe, Obey, Fight: Political Socialization of Youth in Fascist Italy, 1922–1943* (Chapel Hill: University of North Carolina Press, 1985) is also a thorough piece of social history.

In recent years analysing aspects of Fascist culture has become one of the more plied if not always the most revealing of veins for academic exploration. David Forgacs, *Italian Culture in the Industrial Era, 1880–1980: Cultural Industries, Politics and the Public* (Manchester: Manchester University Press, 1990) probed Italian culture and institutional continuities, something that has also interested Marla Stone in *The Patron State: Culture and Politics in Fascist Italy* (Princeton: Princeton University Press, 1998). Unpicking themes, hidden meanings and trajectories in Fascist culture, the major concern of the blending of cultural studies with history in recent years, has been done fruitfully in parts by Ruth Ben-Ghiat, *Fascist Modernities: Italy, 1922–1945* (Berkeley: University of California Press, 2001), and sometimes less convincingly by Jeffrey T. Schnapp, *Staging Fascism: 18 Bl and the Theater of Masses for Masses* (Stanford: Stanford University Press, 1996) and Simonetta Falasca-Zamponi, *Fascist Spectacle: The Aesthetics of Power in Mussolini's Italy* (Berkeley: University of California Press, 1997). Other titles in this genre include: Mabel Berezin, *Making the Fascist Self: The Political Culture of Interwar Italy* (Ithaca, NY: Cornell University Press, 1997); Claudio Fogu, *The Historic Imaginary: Politics of History in Fascist Italy* (Toronto: University of Toronto Press, 2003). Italian Fascist film is engaged with by Marcia Landy, *Fascism in Film: The Italian Commercial Cinema, 1931–1943* (Princeton: Princeton University Press, 1986); Pierre Sorlin, *Italian National Cinema 1896–1996* (London: Routledge, 1996); Jacqueline Reich and Piero Garofalo, *Re-Viewing Fascism: Italian Cinema, 1922–1943* (Bloomington: Indiana University Press, 2002); and Mary P. Wood, *Italian Cinema* (Oxford: Berg, 2005). *Football and Fascism* (Oxford: Berg, 2004) by Simon Martin is a first foray into this subject and is also probed in John Foot, *Calcio: A History of Italian Football* (London: Fourth Estate, 2006).

Racism in Italian Fascist culture has now been studied by Aaron Gillette, *Racial Theories in Fascist Italy* (London: Routledge, 2002). It adds much to the substantial body of literature on the experience of Jews in Fascist Italy, which includes: Meir Michaelis, *Mussolini and the Jews: German–Italian Relations and the Jewish Question in Italy, 1922–1945* (Oxford: Oxford University Press, 1978); Susan Zuccotti, *The Italians and the Holocaust: Persecution, Rescue and Survival* (London: Peter Halban, 1987); Jonathan Steinberg, *All or Nothing: The Axis and the Holocaust, 1941–1943* (London: Routledge, 2002); and Renzo De Felice, *The Jews in Fascist Italy: A History* (New York: Enigma Books, 2001), which is a translation of one of De Felice's first books. Alexander Stille, *Benevolence and Betrayal: Five Italian Jewish Families under Fascism* (New York: Summit Books, 1991) is a moving account perfectly blending historical rigour and narrative power.

On Italian colonialism, military diplomatic histories such as A.J. Barker, *The Civilizing Mission: A History of the Italo-Ethiopian War of 1935–1936* (New York: Dial Press, 1968) or Anthony Mockler, *Haile Selassie's War* (Oxford: Oxford University Press, 1984) have now been added to by studies seeking to understand colonialism as a cultural and social experience: some collected essays can be found in Patrizia Palumbo (ed.), *A Place in the Sun: Africa in Italian Colonial Culture from Post-Unification to the Present* (Berkeley: University of California Press, 2003); Ruth Ben-Ghiat and Mia Fuller (eds), *Italian Colonialism* (New York: Palgrave Macmillan, 2005); and Jacqueline Andall, Derek Duncan (eds) *Italian Colonialism: Legacy and Memory* (London: Peter Lang, 2005). Nicholas Doumanis, *Myth and Memory in the Mediterranean: Remembering Fascism's Empire* (New York: St Martin's Press, 1997) recounts the memory of Italian occupation of the Dodecanese Islands from the Greek viewpoint, and *Legacy of Bitterness: Ethiopia and Fascist Italy, 1935–1941* (Lawrenceville, NJ: Red Sea Press, 1997) brings together some of Alberto Sbacchi's important writings on the subject.

In recent years the work of MacGregor Knox has dominated the telling of Mussolini's foreign policy: *Mussolini Unleashed, 1939–1941: Politics and Strategy in Fascist Italy's Last War* (Cambridge: Cambridge University Press, 1982), *Common Destiny: Dictatorship, Foreign Policy, and War in Fascist Italy and Nazi Germany* (Cambridge: Cambridge University Press, 2000) and *Hitler's Italian Allies: Royal Armed Forces, Fascist Regime, and the War of 1940–1943* (Cambridge: Cambridge University Press, 2000) have been joined by Robert Mallett, whose *The Italian Navy and Fascist Expansionism, 1935–40* (London: Frank Cass, 1998) and *Mussolini and the Origins of the Second World War, 1933–1940* (Basingstoke: Palgrave, 2003), as well as Aristotle Kallis, *Fascist Ideology: Territory and Expansionism in Italy and Germany, 1922–1945* (London: Routledge, 2000), seek to give Italian foreign policy an ideological backing and a social function that was altogether missing in accounts highlighting Mussolinian opportunism, such as Denis Mack Smith, *Mussolini's Roman Empire* (London: Longman, 1976). On the vicissitudes of 1943 and Fascism's first demise see Elena Aga Rossi, *A Nation Collapses: The Italian Surrender of September 1943* (Cambridge: Cambridge University Press, 2000) and Philip Morgan, *The Fall of Mussolini: Italy, the Italians, and the Second World War* (Oxford: Oxford University Press, 2007).

References

'OO' throughout the text stands for Susmel E. and Susmel D. (eds) (1951–62) *Opera Omnia di Benito Mussolini*, 36 volumes, Florence, La Fenice.

Apih E. (1988) *Trieste*, Bari, Laterza.

Bosworth R. (1998) *The Italian Dictatorship*, London, Arnold.

Bosworth R. (2002) *Mussolini*, London, Arnold.

Bosworth R. (2005) *Mussolini's Italy*, London, Penguin.

Brendon P. (2000) *The Dark Valley, a Panorama of the 1930s*, New York, Knopf.

Buonvino O. (1906) *Il giornalismo contemporaneo*, Milan, Sandron.

Burleigh M. (2001) *The Third Reich, a New History*, London, Pan Books.

Burleigh M. and Wippermann W. (1991) *The Racial State*, Cambridge, Cambridge University Press.

Cannadine D. (1992) *G.M. Trevelyan. A Life in History*, London, HarperCollins.

Cannistraro P. (1975) *La fabbrica del consenso*, Bari, Laterza.

Centro Furio Jesi (ed.) (1994) *La menzogna della razza*, Bologna, Grafis.

Chabod F. (1996) *Italian Foreign Policy. The Statecraft of the Founders*, Princeton, Princeton University Press.

Ciano G. (1980) *Diario 1937–1943*, Milan, Rizzoli.

Clark M. (1996) *Modern Italy, 1871–1982*, London, Longman.

Clark M. (2005) *Mussolini*, London, Pearson.

Corner P. (1986) 'Liberalism, pre-Fascism, Fascism' in Forgacs D. (ed.) *Rethinking Italian Fascism*, London, Lawrence & Wishart.

Croce B. (1928) *Storia d'Italia dal 1871 al 1915*, Bari, Laterza.

Croce B. (1929) *A History of Italy 1871–1915*, Oxford, Clarendon Press.

Dall'Orto G. (1994) 'Omosessualità e razzismo fascista' in Centro Furio Jesi (ed.) *La menzogna della razza*, Bologna, Grafis.

Davis J. (1988) *Conflict and Control: Law and Order in Nineteenth Century Italy*, London, Macmillan.

Davis J. (1994) 'Remapping Italy's path to the twentieth century', *Journal of Modern History*, 66, pp. 291–320.

Davis J. (1997) 'Modern Italy – historical perspectives since 1945' in Bentley M. (ed.) *Companion to Historiography*, London, Routledge.

Davis J. (2004) 'Filippo Mazzonis and Italy's monarchy', *Journal of Modern Italian Studies*, 9, 2.

De Bernardi A. and Guarracino S. (eds) (1998) *Il Fascismo*, Milan, Mondadori.

De Felice R. (1965) *Mussolini il Rivoluzionario*, Turin, Einaudi.

De Felice R. (1968) *Mussolini il fascista*, II, Turin, Einaudi.

De Felice R. (1974) *Mussolini il duce*, I: *Gli anni del consenso, 1929–1936*, Turin, Einaudi.

De Felice R. (1981) *Mussolini il duce*, II, Turin, Einaudi.

De Felice R. (1995) *Rosso e Nero*, Milan, Baldini & Castoldi.

De Grand A. (2004) 'Mussolini's follies: Fascism in its imperial and racist phase, 1935–1940', *Contemporary European History*, 13, 2, pp. 127–47.

De Grazia V. (1981) *The Culture of Consent*, Cambridge, Cambridge University Press.

De Grazia V. (1992) *How Fascism Ruled Women*, Berkeley, University of California Press.

Deakin F. (1966) *The Brutal Friendship: Mussolini, Hitler and the Fall of Italian Fascism*, Harmondsworth, Penguin.

Del Boca A. (1992a) *Gli Italiani in Africa Orientale*, I: *Dall'Unità alla marcia su Roma*, Milan, Mondadori.

Del Boca A. (1992b) *Gli Italiani in Africa Orientale*, II: *La conquista dell'Impero*, Milan, Mondadori.

Del Boca A. (ed.) (1991) *Le guerre coloniali del fascismo*, Rome, Laterza.

Del Boca A. (ed.) (1996) *I gas di Mussolini*, Rome, Editori Riuniti.

Del Boca A. (1996b) 'L'impero' in Isnenghi M. (ed.) *I luoghi della memoria, simboli e miti dell'Italia unita*, Rome, Laterza.

Delzell C. (ed.) (1970) *Mediterranean Fascism, 1919–1945*, New York, Walker & Company.

Di Scala S. (1980) *Dilemmas of Italian Socialism*, Amherst, University of Massachusetts Press.

Dogliani P. (1999) *L'Italia Fascista 1922–1940*, Milan, Sansoni.

Duggan, C. (2002) 'Nation-building in 19th-century Italy. The case of Francesco Crispi', *History Today*, 52, 2.

Dunnage J. (1997) *The Italian Police and the Rise of Fascism*, Westport, Praeger.

Eley G. (2002) *The History of the Left in Europe 1850–2000*, Oxford, Oxford University Press.

Falasca-Zamponi S. (1997) *Fascist Spectacle. The Aesthetics of Power in Mussolini's Italy*, Berkeley, University of California Press.

Forgacs D. (1990) *Italian Culture in the Industrial Era 1880–1980: Cultural Industries, Politics and the Public*, Manchester, Manchester University Press.

Galli Della Loggia E. (1996) *La morte della patria*, Rome-Bari, Laterza.

Gentile E. (1996) *The Sacralization of Politics in Fascist Italy*, Cambridge, Mass., Harvard University Press.

Gentile E. (1997) *La grande Italia*, Milan, Mondadori.

Giddens A. (1990) *Sociology*, Cambridge, Cambridge University Press.

Ginsborg P. (2000) *A History of Contemporary Italy*, Harmondsworth, Penguin.

Ginsborg, P. (2003) *Italy and its Discontents: Family, Civil Society, State 1980–2001*, London, Penguin.

Goebbels J. (1943) *Sportpalast* speech (18 February 1943) (available at www.calvin.edu/academic/cas/gpa/goeb36.htm).

Goldhagen D. (1996) *Hitler's Willing Executioners*, New York, Knopf.

Gramsci A. (1967) *Sul Risorgimento*, Rome, Editori Riuniti.

Gregor A.J. (1979) *The Young Mussolini and the Intellectual Origins of Fascism*, Berkeley, University of California Press.

Gregor A.J. (2005) *Mussolini's Intellectuals*, Princeton, Princeton University Press.

Herzstein R. (1979) *The War that Hitler Won: the Most Infamous Propaganda Campaign in History*, Hamilton.

Hilberg R. (1961) *The Destruction of the European Jews*, London, W. H. Allen, 1961.

Hobsbawm E. (1995) *Age of Extremes*, Abacus.

Kallis A. (2000) *Fascist Ideology. Territory and Expansionism in Italy and Germany, 1922–1945*, Routledge.

Kershaw I. (1998) *Hitler, 1889–1936: Hubris*, Harmondsworth, Penguin.

Kershaw I. (2000) *Hitler, 1936–1945: Nemesis*, Harmondsworth, Penguin.

Kitchen M. (1994) *Nazi Germany at War*, London, Longman.

Kitchen M. (2006) *Europe Between the Wars*, Harlow, Pearson Education.

Knox M. (1996) 'Fighting power in Italy and Germany' in Bessel R. *Fascist Italy and Nazi Germany, Comparisons and Contrasts*, Cambridge, Cambridge University Press.

Knox M. (2000) *Common Destiny. Dictatorship, Foreign Policy, and War in Fascist Italy and Nazi Germany*, Cambridge, Cambridge University Press.

Koon T. (1985) *Believe, Obey, Fight*, Chapel Hill, University of North Carolina Press.

Lanaro S. (1988) *Nazione e Lavoro*, Venice, Marsilio.

Lyttelton A. (1973) *The Seizure of Power*, Weidenfeld & Nicolson.

Lyttelton A. (1997) 'La dittatura fascista' in Sabbatucci G. and Vidotto V. (eds) *Storia d'Italia. Guerre e Fascismo*, Rome-Bari, Laterza.

MacDonald R. (1994) *The Language of Empire: Myths and Metaphors of Popular Imperialism, 1880–1918*, Manchester, Manchester University Press.

Mack Smith D. (1958) *Italy: A Modern History*, Ann Arbor, University of Michigan Press.

Mack Smith D. (1975) *Mussolini's Roman Empire*, London, Longman.

Malatesta M. (ed.) (1995) *Society and the Professions in Italy, 1860–1914*, Cambridge, Cambridge University Press.

Mallett R. (2003), *Mussolini and the Origins of the Second World War, 1933–1940*, Basingstoke, Palgrave.

Marazzini C. (1994) *La lingua italiana. Profilo storico*, Bologna, Il Mulino.

Marrus M. (1989) *The Holocaust in History*, New York, New American Library.

Mazower M. (1998) *Dark Continent: Europe's Twentieth Century*, London, Allen Lane.

Michaelis M. (1978) *Mussolini and the Jews: German–Italian Relations and the Jewish Question in Italy, 1922–1945*, Oxford, Oxford University Press.

Mignemi A. (ed.) (1984) *Immagine coordinata per un impero Etiopia 1935–1936*, Turin, Forma.

Milward A. (1977) *War, Economy and Society 1939–1945*, London, Allen Lane.

Molfese F. (1966) *Storia del Brigantaggio dopo l'Unità*, Milan, Feltrinelli.

Momigliano E. (ed.) (1959) *Tutte le encicliche dei sommi Pontefici*, Milan, dall'Oglio.

Morgan P. (2004) *Italian Fascism, 1915–1945*, Basingstoke, Palgrave.

Moseley R. (1999) *Mussolini's Shadow: The Double Life of Count Galeazzo Ciano*, New Haven, Conn., Yale University Press.

Mosse G. (1975) *The Nationalization of the Masses: Political Symbolism and Mass Movements in Germany from the Napoleonic Wars through the Third Reich*, New York, H. Fertig.

Mussolini B. (1939) *My Autobiography*, London, Hutchinson.

Mussolini B. (1998) *My Rise and Fall*, New York, Da Capo Press.

Mussolini e il Fascismo: Il patto d'acciaio (2005), [DVD], Milan, Hobby and Work Publishing.

Newsreel *Giornale Luce B0310* 14 July 1933 (available at www.archivioluce.it).

Orwell G. (1990) *Nineteen Eighty-four*, Harmondsworth, Penguin.

Papal encyclical (29 June 1931) 'On Catholic action in Italy; *Non abbiamo bisogno*' (available at www.papalencyclicals.net/Pius11/P11FAC.HTM).

Papal encyclical (14 March 1937) 'Mit brennender Sorge' (available at www.papalencyclicals.net/Pius11/P11BRENN.HTM).

Passerini L. (1990) *Mussolini Immaginario*, Bari, Laterza.

Patriarca S. (1995) *Numbers and Nationhood. Writing statistics in nineteenth-century Italy*, Cambridge, Cambridge University Press.

Payne S. (1995) *A History of Fascism 1914–1995*, Madison, University of Wisconsin Press.

Perfetti F. (1977) *Il nazionalismo italiano dalle origini alla fusione col fascismo*, Bologna, Il Mulino.

Pini G. and Susmel D. (1973) *Mussolini. L'uomo e l'opera*, II: *Dal fascismo alla dittatura*, Florence, La Fenice.

Pollard J. (1985) *The Vatican and Italian Fascism, 1929–32*, Cambridge, Cambridge University Press.

Preti L. (1968) *Impero fascista, africani, ebrei*, Milan, Mursia.

Rochat G. and Massobrio G. (1978) *Breve storia dell'esercito italiano dal 1861 al 1943*, Turin, Einaudi.

Romanelli R. (1988) *Il comando impossibile. Stato e società nell'Italia liberale*, Bologna, Il Mulino.

Salvatorelli L. and Mira G. (1964) *Storia d'Italia nel periodo fascista*, Turin, Einaudi.

Schnapp J. (ed.) (2000) *A Primer of Italian Fascism*, Lincoln, University of Nebraska Press.

Scipione l'africano (1937) directed by Carmine Gallone.

Schram A. (1997) *Railways and the Formation of the Italian State in the Nineteenth Century*, Cambridge, Cambridge University Press.

Seldes G. (1935) *Sawdust Caesar*, New York, Harper & Brothers.

Snowden F. (1986) *Violence and Great Estates in the South of Italy: Apulia, 1900–1922* Cambridge, Cambridge University Press.

Snowden F. (1989) *The Fascist Revolution in Tuscany, 1919–1922*, Cambridge, Cambridge University Press.

Steinberg J. (2002) *All or Nothing: The Axis and the Holocaust*, London, Routledge.

Sternhell Z. (1987) 'The anti-materialist revision of Marxism as an aspect of the rise of Fascist ideology', *Journal of Contemporary History*, 22, pp. 379–400.

Stevenson D. (2005) *1914–1918 The History of the First World War*, London, Penguin.

Togliatti P. (1973) *Opere*, III, 2 (ed. by Ragionieri E.), Rome, Editori Riuniti.

Trevelyan G.M. (1911) *Garibaldi and the Making of Italy*, London, Longmans.

Williams G. (1975) *Proletarian Order*, London, Photo Press.

Wilson P. (1996) 'Women in Fascist Italy' in Bessel R. *Fascist Italy and Nazi Germany, Comparisons and Contrasts*, Cambridge, Cambridge University Press.

Zamagni V. (1998) 'Italy: How to lose the war and win the peace' in Harrison M. *The Economics of World War II, Six Great Powers in Comparison*, Cambridge, Cambridge University Press.

Zuccotti S. (1987) *The Italians and the Holocaust*, London, Peter Halban.

Index